THE COMPLE
TO
FACILITY
MANAGEMENT

Dan Lowry, MBA, PMP, FMP
www.LearningFM.com

ISBN: 978-1973774891

Published by:
Lowry Digital, LLC
2801 E. Kenosha St. #140120
Broken Arrow, OK, 74014, USA
Email: **lowrydigital@gmail.com**
Internet: **www.LearningFM.com**

To Leslie, Aidan, and Jennings, whose support enables me daily.

Table of Contents

List of Abbreviations

A/E (A-E)	Architect / Engineer
AAR	After Action Review
AC	Actual Cost
ACRS	Accelerated Cost Recovery System
ADA	Americans with Disabilities Act
ADR	Alternative Dispute Resolution
AED	Automated External Defibrillator
AHU	Air Handling Unit
AON	Activity-on-node
BAC	Budget at Completion
BCWP	Budgeted Cost of Work Performed
BCWS	Budgeted Cost of Work Scheduled
BIA	Business Impact Analysis
CBA	Cost-benefit Analysis
CBM	Condition-based Maintenance
CFO	Chief Financial Officer
CFR	Code of Federal Regulations
CGTC	Camp Gruber Training Center
CLSS-HC	Certified Life Safety Specialist for Health Care
CM	Construction Management
CMMS	Computerized Maintenance Management System
CMU	Concrete Masonry Unit
COGS	Cost of Goods Sold
COP	Common Operating Picture
COQ	Cost of Quality
CPA	Certified Public Accountant
CPAF	Cost Plus Award Fee
CPFF	Cost Plus Fixed Fee
CPI	Cost Performance Index
CPIF	Cost Plus Incentive Fee
CPM	Critical Path Method

CPPC	Cost Plus Percentage of Cost
CV	Cost Variance
Cx	Commissioning
CxA	Commissioning Authority
DB	Design-Build
DBB	Design-Bid-Build
EAC	Estimate at Completion
EAP	Emergency Action Plan
EF	Early Finish
EIFS	Exterior Insulation Finishing System
EMS	Energy Management System
EPA	Environmental Protection Agency
ES	Early Start
ETC	Estimate to Complete
EUL	Estimated Useful Life
EV	Earned Value
EVM	Earned Value Management
FAF	Financial Accounting Foundation
FASB	Financial Accounting Standards Board
FCA	Facility Condition Assessment
FCI	Facility Condition Index
FF&E	Furniture, Fixtures, and Equipment
FFP	Firm Fixed Price
FM	Facility Management
FMP	Facility Management Professional
FMP	Facilities Master Plan
FP-EPA	Fixed Price with Economic Price Adjustment
FPIF	Fixed Price Plus Incentive Fee
FV	Future Value
GAAP	Generally Accepted Accounting Principles
GASB	Governmental Accounting Standards Board
GFCI	Ground Fault Circuit Interrupter

GL	General Ledger
GSHP	Ground Source Heat Pump
HAZMAT	Hazardous Materials
HQ	Headquarters
HVAC	Heating, Ventilation, and Air Conditioning
IDIQ	Indefinite Delivery / Indefinite Quantity
IFB	Invitation for Bid
IFMA	International Facility Management Association
IRR	Internal Rate of Return
IT	Information Technology
JHA	Job Hazard Analysis
JSA	Job Safety Analysis
KPI	Key Performance Indicator
kWh	Kilowatt Hour
LCC	Life-cycle Cost
LED	Light Emitting Diode
LF	Late Finish
LHS	Life, Health, Safety
LOTO	Lockout - Tagout
LS	Late Start
MACRS	Modified Accelerated Cost Recovery System
NFPA	National Fire Protection Association
NIBS	National Institute of Building Sciences
NPV	Net Present Value
NTE	Not to Exceed
O&M	Operations and Maintenance
OCS	Officer Candidate School
OSHA	Occupational Safety & Health Administration
P&L	Profit and Loss
PBX	Private Branch Exchange
PdM	Predictive Maintenance
PE	Professional Engineer

PM	Project Manager
PM	Preventative (Preventive) Maintenance
PMB	Performance Measurement Baseline
PMBOK®	Project Management Body of Knowledge
PMI®	Project Management Institute
PMP®	Project Management Professional
POTS	Plain Old Telephone Service
PP&E	Property, Plant, and Equipment
PPE	Personal Protective Equipment
PSTN	Public Switched Telephone Network
PTA	Point of Total Assumption
PU	Packaged Unit
PV	Present Value
PV	Planned Value
QA	Quality Assurance
QC	Quality Control
RACI	Responsible, Accountable, Consult, Inform
RFI	Request for Information
RFP	Request for Proposal
RFQ	Request for Quote
ROA	Return on Assets
ROE	Return on Equity
RPI	Real Property Inventory
RTU	Roof Top Unit
SaaS	Software as a Service
SDS	Safety Data Sheet
SLA	Service Level Agreement
SOFP	Statement of Financial Position
SOP	Standard Operating Procedure
SOW	Statement of Work
SPI	Schedule Performance Index
SV	Schedule Variance

SWOT	Strengths, Weaknesses, Opportunities, Threats
T&M	Time and Materials
TF	Total Float
TOC	Tactical Operations Center
TU	Terminal Unit
VAC	Variance at Completion
VoIP	Voice Over Internet Protocol
WBDG	Whole Building Design Guide
WBS	Work Breakdown Structure
ZBB	Zero-based Budgeting

Introduction

I've come to a conclusion. Most facility management (FM) resources fall into one of two categories: those that read like college textbooks and those directed at marketing products and services to practicing facility managers (or anyone involved in the profession). *Both really annoy me.*

I concede both types of resources have their purpose. While neither is inherently bad, these are not the resources I searched for during the trials and errors of learning this profession. I needed a guide written by facility managers, for facility managers - that wouldn't put me to sleep after two pages of mind-numbing processes and techniques. Before beginning, you need to understand a few things about this book.

First, this book is not your typical guide to facility management. Don't get me wrong, I will explain the processes and techniques you need to be successful, but I also will put them into context. I want to give you information you need and then give you examples in my own stories to illustrate concepts. Depending on your level of experience, some of these principles might seem very basic -- and that is a great thing. Facility management is built on four basic knowledge domains: ***Operations & Maintenance, Project Management, Business Finance, and Leadership***. The more we practice basics, the better we become at executing advanced functions (which we also will discuss).

Second, this book will create value for you by challenging you as a professional. Do not expect to read this book and magically be transformed into an FM genius. Our knowledge areas take time and practice. That said, I promise you anyone can learn how to become an expert in all of them. The primary goal of this book is to give you all of the tools you need to do the following:

Learn facility management and become confident in your craft.

Get a job as a facility manager with the tools to excel far beyond expectations.

Prove to your organization the immense value you bring to it.

Third, this book serves to promote the FM profession. Whether or not you understand it now, facility management is a relatively new vocation. As such, many organizations do not understand the value we bring. We are viewed as an expendable cost center. I mean, who really needs to maintain equipment, right? Sadly, many operations managers think this way and prefer to outsource all the pieces or employ one handyman to take care of everything. It's up to us as FM professionals to teach our organizations the value we bring. It is up to us to increase our worth industry-wide and I challenge you to join me in this effort.

Fourth, if you are looking for a college textbook or encyclopedia of step-by-step instructions on how to maintain various pieces of equipment, close this book and put it back on the shelf. This guide will develop you in all aspects of facility management. If you are looking for marketing material that compares various facility-related widgets and why the round one is better than the square one, don't buy this book. As an active facility manager, I know how many sales calls you are already dealing with and I'm not going to waste your time with more product information. However, if you want an interactive learning experience where we discuss some pretty complex facility management topics in an easy to understand way, then keep reading. This guide will serve to develop you as a well-rounded facility manager with the knowledge to step into any industry and develop specific skills from there.

Finally, I want your feedback. Please, share your thoughts and experiences with me. The best way to find me is through my website at **www.LearningFM.com**. Do us both a favor and sign up for my newsletter so we can keep in touch. I will learn as much from you as you will from me and I really look forward to hearing from you. From there you can connect with me on social media, listen to The Learning FM Podcast, watch the Learning FM videos, and more.

I can also be reached at **dan@learningfm.com**. And yes, I promise I will get back with you.

Thank you so much for reading. Now, let's get started.

About the Author

My name is Dan Lowry and I am currently the Director of Facilities for Southern Hills Country Club in Tulsa, OK. I actually debated for quite a bit on whether to include the name of my current organization, but in the interest of full disclosure (and since you can easily find it on LinkedIn, anyway) I decided to go with it.

I've taken a somewhat circuitous route to end up here. I suppose that's ok since there is no normalized career path laid out for facility management professionals; but, together maybe we can start to change that. This guide takes everything I've learned about facility management, project management, finance and leadership to teach what new facility managers should be, know, and do. Having not set out in college to become a facility manager, I learned along the way through formal education, self-study, experience, and training. This guide is what I wish I had when I first started.

I graduated from the University of Oklahoma in 2002 with a degree in criminology, because I wanted to be a Tulsa police officer. Of course, the Tulsa Police Department was not hiring when I graduated. So, I got a job as the warranty manager for a local home building company. I worked my way up through that business for six years from doing warranty work to managing custom residential projects and finally serving as the vice-president for a small local home builder.

The other life-shaping decision I made early-on came immediately after 9/11, when I joined the Oklahoma Army National Guard as a Private First Class with ambitions of being an officer. After more than 15 years, I am currently a Major and have served the Army, both part-time and full-time, as an engineer in facilities and operations. In fact, the major reason I got out of the residential construction market was due to a year-long deployment to Baghdad in 2008.

When I came back from deployment, the residential construction market was in the toilet, but the Tulsa Police Department was hiring (finally!). It wasn't too long after making it through the TPD Academy and field training that I was laid off. Twice. Yes, twice. As it turns out, the City of Tulsa isn't the best manager of public funds. I realized rather quickly that I needed a different career path. So, I went back to school to get my MBA and found a full-time job managing military facilities with the Army

National Guard. It was there at my first job as a facility manager that I realized I had found my passion and wanted to learn as much as I possibly could.

I now have a Master of Business Administration in Finance, am a certified Project Management Professional (PMP®) through the Project Management Institute (PMI®), and maintain credentials as a Facility Management Professional (FMP) through the International Facility Management Association (IFMA). I belong to the City and Country Club Council of IFMA, my local IFMA chapter, and my local PMI chapter.

Throughout all of this, my favorite part of facility management is the constant quest for knowledge. There are so many facets and components to this ever-evolving environment that we all manage; there is no way that any one person can ever learn it all. It's a fascinating career and I love sharing what I have learned with you.

Preface

As a Company Commander in the Army National Guard, I was responsible for everything my company did or failed to do. Sounds fair, right? So, by that logic if any one Soldier (of the over 100 assigned to the company) didn't pass the physical fitness test or didn't want to re-enlist or do any number of things they were expected to do, then I was to blame.

During my two and a half years as a Company Commander, I had several bosses. One of these was a Lieutenant Colonel Battalion Commander who was both active-duty (he was a full-time officer 365 days per year) and one of the smartest officers that I had met. I was initially excited to have him as my commander, that is until he gave his expectations for the year. The rest of us were part-time (one weekend a month, two weeks a year) and apparently, he forgot that not everyone was active duty. His expectations were absolutely on point, but the sheer number of them would have been nearly impossible for an active-duty battalion (a unit where all Soldiers assigned are full-time, 365 days per year) to accomplish, let alone one that only showed up one weekend a month. The added problem? All expectations seemed to have the same priority: *high*.

Needless to say, everything did not get done. Since there wasn't enough time to do everything, all Company Commanders (myself included) were forced to pick what they thought were the highest priorities, do those, and hope the Battalion Commander was pleased with where the chips fell at the end of the year. What I thought was going to be a great journey under a smart leader turned into a very stressful year.

I relate this story to how I felt when I got my first job as a Facility Manager. To say I was overwhelmed could be considered the understatement of the century. I researched any books and articles I could find, trying to come up with a guide on how to sort through the chaos and figure out what I didn't know. What I found were several resources that seemed to cover everything, but lacked how to really do anything.

For anyone reading this who is new to facility management, you will soon discover that FM is a giant umbrella that many times encompasses "everything else." Everything else will be quickly defined as all other responsibilities at your facility that haven't been expressly assigned to a specific department. Here are a few examples:

- Operations and Maintenance
- Project Management
- Interface with Architects, Engineers, Subcontractors, etc.
- Planning, Programming, and Budget Execution
- Capital Procurement
- Housekeeping
- Laundry
- Inspections (Elevators, Fire Systems, Tax Assessors, etc.)
- Inventory Control
- Energy Management and Sustainability Upgrades
- Safety
- Security
- Training
- Hazardous Materials Management
- Grounds Keeping and Landscaping
- Information Technology (IT) Systems
- Emergency Response and Preparedness
- Space Planning

The list goes on and on.

Now think back to my Army example. If any part of the facility fails to do what it is supposed to do (much like any one Soldier in my company), I am held accountable for that. If any stakeholder in the facility (employee, tenant, member, guest, customer, subcontractor, etc.) has an expectation that the facility cannot meet, I again am held accountable. The stakeholder isn't at fault for expecting the facility to function as it is designed, they are right to do so (much like the Battalion Commander with high expectations). So, to ensure stakeholders' expectations are met; how do facility managers effectively manage their facilities?

As in my earlier example, many facility managers find themselves trying to prioritize a list of everything that needs to be done. The result is we are forced to manage the highest priorities while postponing lower priorities. This guide provides a way to not only overcome being overwhelmed and stressed, but prove to all stakeholders that facility management is a vital function of the organization; and, that you are the right person for the job.

Finally, I said this is *a way* --not *the way*. There are many different management styles and all must be custom tailored to each situation. Your employees will not be the same as mine and your facilities might require a different focus at a different time than mine have needed. So, please feel free to tailor this guide to your needs.

Section 1: What Am I Getting Myself Into?

It was a cold morning in January, more years ago than I care to admit. I waited patiently in my Hyundai Sonata in the far corner of the Tulsa Police Academy parking lot. A lump swelled in my throat as I could only imagine what was in store for us that first morning as new trainees. I had already been through Army basic training and Officer Candidate School, so I knew only too well what these first encounters were like in situations such as this.

I fumbled for my keys as I shut the car door five minutes prior to my report time. It was still pitch black outside and I could barely make out the silhouettes of my classmates as we walked toward the entrance of the brightly lit building.

We entered the back of the theater-style classroom and noticed we each had a nameplate in front of the chairs, midway up from the front in the stadium seating. The two familiar faces of the police recruiters greeted us all with cheery grins and welcomed us to come down to the front of the classroom, where we could help ourselves to hot coffee and donuts.

"Uh-oh," I thought. "This is *not good*."

After going through several Army schools designed to tear you down and then build you back up, I knew a trap when I saw one. Two of my classmates took the bait while the rest of us leered suspiciously at the recruiters, taking our seats behind our respective nameplates.

Rat-at-tat-at-tat!!! The two assault rifles filled the classroom with the deafening echoes of blanks being fired into the air. Two police department drill sergeants, whom we had never seen before, ran into the room, screaming orders to evacuate our seats and run down the hall.

It was at that moment, somewhere between the smell of gun powder and the twinge of regret, that I thought, "What am I getting myself into?"

To be clear, FM is nothing like this story (don't worry, I'll bring it full-circle). As a facility manager, I have learned so many different things about so many different industries that I can't remember ever being bored in this job. However, because there is so much to learn, it can seem overwhelming in the beginning. If you find yourself asking, "What did I get myself into," you are not alone.

There are many great aspects to FM. As the central point of contact for all departments when facility issues arise, I have the opportunity to deal with most of the stakeholders and I love it. Because almost all projects within organizations touch a facility in some way, facility managers are (or should be if they are not) involved in the strategic planning of the future of the facilities they manage. Additionally, no two days are ever the same in FM and that keeps me challenged and interested much of the time.

That said, I would be remiss if I did not warn you about one thing. The Tulsa Police Academy was very clear on the fact that as a police officer, I would be seeing people at their worst. No one likes to see a cop. The fact that you're needing to interact with a police officer for whatever reason, means that something has gone terribly wrong in some form or fashion. Similarly in FM, people only come to me with their problems. They do not call to say how much they love the repair we just spent months on; they call to complain that they are too hot, or that a toilet won't flush, or that they just don't appreciate the paint color in their office. Just understand, FM is rewarding in many ways, but you must also be good at letting things go.

The facility manager's job is never done. Whether you manage facilities that perform 24/7 operations or only operate five days a week for eight hours a day, the facility still exists all the time. At any point, your facility could experience a break-in, a weather-related catastrophe, a utility failure, a fire, or any number of other problems that you will need to respond to whether you are at work, on vacation, or at your kid's soccer game. Just be prepared for the fact that you are now the proud parent of a facility that will need constant attention in some form or fashion.

Chapter 1: What is Facility Management?

The International Facility Management Association (IFMA) defines facility management as *a profession that encompasses multiple disciplines to ensure functionality of the built environment by integrating people, place, process, and technology*[1].

Clear as mud? Let's break it down.

On average, the biggest purchase an individual or family is likely to ever make is their home. Most people purchasing a home don't buy the first one they see. They shop around for it until they find the perfect one (or at least something both suitable and affordable) that allows them as occupants to live their life. The same is true for commercial facilities, which must function in a way that enables the occupants to accomplish their jobs. Now, if you've ever owned a home, how do you define your job as a homeowner? When the dishwasher breaks or a shingle blows off the roof, you have it repaired, correct? When four people need to all take showers at the same time (which puts a strain on the hot water tank and results in cold showers), you set a process for the most efficient way to accomplish this, correct? When your new baby comes home from the hospital, you put certain safety controls in place to protect him or her (for instance, receptacle covers), correct?

Facility managers are the homeowners of their facilities. They do whatever it takes to ensure the users can do their jobs as efficiently as possible. Your job as an FM is to make sure the facility functions as designed in perpetuity. This includes not only the overall facility (the walls, roof, floors, windows, utility lines, parking lots, etc.), but all associated systems of that facility (HVAC, plumbing, electrical, fire suppression, elevators, etc.) and the operations of the facility itself (housekeeping, laundry, maintenance, security, landscaping, internet, safety, phone lines, etc.).

We'll explore this in much more depth as we go along, but you can probably start to see the expanse and scope of your responsibilities.

Chapter 2: How Does Someone Become a Facility Manager?

Traditionally, facility management has not been seen as its own profession. In many cases, FM responsibilities were given to the maintenance person as additional duties. FM evolved over the years from a void in the management of commercial facilities. It is becoming more and more rare to see the maintenance technician who has been in a particular facility for longer than anyone can remember, acting as the adjunct facility manager. Increasingly, private and governmental organizations are requiring FM professionals to have degrees, certifications, and actual experience in order to be considered for FM jobs.

To be honest, this is a great thing! With the void in management came a credibility to our profession that had not existed before, which was intensified by aging infrastructure. Executives began to recognize the need for a knowledgeable FM, which you will use to become the most valuable employee your facility has. However, this also means facility managers must become true professionals through degree programs, continuing education, on-the-job training, and past experience.

Education

So, what is required? Undergraduate degree programs in FM are now being offered in colleges, but this is still a fairly new thing. If you have one of these degrees, congratulations! Many job postings for Facility Managers or Directors of Facilities positions currently require undergraduate/graduate education in one of four disciplines: construction management, engineering, architecture, or business. Let's look at each one of these in more detail.

- Construction Management (CM) – This degree specializes in principles of managing commercial construction projects and includes courses in blueprints, building materials, estimating, etc. This is a very good degree to gain valuable project management lessons and a broad base of knowledge that will be very useful in commercial facilities.

- Engineering – This degree requires the student to specialize in a branch of engineering, such as mechanical, civil, electrical, geotechnical, etc. This is extremely specialized. In my opinion, it's not the ideal degree to obtain if you want to get involved in FM. It's not a bad degree, don't get me wrong. However, on the occasions when I will need a specialized engineer, I will just hire a Professional Engineer (PE) that has been licensed in their specific specialty. I have never felt the need to hold this degree. Nevertheless, if you are looking to manage facilities that have a highly technical maintenance or design team (such as a theme park with thrill rides), you will find a requirement for an engineering degree.

- Architecture – This degree obviously sets you on course to become a certified architect. Again, in my opinion (because it is so specialized), I would only pursue this degree if I wanted to be a certified architect. That said, it will look great on the resume if you have an architecture degree and want to start a career in FM.

- Business – Okay, I may be a little biased here since I have a MBA in finance, but having a strong foundation in business is vital to excelling as a facility manager. There are many facets of FM that require strong business acumen such as programming, budget creation, capital expenditures, forecasting, statistical analysis, etc. I have found this to be a useful degree to have when coupled with experience in FM.

If I had to do it all over again and I knew that FM was where I wanted my career to go, I would first look at FM degree options. Then if none of those suited me, I would study CM in undergrad and still get an MBA in finance. As it stands, I've had to learn project management and commercial construction practices on the job.

Certifications and Experience

Certifications and experience will round out your resume. In my opinion, you should focus on getting the most experience you can and add certifications as you go. Experience managing facilities in the industry where you would like to work will be key to finding a job as an FM.

Resume

Start putting together your resume now. You can find thousands of different formats online and just as many people offering their opinions on how to put them together. To be honest, the format doesn't matter near as much as the content. The most important thing to remember when putting together your resume is this: ***So, What?***

So, what? Who cares? In everything you put on your resume, ask yourself why your intended audience should care about what you write. Here's the key: ***show them how you bring value***. This is a common theme in this book, and it is a vital one to understand. Few hiring managers care only about where you worked or went to school. They only care about how any of that translates into value for them and their organization. Here's an example:

> Let's suppose I'm the hiring manager over a chain of fast-food restaurants and I'm looking for a new manager at one of them. I don't care that you have seven years of experience working at fast-food restaurants on your resume. Why would I? Really, that shows that you haven't been that motivated to do anything else the last seven years. Now, suppose your resume says that in your previous work experience, you were able to save your restaurant money by reducing labor costs by 10% after implementing a new process. Or maybe you were able to increase the revenue at your old job by 15% as a result of coming up with a new marketing campaign.
>
> That shows how you bring value in actual dollars, using your previous employer as an example. This is tangible value.

Value comes in two forms for an organization: tangible and intangible.

Tangible value is quantifiable. Essentially, it is saving money or bringing in more revenue. Intangible value is bringing benefits to an organization that are not easily quantifiable. An example of intangible value is teaching others how to be more efficient or mentoring someone as they develop into a leader within the company.

Are you asking yourself, "Self…what if I didn't do anything that brought value to my employer to use as an example?"

I've coached a lot of people on how to craft their resumes and I have heard this question more than a few times. My answer is always the same. If you really didn't bring any value whatsoever to your employer, why did they keep you around. You should have been fired long ago. I would be willing to bet that you brought real value and you just need to find it.

This is what you need to keep in mind as we move forward in this book. Proving your value to your organization is essential for getting a job, keeping a job, excelling in your job, and developing as an FM professional.

Chapter 3: What is Facility Management Like?

Whenever friends or business acquaintances ask me what I do for a living, I tell them I'm a facility manager. Inevitably, I get a questioning look followed by, "What is that?" I promptly respond with, *"it's a profession that encompasses multiple disciplines to ensure functionality…"* Just kidding. That really doesn't make sense to anyone and certainly doesn't describe what it is that I do on a daily basis.

I generally respond along the lines of "building maintenance" or "project management" at my facility and leave it at that. That's at least something that a layperson can understand and doesn't lead me into some long explanation of efficiencies and processes while I watch my captive's eyes glaze over and roll back in his or her head.

But it's sad I can't explain any better, because FM is critically important to successful organizations and it has become more rewarding than any career I could have imagined. I think describing what the job is like can best be accomplished with a discussion of the characteristics I believe all facility managers should have.

Chapter 4: What Characteristics Should a Facility Manager Have?

Leadership is the art of getting someone else to do something you want done because he wants to do it.

~ Dwight D. Eisenhower

Leader – In my humble opinion, this is far and away the most important attribute. I was caught off guard in my first FM interview when one of the three colonels on my hiring board asked me if I was a leader or a manager. I knew what the right answer was, but it took me a second to figure out why. It was ironic that even though I was interviewing to be the facility *manager* of the Army installation, I knew I needed to be both a leader and a manager. A leader influences and motivates his/her followers to accomplish a common goal. A manager is adept at controlling resources to accomplish given tasks. You need to do both to be successful in FM.

Problem Solver – Problem solving comes in as a close second to leadership. I firmly believe that one reason I enjoy and excel at FM is that I love puzzles. I like figuring out causes behind problems and then solutions that work best for everyone. Trust me, there are many problems to fix in FM. During my days of building custom homes, I could build the same house 10 times and run into different problems each time. It can be frustrating, but it's also exciting and fun. You have to love to solve problems. Murphy's Law states that whatever *can* go wrong, *will* go wrong. It never fails that the one critical asset that has to work will break at the least opportune time. It takes a great problem solver to stay calm under stress to get through those challenges.

Perpetual Student – The one constant in the FM industry is change. The built environment is constantly shifting and evolving. In order to stay relevant, we must learn to evolve with it. There is a reason there are so many credentials available to obtain, symposiums to attend, seminars to catch, and industry updates to read. Many of the facets of FM are driven by changing technologies and it is our job to inform our stakeholders how to improve the facilities we manage.

Adaptable – Hand-in-hand with a thirst for knowledge comes adaptability. Because many facets of FM change so often, it is incumbent on us to change with them. I remember a $32mm dollar new construction project I helped design in the military, which took nearly four years to complete. By the time the design was finished, part of it was so out of date it had to be changed. Adaptability also has to be thought of in terms of ever-changing preferences of your stakeholders. More than once, I have completed a renovation only to change part of it weeks later because the outcome didn't satisfy the needs of the stakeholders, even though the specifications were followed exactly.

Communicator – A colleague once told me that when he received a request by email, he deleted it. It was only after the request was resent that he acted on it because, "only requests worth asking twice are worth answering." Obviously, this is completely unacceptable. But, I will never for the life of me understand why, in today's era of modern communication equipment, it still takes some "professionals" days to address emails, return phone calls, and act on formal requests. Route all of these communications to your cell phone, keep it on you, and answer them the same day. As a facility manager, you have to communicate with everyone. You must be able to walk into a board meeting and present problems and solutions. You must be able to direct vendors, contractors, and employees. You must be able to negotiate with suppliers and work with peers within the facility to hear their problems and solve them within budget and also meet their needs.

Storyteller – You might see this and wonder where I could possibly be going here. However, you'll find out that the ability to tell the story of your facility will be an invaluable characteristic that you will rely on time and time again. Keep in mind that FMs have a hard time explaining exactly what we do in generally descriptive terms. You must be able to pinpoint how all aspects of your facilities are working synergistically with one another and what you've done to improve their efficiencies. Describing how your efforts improve the stakeholders' experience will go a long way to increasing your perceived value within the organization.

Chapter 5: Who Needs Facility Managers?

This is a great question because the answers are so varied. The real answer is anyone who owns or operates a facility, whether it's a house or a skyscraper, needs someone to manage it. The reality though, is that many smaller operations place the importance of FM at the bottom and let their facilities age and fall apart. It's a sad thing to see facilities neglected over time, but it happens more often than you think.

That said, many larger industries just cannot function without full-time facility personnel on staff to take care of daily operations and maintenance at an absolute minimum. Here are a few examples of industries that actively look for FM professionals:

- Government facilities
- Hospitals/medical systems
- Colleges/universities/school systems
- Restaurant chains
- Manufacturing
- Hospitality (hotels, theme parks, country clubs)
- Facility management firms

The countless needs of facilities within these diverse industries can be so different that specifying exactly what you need to know as an FM becomes muddy. For instance, I know firsthand that the emphasis in managing government facilities is on energy reduction and budget execution. Because of this, the end user's satisfaction in many cases falls by the wayside. This is in direct contrast to facilities in the hospitality industry where the end user's satisfaction is the highest priority because it has a direct impact on the organization's revenue stream. For the medical industry, much emphasis is placed on regulations and requirements from accrediting bodies, such as the Joint Commission on Accreditation of Healthcare Organizations (JCAHO).

That last one in the list above is an industry of particular interest. Several firms provide outsourced facilities-management solutions to clients who choose not to keep full-time FM employees on the payroll. Some of these firms include CBRE, JLL, and Sodexo. These are great organizations where you can establish and develop an FM career. A quick search on the internet can yield more results.

One other thing to note here. The term "Facility Manager" is not universal. It would be nice if you could go to a job board or search engine and return all available postings by simply searching these two words. However, terms such as Director of Facilities, Facility Engineer, Manager of Engineering, Facility Director, Facilities Manager, Maintenance Manager, Chief Engineer, and Director of Engineering all have been used interchangeably. I've even been referred to as the Operations Manager, but that typically indicates a different skillset. Play with the search terms and see what you can find. It's interesting to see what comes up.

Section Summary

The reason facility management has historically been neglected in the budget is simple. Facility management is a cost center, not a revenue stream. We don't make the organization money. So the key is to prove your value and show how you can increase the organization's bottom line through your management efforts. That really is the key for all of us in the industry. It is critical for us to educate ourselves on bringing value to the industry and then prove that worth to everyone else.

If you get nothing else out of this section, remember it's all about value. If you bring value, which you absolutely will if you are an effective FM, you will be a crucial member of your organization. The more that industries realize the worth of facility management, the more our profession will grow. I look forward to growing this profession with you.

What Happens Now That I am a Facility Manager?

This is the question that the rest of this book will answer. After getting my first FM job, I was terrified of what I didn't know. I knew there was a lot to learn, but I had no idea what that was. My biggest question was where to begin.

Next, we will address just that.

Section 2: Where to Begin

Determining where to start was the hardest part of my first facility management job. I mean, operations were ongoing and had been for quite some time. Not only did I have to learn what I was doing, but I had to maintain a lot of operating facilities at the same time. First, I knew I had to focus on key areas to learn how to maximize my time. Then, I could learn all of the details about efficiencies and process improvements at a later time. But what were those key areas?

When you start a new job in FM, it really helps to know the previous facility manager and ask where you should begin. They intimately know the facilities, users and operations that you now must support. Knowing all three is essential to being great at your job. That said, if you have a new facility or have no clue who the last facility manager was (or even worse, the organization never had a facility manager before), there is a step-by-step process for where to begin. This section will go through that process and why; but first we need to think about and understand how we learn.

Chapter 1: Know What You Don't Know

First introduced by Noel Burch of Gordon Training International in the 1970's, the conscious competence learning model *is described as the psychological states that are involved in transforming skill incompetence to competence or outright mastery*[2] (See Figure 1). This learning model is what you must go through to master any new job where you're not certain how to begin. It consists of these four stages individuals go through in a cycle as they learn any new skill:

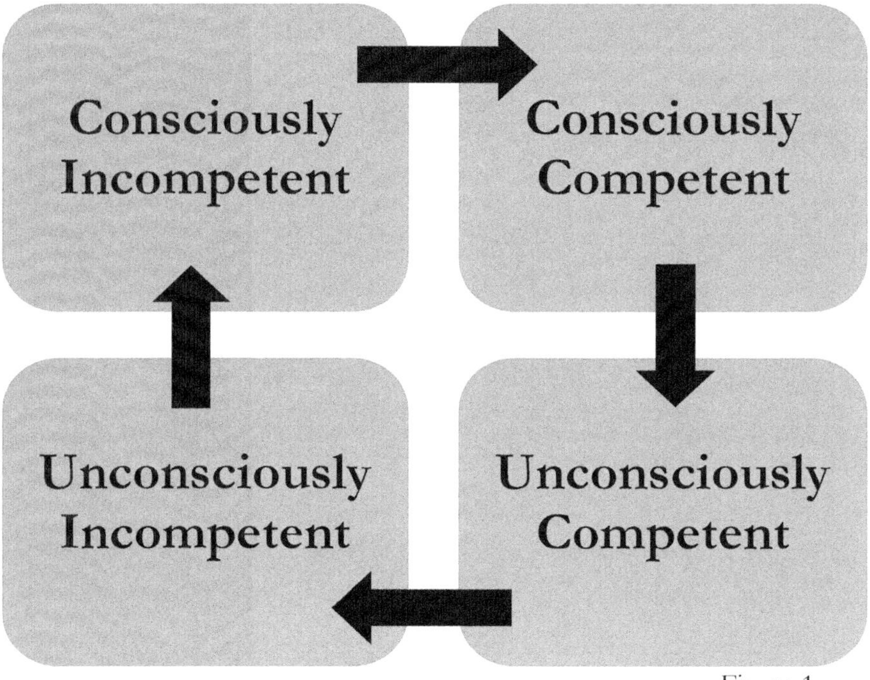

Figure 1

- The first stage is being unconsciously incompetent. This is where the professional doesn't know what they don't know. They understand that they have a lot to learn, but they have no idea where to start. In this stage, you are completely worthless to the organization because you are not doing anything to improve.
- The second stage is being consciously incompetent. Here the professional understands everything they don't know, but they

don't know how to do it. In the case of FM, you might have read a list of responsibilities but still have no idea about practical application at your facility. In this stage, you start to build value because you know what you need to learn and you actively study it.

- From there, the professional will progress into the third stage of being consciously competent. Now they understand what is expected and can perform these new skills deliberately. They will still need to reference resources, checklists, and training aids, but they can function at their jobs.

- The final stage in the progression is unconscious competence. Here the professional has truly mastered their skill and can perform more like a reflex rather than thinking about many specifics. This is where you are truly valuable to the organization. In this stage, you are so proficient you can get the work done and simultaneously focus on improving the organization and leading your department strategically.

Bear with me, I'm bringing this full circle. Knowing that all new facility managers are unconsciously incompetent when they begin, it is vital to figure out as quickly as possible how to move to the second stage and understand what you need to learn. The longer you stay in stage one, the less valuable you are to the organization -- and we already know the importance of building value within our organizations. Also, understand that any professional will begin the cycle again when they are presented with something new. This can be a new career opportunity, a new facility or environment, or development of a new skillset.

I have yet to talk to a facility manager who was handed everything they needed to know their first day on the job. This has a large part to do with the fact that there probably isn't anyone else there (unless the old FM got promoted) who really understands what the job entails, let alone knows what information to pass on to you. As problem solvers, we need to quickly overcome that and I'll explain how next.

Chapter 2: Real Property Inventory

Know from whence you came. If you know whence you came, there are absolutely no limitations to where you can go.

~ James Baldwin

The National Institute of Building Sciences (NIBS) is *a non-profit, non-governmental organization that successfully brings together representatives of government, the professions, industry, labor and consumer interests, and regulatory agencies to focus on the identification and resolution of problems and potential problems that hamper the construction of safe, affordable structures for housing, commerce, and industry throughout the United States.*[3] As a program of the NIBS, the Whole Building Design Guide (WBDG) provides information on building-related guidance, criteria, and technology to practitioners in government and the industry.

The WBDG defines a Real Property Inventory (RPI) as *a record of an organization's real property assets*, which includes *land and anything permanently affixed to it, such as buildings, their installed systems, building equipment, and can include roads, parking facilities, fences, utility systems, structures, etc.*[4]

So where do you start? The RPI.

The RPI tells you "where your facilities have been." As a facility manager, you must know what you have in order to know where you go from there. To even begin to know what direction your facilities will go, FMs must have a firm understanding of what their facilities consist of, which is everything the FM will be responsible to manage.

Not every organization will call the RPI by this name. They should, however, all include the same basic information about all fixed assets. The RPI is nothing more than a list (hopefully maintained in a backed-up digital format that can be easily queried) of all assets owned and maintained by the organization. The bottom line is that you have to know all key information about your facilities. Here is the minimum information you need to keep track of in the RPI for each fixed asset:

- Asset name
- Size (square footage of building, linear feet of sidewalks/utilities, tonnage of HVAC, etc.)
- Placed-in-service dates

- Estimated useful life
- Initial costs
- Costs assigned to the asset during its life
- Identifying information (location, model number, serial number, etc.)

If you are lucky enough to already have an RPI with this information, congratulations! Certain organizations are more diligent about record keeping than others. If you aren't that lucky, you are not alone. I've inherited poor RPIs and no RPIs and had to go from there. How we operate as an FM will build upon this information, so we need to be as accurate as possible in collecting it.

The asset name, size, and identifying information can usually be found easily enough. Look for data plates in the cases of building equipment or plans/blueprints in the cases of larger structures. From there, you will have to do more digging on the rest of the data. Typically, you can get help from your accounting department on costs and placed-in-service dates. You can find estimated useful life information on the internet by asset, but we will talk more about life-cycle analysis and replacements later.

As you gather the pertinent information, make sure your RPI is kept in a secure environment that is easily updated. I've seen everything from spreadsheets to complex cloud-based asset inventory systems. The bottom line: use what will work for you and what your organization can afford.

Chapter 3: Facility Condition Assessment

Now that you understand what you have, you need to understand what condition it is in. But how do we do that for every asset in every facility? For everything within the RPI, you need to compare its current condition with the baseline condition of when it was first put into service (when it was new, regardless of if that is when your organization first put it into service). This will give you a record of its condition and a working knowledge of what needs to be done to maintain the equipment over the course of its useful life. This will also tell you when that equipment might need to be replaced. The result is your new baseline and the process is called a Facility Condition Assessment.

A Facility Condition Assessment (FCA) is a thorough inspection of the facility or group of facilities to determine current condition. The FCA is only a snapshot of the condition of all facilities at one point in time, because conditions constantly change with continued use. The moment you "take the snapshot," each asset's condition begins to change, so keep that in mind.

The FCA is most easily accomplished through a team of specialists coming to your facility and conducting hands-on examinations of all identified real property assets. While it is possible to conduct the FCA in-house, I highly recommend hiring a professional team to do this. First, you need an in-depth knowledge of each system to accurately assess its condition and FMs typically don't have specialized expertise in all building systems. Second, a professionally packaged FCA will carry credibility when you use it to argue for funding. And third, the FCA takes some time to conduct and put together. I don't know of any FMs who can neglect all aspects of a job that requires constant attention to focus on conducting and completing a full FCA. That said, using a professional team costs money and if you don't have the funding, an in-house condition assessment is preferable to no assessment at all.

The most sensible way to put an FCA together is to group building systems by type (for instance parking lots in one section, roofs in another, and so on). Here is how my last FCA was organized:

- Executive Summary of the property, general findings
- Building types on property

- Condition of site improvements
    - Utilities
    - Parking lots and paving
    - Drainage systems
    - Topography and landscapes
    - General site improvements (fencing, exterior lighting, pools, etc.)
- Architectural and structural systems
    - Foundations
    - Building superstructure
    - Roofing
    - Envelope (walls, doors) and stairways
    - Patios and balconies
    - Circulation (corridors, common areas, etc.)
- Mechanical and plumbing systems
    - HVAC
    - Plumbing and domestic hot water
    - Gas distribution
    - Electrical
    - Elevators
    - Fire protection systems
    - Security systems
- Interior systems
    - Finishes (floor and wall coverings, paint, etc.)
    - Furniture, Fixtures, and Equipment (FF&E)
        - Customer furniture
        - Administrative furniture
        - Kitchen equipment
        - Light fixtures
- Other as appropriate

From there, each section was broken down by facility. For example, under roofing there would be a general assessment of the condition of each roof on each of the 13 buildings on site. It is beneficial to take a photographic record and include this as part of the FCA. As an FM, it helps to compare pictures from an older FCA to current conditions to determine how the facilities are aging. Not to mention, pictures sell better in the board room when you go to request funding for maintenance and repairs.

Finally, the FCA should include a recommendations section. The format is not as important as the information it contains. There should be a list of short-term recommendations, which are facility systems that must be addressed, typically within the next year. This should be followed by a list of long-term recommendations. We will get more into long-term planning in the next chapter, but the FCA should cover an estimation of repair and replacement activities (timeframe and cost) of all building systems over a period of time in the future with which you are comfortable. I use a 20-year timeframe and it will directly feed my 20-year capital plan.

Chapter 4: Facilities Master Plan

Now that you know the current condition of what you have, you can plan where to go in the future.

The Facilities Master Plan (FMP) is a long-term plan that describes the vision and direction of the organization, specifically in terms of facilities. The FMPs I have worked on projected one to two decades into the future. These plans are not created in a bubble or vacuum, however. The direction of the FMP will be steered through a larger vision (such as a strategic plan) at the organizational level.

Once again, this plan can be created by a team of professionals, which might be required depending on the scope and size of your facilities.

This plan differs from the recommendations in the FCA in several ways.

First, it examines how the existing facilities meet the requirements of all stakeholders now compared to the future. For instance, if the organization's strategic plan calls for unparalleled growth that will double the number of occupants in the facilities, the FMP will study what will be required to meet the increased demand. These requirements will probably include more building space and might also include things like IT infrastructure improvement, increased parking capacity, and a traffic study to name a few.

Second, the FMP will propose major projects to remedy identified facility shortfalls (for instance building expansions as identified in the scenario above). Other projects will be identified through interviews with stakeholders and surveys to determine future requirements apart from those already identified. For instance, the FMP might determine a completely new structure will be required to accommodate a new service offering like a fitness or daycare center.

Finally, the FMP will paint a picture of what the facilities look like when all plans have been accomplished. If the FMP is larger and includes a number of projects that will have to be accomplished over time, these can be broken down into phases as desired.

Large-scale FMP projects are generally contracted for large campus settings (i.e., college campus, military installations, government facilities, etc.), but the concept can be tailored to any FM operation, in any industry, at any level. There are numerous examples on the internet of completed FMPs and what they entail. Remember that the FMP is an evolving document and will change as requirements change. No matter what the scope of the master plan is, there has to be representation from all stakeholders during the planning process. This is typically accomplished by establishing a leadership team that meets during each stage of the FMP process.

Section Summary

Status quo, you know, is Latin for "the mess we're in".

~ *Ronald Reagan*

> The most successful facility manager I've ever met was a Colonel in charge of all FM activities for the Oklahoma National Guard. He accomplished more in advancing the future of Oklahoma's military facilities than any of his predecessors for one reason only: He refused to accept the status quo.
>
> He used a portion of the budget that was allocated to him from the National Guard Bureau every year to engage and finish small, medium, and large project designs. He did this because he knew a handful of states across America would not be able to execute all of their allotment each year, and he could take advantage of that. Instead of accepting the fact that his allotment of money for each fiscal year was a fixed amount, he was able to take his finished designs to National Guard Bureau and show them he could use the money the other states were giving back.
>
> It worked. He got additional money year after year and drastically improved the facilities for the state simply by refusing to accept the answer, "because it has always been done that way."

This section focused your attention on three basic steps: establish your RPI, conduct an FCA, and establish an FMP. I used terms that you may or may not be familiar with, but keep in mind it all boils down to identifying what you have, what condition it is in, and where to go moving forward. As long as you focus on these three things, you will set yourself up for success in managing your facility.

Of the three steps, the key to keep in mind is knowing where your organization is going in the future. Even if you know there is no room in your budget to outsource planning and there won't be any extra room in the coming budgets for capital improvements, it is still vital to have a plan with recommendations so that you can present them to your organization's decision makers when the time comes.

Maintaining the status quo is a recipe for failure. That's especially true in facilities because there is no status quo – everything is constantly changing. Even if you do the bare minimum and just make sure your equipment and facilities are running, they are getting one day closer to the end of their useful life for each day that goes by. Proactively managing facilities is vital to being a successful FM and that's what we will discuss next.

Section 3: Operations and Maintenance

Congratulations, now you know where your facility has been and where it's going. This is what I think of as macro-facility management. This is on the strategic level and it's what we always work toward. But what about the micro-level? What about those day-to-day operations we must accomplish that really don't have any direct impact on whether or not the strategic plan is accomplished?

Before we move forward, you need to understand what your facilities' end-users expect to get out of the facilities. What can the facility do for them? If you manage a medical facility, your end-users will expect vastly different things and have a different expectation of quality than if you manage a high-end travel destination in the hospitality industry.

What's the best way to figure this out? Ask.

I start with the workers in the facility. First, ask them what they do on a daily basis and how the facility could change to enable them to improve in their job performance. Second, ask them for feedback from customers they serve (I'm assuming the organization has customers who also use the facilities). Next, ask employees for recommendations. I don't care how great the past facility manager was, there is always room for improvement. Finally, incorporate guidance from your superiors, and don't be afraid to ask for clarification when it contradicts something you've learned from another stakeholder. Sometimes end-users and bosses don't really know what they want until they hear it from someone else. Knowing this, I like to steer the direction of the conversation whenever possible. Let them tell you what they need to accomplish in their job and then you make recommendations on how the facility can support that.

Now that we know what daily operations our facilities must support, we can tackle operations and maintenance.

Chapter 1: The Future of Maintenance

> My favorite vehicle I've ever owned was a 1985 Toyota Land Cruiser. I loved the smell of it and the feel of the manual transmission, both in-town and off-road. I remember pulling into my driveway, throwing it on some jack stands and changing the oil. I'm in no way, shape, or form an automobile mechanic. But with the Land Cruiser and a 1978 Chevy I had, I was able to do some basic repairs: new starter, new alternator, light transmission work, etc.
>
> I now drive a late model F-250 and I honestly don't think I could point to the starter to save my life. I wouldn't even take the thing to an independent mechanic. New vehicles these days are so complex we're forced to take them to the dealership where trained mechanics have the knowledge to maintain them (not to mention the specialty diagnostic systems and tools). As technology advances and our lives improve with convenience and efficiencies, equipment becomes harder to maintain. Facilities are becoming just like new cars.

Facility managers have a couple of problems now that we will continue to face more and more in the coming years. First, the institutional knowledge that has organically grown in these aging facilities will leave as maintenance personnel who have been around for decades retire. This presents a huge problem because they were there when the buildings were built or the utilities were laid or the equipment was installed and they know how to fix the things that break because they've worked on them countless times before. Gone are the days of maintenance technicians beginning a job at a facility and spending their entire career there. Really, this is a trend that is shifting across all industries as new generations enter the work force. I'm not an expert on generation gaps and work ethic; but, the desire for workers to stay at the same job for 30 years or more is fading as generations evolve.

Second, our facilities are going the way of the new cars. As technology pervades this profession more and more, we must embrace new ways to conduct maintenance and repair activities. For example, I use an Energy Management System (EMS) to monitor and control HVAC operations in two of my biggest facilities. This system allows me to remotely control all HVAC units and keep tighter parameters on energy management than with traditional thermostats. I whole-heartedly embrace the benefits of this system, but when any part of it goes down, I can't fix it. I am forced to call the EMS provider and they send a technician with specialized training in that system. Technology is starting to out-pace our abilities as facility managers to maintain and repair newer components with on-site personnel.

So, should we all panic? No of course not, but we should learn how to adapt to the changing environment. Just understand as you install systems that rely heavily on emerging technology, you will need to outsource certain repair activities. After all, changing and adapting is what we do as FMs.

Chapter 2: The Basics of O&M

About a week after I started my first full-time facility manager job with the Army, I accompanied my boss on a trip to National Guard Bureau to get the lay of the land. National Guard Bureau controls all of the money for federal facilities in the individual states for the National Guard. After being introduced to one particular program manager, she looked at me and asked, "Are you going to be focusing on O&M?"

I ever so eloquently replied, "uhhhhhhh……," with what I can only imagine was a look of complete befuddlement.

My boss chuckled and said, "Yes. He will be focusing on Operations and Maintenance."

This was not my proudest moment.

The term "operations" implies that the facility's infrastructure is used to create the environment that it was built to create. And the term "maintenance" implies the infrastructure is serviced so it operates consistently and safely, enabling the operations to continue. According to the WBDG, *operations and maintenance typically includes the day-to-day activities necessary for the building and its systems and equipment to perform their intended function. Operations and maintenance are combined into the common term O&M because a facility cannot operate at peak efficiency without being maintained; therefore, the two are discussed as one.*[5]

Maintenance activities consist of two types: planned and unplanned. Planned maintenance is any maintenance activity with a scheduled process where all costs, materials, and tools associated with it are available prior to beginning. Unplanned maintenance covers all other maintenance activities. Unplanned maintenance is typically the result of repairing a failed component or poor service quality. In FM, you will never eliminate unplanned maintenance. However, the goal should be to incorporate a comprehensive preventative maintenance strategy to reduce and limit repairs that occur at your facility. Preventative maintenance is regularly planned maintenance conducted on a schedule on equipment still in working condition to prevent it from failing unexpectedly.

Examples of preventative maintenance include anything from replacing filters in HVAC systems to lubricating required components of larger systems. If you are not familiar with how to set up a preventative maintenance system and your facility does not have one, a good place to start is with O&M manuals for each piece of equipment you maintain. These manuals include recommended maintenance schedules from the manufacturer. If you can't find the O&M manuals, try getting the model number from the equipment's data plate and searching it on the internet. Most O&M manuals are digitized and available online. If that doesn't work call the manufacturer, who will be able to point you in the right direction.

Legal Requirements

An important, but sometimes overlooked and never simple task for FMs, is to determine what legal requirements govern how you will manage your facilities. These requirements vary based on the type of facility, your industry, and the characteristics of your built environment.

> As the Facility Manager of a military installation, I could not for the life of me understand why certain buildings on post were required to conform to Americans with Disabilities Act (ADA) standards. Not that I have anything against ADA requirements, I just thought it was bizarre that the military refuses to allow individuals to serve who have certain limiting disabilities, but then requires its buildings to accommodate those standards. So, how in the world would anyone with a disability even be using the facilities on the military installation to begin with, if they weren't allowed to be in the military? But, ADA compliance is required and this was one set of requirements that I wasn't getting around.
>
> Alas…it wouldn't be the last time in my career that I would be wrong about something. Just because you can't belong to the military if you have certain disabilities doesn't mean that you can't be the family member of a service person and have a disability. And now after more than a decade of contingency operations, there are absolutely veterans who are disabled that were not when they joined the service.

The takeaway here is don't assume anything. Do your homework and err on the side of caution. If you have to assume, make the assumption that the law, regulation, or code applies to your facility – not the other way around.

The best way that I can tell a facility manager to go about doing this is to start small and expand. What I mean is start at the local level, look at the state level, and move to the national/federal level when looking at regulations, codes, and standards. Look at each type of facility that you maintain. If there is any chance it has an impact on public safety, it is covered. If you have a kitchen, there will be a health department. If you have an elevator, it will be inspected. If you have occupancy, you will most assuredly have fire detection and suppression systems (both of which require routine inspections and preventative maintenance). Remember to pay attention to environmental regulations. Occupational Safety & Health Administration (OSHA) law and regulations pertain to everyone. This will be discussed later in the safety chapter.

The good news is that your facility would not have existed before you without conforming to certain legal requirements. Look internally, ask questions, and go from there. No one has ever learned all applicable requirements overnight. Be diligent and don't give up.

One more thing you should consider is to really check legal requirements thoroughly when renovating a space. Obviously, you need to understand legal requirements during new construction, but renovations are sometimes overlooked. You might be grand-fathered now (meaning a new regulation has come out, which doesn't apply to you, since your facility existed before the requirement), but you won't be once you renovate. The good news is that most renovations require the use of engineers and/or architects who will also be researching applicable legal requirements as they design new spaces.

Chapter 3: Computerized Maintenance Management System

A computerized maintenance management system (CMMS) is a software package that maintains and manages information about the facility's maintenance operation. The CMMS can be hosted locally or on the web. Local hosting of the CMMS typically requires the end-user to purchase the software, install it on their servers, and maintain the system throughout its useful life. In contrast, web-hosted programs are hosted on an external server and maintained by the CMMS company.

I've used different CMMS options and there are advantages and disadvantages to both. The primary advantage for a web-hosted solution is that it can be more cost-effective with lower up-front costs. The biggest disadvantage is that all of your maintenance information is out of your control. Also, while it is cheaper in the near-term, keep in mind that you pay a monthly charge for the service for as long as you use it. I currently use a web-hosted software as a service (SaaS) application in which I had a very small up-front cost to set up the system, but pay a recurring monthly cost for hosting and support. I prefer this option because all upgrade and server maintenance is performed by the CMMS company.

Do you need a CMMS?

The short answer is absolutely. However, it really depends on how efficient you want to be. It is technically possible to be a facility manager without one, but these software packages make your job *much* more manageable. The basic functions of a CMMS are work order management, asset management, planned maintenance scheduling, and other modules that can be beneficial depending on which service you choose. In addition to managing these processes with considerably more efficiency, the major benefit to using a CMMS is the ability to pull reports on any of the functions it manages.

For instance, if I only use the work order management and asset management modules, I can assign the costs of labor and materials from each work order to a specific asset. I can then run a report and filter by asset type, location, dates, etc., to analyze and report to management how we are spending maintenance dollars. I also use this information in my life-cycle analysis to recommend an asset replacement strategy based off of a facility condition index (which we will cover later). Let's look at these modules in a little greater detail.

Work Order Management

This is the heart of the CMMS and will greatly aid in your success. This module is a portal where work orders are requested, managed, and closed through a web interface or smartphone app. The facility's work order manager (or FM if you don't have one) authorizes users and sets their level of responsibility.

For instance, I give every manager in our facility access to request maintenance work in their area of responsibility (the fitness manager sends in work orders for the fitness center, the tennis manager sends in work orders for the tennis center, etc.). The CMMS automatically emails me to let me know a work order has been scheduled. The work order then gets automatically routed and assigned to one of the maintenance technicians depending on the type of work order it is (lighting goes to one person, kitchen equipment goes to another, etc.).

The maintenance tech then opens the work order and responds accordingly. They have the option of adding notes (for instance if parts had to be ordered), adding their time and materials (if they had to repair it), and closing the work order when finished. When the work order is closed, it automatically emails the requester to let them know it has been completed. Assuming the work was performed on a building asset with a serial number, the costs are assigned to that asset for tracking and future reporting. This allows you to pinpoint exactly which pieces of equipment are costing the organization money when it comes time to recommend capital purchases.

Prior to this implementation, my facility used a system where a manager requesting a work order would need to call the receptionist, who would email a lady in accounting, who would print off an excel form with the information for the FM, who would give it to a technician, who would record time and materials on it and give it back to the FM when complete. As far as I can tell, the information was never tracked or recorded beyond that point.

Needless to say, our CMMS has been beneficial to the maintenance department. You want to know how much money we spent last year for HVAC repair in the main building? No problem. You want to know how much money we spent on materials for plumbing repair two years ago?

Easy. And yes, that type of information comes in very useful at times.

The work order module is the most important part of the CMMS (in my humble opinion). The different systems that I've worked with all record much of the same information, but you will want to make sure the modules you need are included in a CMMS before purchasing.

Also, be sure to evaluate and compare the ease of use when looking at purchasing a CMMS. The one I used at Camp Gruber took between five and 10 minutes just to close a work order. The CMMS I use now takes 30 seconds. While the one at Camp Gruber included more modules like budgeting and project management, I don't need those here. You can imagine how frustrating it would be to spend all of your time opening and closing work orders. At Camp Gruber, we hired a full-time work order administrator and it was still frustrating.

Asset Management

Not every CMMS has an asset management database integrated into it. That said, I would highly recommend getting one that does. You already know you need to keep an asset inventory. It just makes sense to keep it in the same program the facility uses to manage work orders so costs can be automatically assigned.

That said, I actually keep mine in two places for redundancy. The other system I use lets me geo-locate the assets on a series of digital floorplans as icons. I can turn each type of building system on visually by turning the individual layers off and on. To get more information about an asset, I simply click on the icon and the detailed information such as model/serial numbers, power requirements, photos, and O&M manuals pops up on the screen. It's pretty handy, but not necessary if you don't have the time or money to get a secondary system like this.

Planned Maintenance Scheduling

Putting your preventative maintenance strategy in a calendar helps to visualize what needs to be done and when. This module lets you put information into a digital calendar and assign it to an employee. When it's time for that employee to conduct the maintenance, the CMMS will automatically generate a work order and send it to the employee, give them a place to record their time and materials, and give you a record of the maintenance being performed. It takes some effort to set up initially, but will save you time in the long-run.

Other Modules

Other modules that might or might not benefit you as an FM are inventory management, budgeting forecasts, project requests, and more. If your facility does not currently have a CMMS and you intend to get one, start your search with work order management, asset management, and scheduling. Then, narrow down with additional modules that will benefit you in the future.

The biggest key with implementing a CMMS is to require its use by all employees. Be diligent, as it might take some time to change the habits of all employees, but it will pay off when they do. Don't allow them to fall into old habits such as calling in a work order or not closing one out. Implement the process and then stick to it.

Building Information Modeling

If your facilities are large and complex enough and you have the budget, an increasing presence in the industry is building information modeling (BIM). According to the National Building Information Model Standard Project Committee, BIM is *a digital representation of physical and functional characteristics of a facility. BIM is a shared knowledge resource for information about a facility forming a reliable basis for decisions during its life-cycle; defined as existing from earliest conception to demolition.*[6]

Think of BIM as a 3-D digital model of all facilities and systems contained therein that give the user information about the individual systems and allows the user to see how they relate to each other and the facility as a whole. While not essential for facility operations, it would be worth your time to look at BIM to see how technology is shaping the industry.

Chapter 4: Types of Services

Up until this point, we have learned O&M from the management side of things. Next, we need to put that into context with what the actual services are that comprise operations and maintenance activities. We will look at the two types of facility management services: hard services and soft services.

Hard services are those for the fixed asset systems of the facility that cannot be removed or separated from it. These systems include utilities, HVAC systems, the building envelope, etc. Soft services are those that satisfy the needs of the occupants. These are things like housekeeping, waste management, pest control, security, and emergency preparedness.

Management of Hard Services

These services will be a major focus for your facility management team as it is your responsibility as the FM to operate and maintain the fixed assets from acquisition to disposal (the asset's life-cycle). To the best of your ability, get involved in the acquisition process early. The earlier you are involved in acquisition, the more input you will have on the design of the asset. This will have a direct effect on how you will maintain the asset over the course of its useful life.

For instance, if you can be involved in the design and specifications of a new construction project, you will have input on what types of systems are installed. If you know one particular manufacturer's equipment is easier to maintain and less costly over the long-run, ask the designers to specify that manufacturer over the competition. This may sound crazy, but architects and interior designers don't typically pay much attention to the maintenance of building systems that must be performed after the project is complete. I've never understood this because the maintenance phase constitutes the vast majority of the asset's life-cycle. In contrast, professional engineers are generally better at designing systems with ongoing maintenance in mind, but it's always good to remind them along the way.

Asset Life-cycle

Every asset has a life-cycle, which is its useful life from acquisition to disposal. Inevitably, the facilities we manage will outlive their building systems. The facility manager is responsible for managing not only the maintenance, but also the replacement of these systems. Additionally, FMs replace components and systems for the purpose of improving performance or efficiency, which might occur prior to the end of the asset's useful life. Regardless of the reason, all replacement projections are put into a strategy referred to as a long-term capital renewal plan, which aids the FM in their budget forecasts and requests. There are three stages in the life-cycle:

- Acquisition – this begins the life-cycle of the asset. Once the asset is designed, procured, and installed according to specifications, it is placed in the RPI. Here, it is tracked through its useful life.

- Useful life – this stage encompasses the vast majority of the life-cycle. All O&M activities are performed and tracked during the useful life stage in the life-cycle. When the asset has reached the end of its useful life, it is disposed.

- Disposal – at the end of the asset's useful life, it is removed from service and sold, repurposed, thrown away, or recycled. If there is still an operational need for the disposed asset's purpose, the life-cycle begins again with acquisition of a replacement.

The useful life of an asset refers to two things. First is an asset's ***condition of service***. An asset is still within its useful life if it is functioning properly. If the asset is not functioning and cannot be repaired, it has reached the end of its useful life. Second is the asset's ***intended use***. Assuming it is functioning properly, an asset that is still meeting its intended purpose is within its useful life. If operations have changed and the asset no longer meets its intended use, it is no longer within its useful life.

Every asset has an estimated useful life (EUL). One easy reference for determining the EUL of building assets is by using EUL tables. If your department does not currently have an estimated useful life table for your existing assets, you can find examples on the internet. These are often used by accountants to determine how long to depreciate assets. FMs can use the EUL in conjunction with other tools to determine when assets will likely need to be replaced. This process is called life-cycle analysis. One tool that I have used many times in life-cycle analysis is the Facility

Condition Index (FCI).

Facility Condition Index

When I first became the facility manager in my current position, a 20-year capital plan had already been created. I thought that was a great starting place and it would point me in the right direction to modify and suggest alternatives to the current procurement strategy. However, I pretty quickly realized that the vast majority of the 20-year capital plan was not being followed.

The plan wasn't a bad one, there were just different priorities that would present themselves through the years and there was only a certain amount of money to go around to the various departments. Of all the departments, the FM department was not the biggest. So, what could we do about this? I knew that there was no way these competing demands would slow down over time, but there had to be a middle ground. I needed a tool to justify asset replacements and get the funding. The FCI is a great tool to help you with this.

The FCI is an equation that yields a ratio, quantifying the condition of a particular facility asset. The ratio is then given a rating of either good, fair, or poor and used in conjunction with the EUL to determine when to replace an asset. First published in the book *Managing the Facilities Portfolio* by the National Association of College and University Business Officers in 1991, the FCI rating scale identifies the ratings as good (< .05), fair (between .05 and .10) and poor (>.10).

The FCI is a very basic equation that compares repair costs to replacement costs. Here is the FCI formula:

FCI Ratio = Current Year Repair Costs of Asset ÷ Replacement Cost of Asset

As an example, if our department spent $500 to repair a fan motor and $500 to replace a condenser in June on one particular HVAC split system that would cost $6,200 to replace, the equation would look like this:

FCI = ($500 + $500) ÷ $6,200

FCI = .16

That is a poor FCI because .16 is greater than .10 in the FCI rating scale. However, that doesn't necessarily mean I'm going to replace the asset immediately. I use the FCI in conjunction with other information in order to make my recommendations for asset replacement. If that split system was beyond its estimated useful life and it was an inefficient system, chances are good I would recommend replacement. However, if the fan repair happened because of an external cause to the system (it was damaged by something) and the asset still had over half its useful life left, I would wait on recommending replacement.

So, looking back at the 20-year capital plan I inherited, I reworked the capital plan and updated it with the assets that had been overlooked and came up with a new timeline based on a budget amount that was realistic. I took some assets out that I knew would be replaced with major renovation projects that were already scheduled and gave everything else a replacement year in the budget. Now, every year when it comes time to finalize the capital budget, we look at the 20-year plan and conduct an FCI analysis. Based on the rating from the FCI ratio, we make decisions on whether or not to accept the replacement as planned or push the replacement into a future year. This gives me a great balance and a helpful management tool to argue why something needs to be replaced or how it could be delayed if another department has a valid requirement that wasn't previously forecasted.

Life-cycle Cost

Life-cycle cost (LCC) is the total cost of ownership of an asset during the entire life-cycle. This includes acquisition, operation, maintenance, support, and disposal and should be considered along with other tools (such as the FCI) when determining replacement. Examples of LCC costs include the initial capital investment (design, procurement, construction, etc.) and all recurring costs (O&M, energy consumption, consumable goods, etc.). Additionally, the FM should consider value-added items with LCC. An example of a value-added item would be if the asset increases productivity or adds to safety measures, which lowers insurance premiums.

When considering acquisition of a new asset, the FM needs to consider space requirements and potential for the new asset to meet growing demand as the business expands in addition to LCC. It might make more sense to spend more now to purchase an asset with more capacity than the current demand rather than purchase a bigger replacement asset later when the demand grows, but before the end of its useful life. Similarly, the FM should consider how important any given asset is to the operation when considering life-cycle replacements. If an asset is critical, it might move up in the priority of replacement over something that is not critical but has a higher FCI and is already past its useful life. Confidence in building systems is important for operations.

Once a determination has been made to replace an asset or acquire a new one, care should be taken to procure what is needed. This may or may not be the same thing that the end-user thinks they need. Determine what the operational need is first. Once you know the need, you can either source it directly or contract with professional services to engineer or design the solution. Keep in mind, if the need is new or has changed, there might be infrastructure changes required to place the asset in service. For example, if a larger piece of equipment is needed to meet growing demand, the facility might require upgrading part of the electrical system to accommodate the project.

Planned Maintenance

Planned maintenance is any scheduled maintenance activity to ensure an asset or system is currently operating correctly, avoiding unplanned maintenance activities. There are two types of planned maintenance: preventative (or preventive) and predictive.

Preventative maintenance (PM) – PM is servicing facility components that are currently in operating condition by allocating systematic inspection and correction of failures before they occur. PM includes activities such as routine inspections, grease/lubrication, filter replacements, etc. PM is planned based on time.

Predictive Maintenance (PdM) – PdM is the use of technology to determine the current operating condition of in-service systems to predict when maintenance should be scheduled. PdM can save costs over PM because maintenance is only performed when it is needed. However, the cost of technology used to evaluate the conditions must be considered as well as the cost to train staff in its use. PdM has been used synonymously with condition-based maintenance (CBM) in the industry. PdM activities include thermal analysis/IR imaging, oil analysis, etc. PdM is planned based on need.

To better understand the difference in the two, consider the car you drive. If you stick with the manufacturer's recommendations and get an oil change every 5,000 miles, you are performing PM by changing the oil at scheduled intervals (regardless of if it needs it or not, because sooner or later it will need it). If, however, you draw a sample of the oil every so often to evaluate its condition and perform the oil change only when it is required (regardless of the number of miles you have driven), you are performing PdM.

Unplanned Maintenance

Also known as reactive maintenance, unplanned maintenance is any maintenance activity that has not been scheduled and is triggered by a breakdown of some sort. Unplanned maintenance encompasses normal corrective actions, run-to-failures, and emergency maintenance. Corrective actions are repairs to systems that have failed or are in the process of failing (either a component or the system as a whole). Run-to-failure involves a conscious decision to not perform maintenance on the piece of equipment until correct maintenance is required. Run-to-failure is appropriate for situations that do not involve critical systems or components and where the cost to perform maintenance outweighs the benefit. An example of this would be a door closer that you replace when it fails. Emergency maintenance involves a corrective action to a critical component in the facility that would endanger people, processes, or facilities. An example of this would be a broken water supply line that would cause water damage within a facility if not repaired immediately.

It is up to each FM to try and balance planned an unplanned maintenance at their facility. You will never be able to completely eliminate unplanned maintenance, but you should be spending more time on planned maintenance to reduce the occurrences of repair activities. That said, more planned maintenance than is necessary would waste resources. It's up to the FM to understand their facilities, services, end-users, employees, and budgets well enough to balance the two.

Part of balancing maintenance is prioritizing efforts across facility management goals and responsibilities. To be sure, if you ever find yourself thinking that all maintenance is complete in your facility, it isn't. There is a never-ending list of tasks that need to be performed by the facility management team and these must be prioritized and done accordingly. In the same vein, the assets and building systems must be prioritized and maintained. This is part of recognizing and assigning work to your team. If necessary work extends beyond the capabilities of the internal FM team, you will need to determine whether hiring more employees is justified or whether you can contract the work to external organizations. That becomes a balancing act of its own.

So now that we understand the management processes of O&M, we need to get a basic understanding of the major types of facility systems that facility managers deal with on a day-to-day basis. I will first cover hard services for both grounds maintenance and building maintenance and then soft services for FM.

Hard Services – Grounds

Camp Gruber was eye-opening in many ways. The day I interviewed for the FM position there, I was already on the base for a training exercise. This exercise required the largest Army unit in the state to go to Camp Gruber, set up all of their giant tents, and conduct mission planning for two weeks straight. That alone sounds pretty normal, but what was weird was the fact that they set up their tents in the biggest parking lot on post.

You might not think anything of this, but these tents have to be staked down with long rebar stakes to keep them from blowing away. Follow me here. Camp Gruber allowed this unit to come in and drive countless rebar stakes into the asphalt parking lot.

In my interview, I couldn't stop thinking about those stakes and why they would allow that. I finally couldn't take it anymore.

After being asked what I would do to improve the facilities, I said, "Fill in the stake holes from the tents you have out there in the parking lot and not let them do it again."

As it turns out, the officer who had given them permission was one of my three interviewers.

I walked out of the interview, sure that I had screwed it up.

Luckily, I must have impressed in other areas because I got the job. That said, there were no more tents in parking lots for the next three years while I was there.

In this section when I refer to grounds, I am referring to facility systems outside of the building envelope. These include various forms of horizontal construction such as roadways and parking lots, utilities, street lights, road signs, fencing, pools, decorative structures, earthworks, bridges, waterways, etc. However, for the purposes of this guide, I'm going to focus on those systems that the majority of facility professionals can expect to maintain.

Horizontal Construction

> Horizontal construction is a term I learned in the military and for this guide it will encompass paved and unpaved surfaces constructed with earth-moving equipment. We don't readily think of roads and parking lots first when we discuss FM, but these are often the first impression users get at our facilities. They can also leave a very poor impression if a lack of maintenance has led to potholes in the pavement that damage cars. When I first arrived at Camp Gruber, we had a lot of gravel roads, some chip seal (combination of asphalt and fine aggregate), and some asphalt. Most of these were in poor condition because these types of surfaces require a lot of maintenance, especially with heavy military equipment using them. One of our higher priorities was replacing these deteriorating roads as quickly as possible. To do this, we needed to produce construction drawings through a civil engineer, bid the projects and construct them. I'll talk more about project management later, but we had the engineer design asphalt with an option for concrete and that's how they were bid. Each time after the bids came in, we were lucky enough to replace most of the roads in the main cantonment area with concrete over the next three years. We were able to do this because the costs for the concrete options were not that much more than the base asphalt bids. Horizontal construction is expensive and you absolutely want to get the most useful life out of it. It can be difficult to get money for this type of maintenance, but it will pay off in the long run if you fight for it.

A visual inspection of these surfaces will tell you how well they are being maintained. Concrete is very durable and requires little preventative maintenance. It should be kept clean when possible, free from harsh acids or de-icing chemicals, and can be sealed, if so desired. Asphalt, on the other hand, requires routine maintenance. Look for cracks, heaving, signs of potholes starting to form, etc. Asphalt surfaces should be sealed and cracks should be filled to lengthen the life. Depending on how much traffic the asphalt has seen, sealing every three to five years is a good rule of thumb. You will learn to know when it's time, but if you're not sure, get an opinion from a professional. If you see major signs of deterioration or settling, it might be time to repair part of the surface or replace it entirely. First, for signs of settling, you will want to get an opinion from a geotechnical engineer on whether or not the subgrade needs repair. Once you're confident in the subgrade, asphalt is laid in lifts where a lay-down machine makes passes along the road laying a set thickness of asphalt one pass at a time. Replacement options with lifts include placing a new lift on top of the existing surface as an overlay (1.5-2" thick), milling the top (removing the top of the asphalt surface to a set depth) and installing an overlay, or complete removal and replacement. Single potholes can be cut out and repaired individually.

Utilities

The first step in the maintenance of underground utility lines is to determine where your facility's responsibilities stop and where the utility company accepts responsibility for maintenance of the line. Typically, this is at the meter, but does not have to be. As an example, our facility purchased all of the switchgears and transformers on our property. Even though these are not on the utility company's side of the meter, the power company would ordinarily maintain them. However, we get a lower cost per kWh because we own and must maintain the equipment. If there is not a meter (as in sewer lines), there will be a point where responsibility shifts such as when the branch line on your property connects to the utility's main line.

The second step is determining your organization's strategy for maintaining the utilities. I use PdM for sewer lines and contract with the local utilities for maintenance on natural gas and electric lines (to include the switch gears and transformers that we own). PdM consists of routine inspections of manholes (check grouting and signs of deterioration) and smoke tests (looking for points of inflow and infiltration) for sewer lines. Inflow is when storm water enters the sanitary sewer system when it should be entering the storm water sewer system. Infiltration is groundwater that gets into the sanitary sewer system through leaks or cracks in the line. We perform yearly flow tests at fire hydrants and will do corrective maintenance on underground water lines when required.

These are examples of typical utilities you might be in charge of at your facilities:

- Electrical transmission systems (lines, switch gears, transformers, etc.)
- Fuel (natural gas, liquid propane, etc.)
- Potable water (drinkable, treated water supplying your facility)
- Sanitary sewer (sewer that treats waste water)
- Storm sewer (sewer that manages runoff from rain)
- Communications (phone lines, fiber optics, etc.)

Each system requires a different degree of maintenance and inspections. Like other real property assets, become familiar with what you have, where they are, and what their condition is first. Then research how to maintain them.

Other Exterior Real Property

Routine inspections should be performed by qualified FM staff to annotate the status of exterior real property such as signage, fences, decorative structures, lighting, etc. Look for signs of deterioration and failures. Incorporate PM activities to any site-specific systems that your facility employs (for example, we have gates for access control that must be maintained).

You also might be responsible for exterior equipment that requires maintenance contracts with specialized technicians. For example, I have had lightning detection systems at several facilities that required service level agreements (covered later) due to the training required to ensure operability of these safety systems.

Hard Services – Buildings

This section will focus on systems FMs will maintain inside (or as part of) the building envelope. Because the complexity of the various systems in the many different industries we maintain can vary greatly, I'm going to focus on principles of the most common systems you are likely to encounter.

Roofs

Roofing systems fall into one of two categories: pitched (those having a steep slope) or low-slope (commonly referred to as "flat"). Commercial pitched roof systems will commonly consist of shingles, metal, tile, etc. Many commercial facilities, however, employ low-slope roofs. These flat roofs are excellent places to hide other types of commercial building equipment to save valuable space inside the facility (such as HVAC equipment, generators, condensers, etc.). There are many different types of flat-roof systems, so I suggest having your roof inspected by a professional that can tell you its current condition and suggest a plan of maintenance for you.

That said, always look for tell-tale signs of weakening or failing roof systems. These can include cracks, blisters, shrinkage, loss of protective layer, damage other than normal wear, poor installation of other systems (points of penetration), leaking in rain (obviously), etc. The worst sign of a failing roofing component is a water leak. A water leak can be one of the most challenging things to repair simply because it is so hard to pinpoint a source. Then after you think you have it repaired, you won't really know until it rains again. One thing you can do, however, is water test your repair with a hose. That said, it is often hard to simulate the effects of rain combined with heavy winds in a thunderstorm.

HVAC

Heating, ventilation, and air conditioning (HVAC) systems regulate a space's temperature, humidity, and air quality. The basic theory is that there is some form of heat exchange between the system and the air to either remove heat from the air ("cool") or add heat to it. There are several different types of HVAC systems and I will cover the most common.

- Air Handling Unit (AHU) – this is a large metal enclosure that helps condition and circulate air to create a particular kind of atmosphere as part of the HVAC system. It usually contains a blower, heating or cooling elements, filters, dampers, and sound attenuators. This is then connected to ductwork used to distribute the air to the space (supply duct) and return the air back to the AHU (return duct).

- Makeup Air Unit (MAU) – a large AHU that conditions 100% outside air (does not recirculate any air). These are typically used in spaces where you cannot recirculate the air. Examples include hospital surgical rooms, commercial kitchen exhausts, and commercial paint booths.

- Packaged Unit (PU) – an AHU designed for outdoor use. A PU will contain all of its parts within one unit (heating and cooling).

- Roof Top Unit (RTU) – a PU designed to sit on the roof.

- Terminal Unit (TU) – a small system used to control the temperature of a single room. It contains a heating coil, cooling coil, and damper or a combination thereof. Think of these as those all-in-one wall units you may have seen in a motel room.

- Split System – a two component system, where the AHU is located inside and the condensing unit is located outside. Refrigerant lines run between the two. These are used commonly in modern residential construction for central heat and air.

There are many different components of the HVAC systems. Here are just a few:

- Boiler – heats water to generate steam for distribution. These are licensed and routinely inspected.
- Furnace – burns fuel to heat water or air for distribution.
- Heat Exchanger – transfers heat from one material to another.
- Chiller – a machine that removes heat from a liquid.
- Compressor – compresses refrigerant to the right pressure and temperature before passing it through the coil.
- Cooling tower – a heat exchanger that uses evaporation to reduce the water's temperature.
- Geothermal / Ground Source Heat Pump (GSHP) – a heat exchanger that uses the relatively constant temperature of the earth and a series of buried pipes as part of the HVAC system.

Ensure a qualified, licensed technician conducts the O&M activities on mechanical systems (aside from the owner's level of maintenance such as replacing filters). In addition to knowing how to service the system, anyone that handles refrigerant must be certified through the Environmental Protection Agency (EPA). Identify the types of systems in your facility and what maintenance options you have. From there, you can set your O&M strategy for HVAC.

Plumbing

Plumbing systems do two things: distribute liquids and gas and remove waste. O&M of plumbing systems is vital because the majority of the system is hidden and when a problem occurs, it can potentially cause a lot of damage. Again, qualified and licensed professionals should maintain these systems. There are potential safety hazards inherent in plumbing systems and knowledge of codes and maintenance practices is vital for success.

Examples of distribution components include:

- Sinks/Fixtures providing potable water (water that is suitable for consumption)
- Gas lines for fuel
- Fire suppression systems
- Water lines for certain HVAC equipment
- Fire hydrants
- Irrigation systems
- Valves and pressure regulators
- Water heaters
- Backflow preventers
- Booster pumps

Examples of waste components include:

- Sanitary sewer lines (for removal of sanitary or "black" waste)
- Storm sewer lines (for removal of rain/groundwater or "gray" water)
- Grease traps (these prevent grease and solids from getting into the sewer system and must be emptied periodically)
- Sink drains, floor drains, manholes, cleanouts
- Vents
- Lift stations

Conduct periodic routine inspections looking for small drips/leaks, signs of corrosion, safe temperatures, cracks, etc. of the distribution system where visible. Ensure leaks are reported and corrected immediately. Ensure grease traps are emptied routinely and check for unwanted sewer smells during walk-throughs (could be a sign of an empty p-trap or something more serious like a broken sewer line).

Electrical

Electrical systems generate and distribute power. Only qualified, licensed technicians should maintain these systems. Safety is paramount when working on an electrical system. As the FM, ensure that anyone working on an electrical system uses a lockout-tagout (LOTO) procedure. LOTO is a safety procedure that safeguards workers from coming in contact with hazardous electrical energy while working on a piece of equipment or component of an electrical system. You can find OSHA's standard for LOTO in 29 CFR 1910.147.

There are many potential components of an electrical distribution system, but here are some of the most common:

- Switchgears
- Transformers
- Meters
- Wiring, panels, receptacles, switches
- Protection devices – circuit breakers, GFCIs
- Lights/Emergency lights
- Generators

PM is very important for electrical components and PdM (such as IR technology to see if circuits are overheating) can help you detect potential failures before they occur. Routine inspections should include looking for any moisture intrusion, proper grounding, proper connections, corrosion, clean equipment, overloaded circuits, etc. I will talk about ways to reduce electric consumption in a later section.

One additional thing you can do to increase safety around electrical equipment is to have an arc flash hazard analysis. An arc flash is the light and heat produced from an electric arc. This is a rapid release of energy caused by an arcing fault between a phase bus bar and neutral, ground, or other bus bar. I mention it because it can cause severe injuries. The arc flash analysis will label the electrical equipment with potential energy ratings and personal protective equipment required when working on them. Consult NFPA 70E for more information.

Conveyance

Conveyance systems include elevators, escalators, moving walkways, etc. They also include conveyance for things and goods such as conveyor belts in manufacturing. Because of the safety and permit requirements of some of these systems, I find that a maintenance contract is of great benefit to our facility. Whether or not you decide to go this route, routine maintenance absolutely has to be performed on these systems and care must be taken to ensure the safety precautions are in place in the event of an emergency. For elevators, communications equipment must be installed and functional for permitted use. Depending on the size of your facility, elevators will be programmed to respond a certain way in the event of an emergency. Generally, these will need to go into a fire service mode where they automatically return to a fire recall floor (such as the ground floor) when a trigger such as a smoke sensor is activated.

Building Envelope

By the term "building envelope," I'm referring to the walls, doors, windows, stairs, roof (the structure, not the waterproofing application), façade, etc. Periodic inspections for façade cracks and separation at the ridges and soffits can indicate foundation movement. Exterior painting and sealing must be maintained for aesthetics and functionality. Also, check waterproofing elements around penetrations for deterioration. Windows should be caulked and cleaned and checked for seal failures and cracks. Door systems should be checked for operability, functional latching systems, leaking closers, and lubrication. Automatic door sensors and buttons might also need adjustments. Guttering should be free from debris and intact.

Communications and IT

These systems are critical systems for your facilities. When your users and systems cannot communicate, they must be fixed as soon as possible. They include phone (POTS or VoIP), fiber optics, internet, data centers and servers, radio transmission, cellular service, satellite, lightning detection, fire alarm systems, audio-video equipment, etc. These systems can be very simple to very complex. Technology in this industry is constantly improving and changing. These systems are also very likely the backbone of many of your FM processes from maintaining a CMMS to controlling HVAC equipment through an EMS.

In regards to the phone system, I will cover three types. The first is POTS, or plain old telephone service. This was the standard in homes for many years and can still be found in many homes today. However, this is not suitable for commercial purposes. The second type is the public switched telephone network (PSTN) that runs on traditional copper wiring. This is similarly reliable, but requires an on-premises PBX (private branch exchange) in order to enable features such as call forwarding between offices and call directories.

The problem is that many phone companies are moving away from these in order to sell their more expensive cloud-hosted solutions. This brings me to the third type, VoIP, or voice over internet protocol. VoIP is essentially a phone service using your internet. These systems do have benefits such as ease of use and added features, but they are typically expensive to operate (these usually now require a hosting and maintenance agreement with your service provider) and are less reliable. If you lose internet, you lose phone service. Also, they eat bandwidth, so make sure you have enough before going this route or your data speeds for computers will slow down considerably.

These systems may or may not fall under your control as an FM. In my current position, I control part of these systems, but not all of them. At Camp Gruber, an IT staff provided most of these services and I only controlled those communications systems specific to FM (such as the mass notification system as part of the fire alarm system). While larger facilities will probably have IT staff to either completely control or greatly help maintenance of these systems, it is important to understand all communications systems that your facility has and who is responsible for maintenance. Even if you are not directly responsible for communications, chances are you are responsible for the facility that the equipment is in. Thus, you will need to have an understanding of what there is and who to speak with when issues arise.

Furniture, Fixtures, and Equipment

Facility managers can't forget about all of the FF&E in their facility that is not permanently affixed. The maintenance of these assets will vary greatly and will depend on what their intended function is, what the manufacturer recommends, and to what condition your organization expects all of these assets should be maintained. I will go more into FF&E later, but understand this maintenance also falls under hard services for buildings.

Management of Soft Services

Once again, soft services are those services that satisfy the needs of your facility's occupants. They fall underneath O&M because these are the services that revolve around the real property and building systems belonging to your facility. Soft services occur largely in the background and as such, many FMs ascribe to the "no news is good news" philosophy as far as feedback from end-users. That means, if no one is complaining about it, then there's a good chance you are satisfying the needs of your occupants. Examples of soft services that you might be responsible for include:

- Groundskeeping
- Custodial work
- Waste management
- Security
- Emergency management
- Laundry
- Fleet management

While hard services can also be contracted out, it is common to outsource a bulk of these soft services in many facilities. Third-party companies can be contracted to perform one or more service, which can be a great force multiplier for your facility's needs. Benefits include paying one lump sum for a service and letting the third-party manage employee issues such as staffing levels during peak season and administrative details. One possible negative, however, might be that outsourced labor won't fit in with the culture of your organization. This could lead to a negative perception of these services if they are not meeting the occupants' needs. Deciding whether or not to outsource facility management soft services should be determined by your organization, occupant expectations, and budget.

Contracting outside services is conducted through use of service level agreements (SLA). SLAs are official commitments between some form of service provider and a customer. They contain a statement of work and specifications that detail the quantity, quality, and responsibilities of the provider. The SLA is the governing document you will use as the facility manager to ensure you are getting the specified level of service. You should ensure that the SLA is thorough and specific. SLA templates can be found online, but chances are your organization will have its own version if it has contracted services before.

Groundskeeping

Eyes wide as dinner plates, I listened as the outgoing facility manager explained how it was now my responsibility to maintain the 33,027 acres Camp Gruber enveloped. I thought there would be no way in the world I would be able to keep up with that as I pictured eating, sleeping, and dreaming about mowing grass.

But, sure enough it had been done before and I was able to manage. Truth be told, the vast majority of that acreage is comprised of training areas that are wooded and don't require much maintenance except for the gravel roads that connect them and the occasional controlled burn. On top of that, there were many ranges that were maintained by a different group on post, solely responsible for range maintenance. When it came down to it, there were only a few hundred acres that we really had to be diligent about and I was able to hire seasonal workers during the growing season to help control the landscape.

I relate this to reiterate one point in particular. Facility management can appear daunting, especially if you've really never done something that's all encompassing like the FM role is. That said, it is not too big of a task for anyone. Depending on what your particular functions are as an FM, you will be able to analyze and choose the strategies and means that work best for you in your organization.

For this guide, I will define groundskeeping as the act of maintaining an outdoor area for function or aesthetics. Sometimes referred to as landscaping, groundskeeping encompasses some of the following:

- Mowing and trimming

- Pruning trees
- Planting flowers, plants, etc.
- Irrigation activities
- Snow and ice removal
- Picking up debris

Whether you outsource groundskeeping or use in-house labor, it is a very important aspect of maintaining the built environment. It is often the most noticeable and first thing visitors see when arriving at your facility. Even if you work in a facility where aesthetics are not as important to the operations as mine, you will still want to place an emphasis on effective groundskeeping procedures. Groundskeeping also serves to help with rodent control, fire prevention, and safety measures. It is also helpful to ask your groundskeepers to keep an eye out for irregularities in other systems while they are performing their daily duties (e.g., exterior water leaks).

Custodial Work

The cleanliness of a facility will be an FM priority regardless of the industry you are in. The level of service, required duties, frequency, and scope will vary greatly, however. Some examples of possible custodial duties include the following:

- Sweeping, mopping, vacuuming
- Dusting
- Cleaning windows
- Emptying trash cans
- Restocking supplies (hand towels and tissue paper in restrooms, for example)
- Changing linens
- Cleaning equipment used by occupants

Waste management activities can fall underneath the custodial umbrella or might be their own separate department. Waste management encompasses garbage disposal, waste management (such as the emptying of a grease trap or the disposal of chemicals), and recycling services for the facility. Key to this soft service is the proper disposal of these types of waste. If you're not sure how to dispose of certain materials (like old paint), ask local sources.

Checklists are extremely helpful for custodial work. These tasks tend to get monotonous and some things are easily overlooked or skipped intentionally. If you incorporate checklists into employee procedures, they will know exactly what is expected and you will know if it has been done by looking at the list.

Security

While any security equipment (such as cameras, fences, locks, etc.) will likely fall in the facility manager's hands to maintain, the scope of security services might or might not. It is important to understand the needs of the organization with respect to security (for instance, how sensitive the organization's mission is) before planning security operations. Security planning begins with conducting a threat assessment, which looks at likely threats to the facility, determines the seriousness of those threats, and then mitigates them through intervening measures, processes, and security tools to provide both proactive and reactive security measures.

Proactive security measures consist of activities that actively prevent breeches in security. Examples of these types of measures include foot patrols of the campus, guards checking identification at a gate prior to allowing access, and actively monitoring security cameras to detect security threats in real-time. Reactive security measures consist of those activities that allow a response after a security threat has occurred. Examples of this include a passive alarm system or recording security camera feeds that can be accessed after they have recorded an incident in the past.

Because all people want security to some degree, your organization will have some form of security measures in place. One thing to remember if asked to recommend security measures for potential threats is this: as you increase security, you tend to lose freedom. If you install a gate with a guard at the entrance to your property, it will slow down every user at your facility while they attempt to gain access. If you create a stand-off distance from the facility to the parking lot, that is a longer walk every occupant will have to make each time they come and go. Just like we lose freedoms in society as national security measures are tightened for various reasons (like airport security protocols), so too will your occupants lose freedoms as the facility's security increases.

Once you determine the security needs of your facility, you must document all processes and use of security tools in a standard operating procedure (SOP). An SOP is a document that governs (barring any special circumstances or orders) how the personnel charged with executing the security mission of the facility will do their job. It should include everything from conduct, uniform, and training to checklists, reporting, and use of force. Emergencies must be included either as part of the security SOP or in reference to the organization's emergency action plan. That said, security must know exactly what they should do when an emergency occurs, because many occupants will look to them as the on-site first responders.

Security is a vital function within an organization and it must be considered hand-in-hand with emergency operations. As the facility manager, you will definitely have input on emergency operations of your organization. We will cover emergency management as part of the next chapter.

Chapter 5: Life, Health, Safety

Life, Health, Safety (LHS) refers to all of the facility's systems that preserve and protect the life, health, and safety of the occupants and facilities you manage. Your scope in LHS as a facility manager can vary greatly. If you have a safety department in your organization, your involvement might be limited to consultation on building systems. Other FMs will be directly responsible for all safety practices and serve on or lead their organization's safety committee. Health care facility managers have their own certification through the National Fire Protection Association (NFPA) called the Certified Life Safety Specialist (CLSS-HC) for Health Care Facility Managers. Building systems that have a major impact on LHS can include the following:

- Ingress/egress of the facility
- Emergency lighting
- Fire alarms
- Fire suppression
- Fire extinguishers
- Automated external defibrillator (AED) devices
- Exhaust fans
- Personal protective equipment (PPE)
- HAZMAT storage and disposal
- Compressed gas
- Fall protection
- Security systems (cameras, access control, etc.)

This list is not all-inclusive, but gives a good idea of what systems to consider when looking at LHS. Many safety systems fall underneath the umbrella of security.

A great place to start with LHS is the NFPA 101: Life Safety Code®. This is a standard that covers *strategies to protect people based on building construction, protection, and occupancy features that minimize the effects of fire and related hazards.*[7] The NFPA 101 is also beneficial because it covers both new and existing structures. It addresses provisions for *all types of occupancies, with requirements for egress, features of fire protection, sprinkler systems, alarms, emergency lighting, smoke barriers, and special hazard protection.*[8]

The next resource to look at with respect to LHS is OSHA. OSHA was created by the Occupational Safety and Health Act, signed by President Richard Nixon on December 29, 1970. The goal of the act is to ensure private and public employers provide their employees with a safe and healthful environment. OSHA has spelled out many specific safety requirements in a list of standards that you can find at **https://www.osha.gov/law-regs.html**. Examples of specific standards are head protection, foot protection, PPE, fall protection, etc. In addition to all of the OSHA standards, *employers must comply with the General Duty Clause of the OSH Act, which requires employers to keep their workplace free of serious recognized hazards.*[9] The General Duty Clause is essentially a catch-all that is used in inspections where a hazard is present, but not specifically covered under other OSHA standards.

Any FMs would also benefit from attending an OSHA training course. These are offered as 10-hour and 30-hour courses in both construction and general industry. The 10-hour courses are designed for more of an entry-level employee with the 30-hour courses geared more toward supervisors with a role in safety. I have never done the 10-hour course, but the 30-hour course will cover in detail OSHA, their inspection process, regulations, citations and penalties, establishing a safety program, and specific topics in depth such as LOTO, fall protection, confined spaces, noise exposure, HAZMAT, bloodborne pathogens, etc.

For hard services maintenance on LHS systems, code will dictate a lot of what we do as FMs. Fire systems must be inspected and tagged on a routine basis. AEDs have manufacturer specific expiration dates for pads and batteries must be checked routinely. Ingress/egress requirements are dictated by code. The list goes on and on. The two resources above will point you in the right direction with respect to LHS and your systems. From there, identify what you have and how they will be maintained as part of your overall FM strategy.

One requirement from OSHA is that the employer must conduct a hazard assessment. The tool to use in order to meet this requirement is called a job hazard analysis (JHA) (sometimes also called a job safety analysis (JSA)). I've seen different formats for this and in the military, we use something called a deliberate risk assessment worksheet. Regardless, the process is essentially the same. The JHA focuses on the worker (the individual who could potentially be injured), what they are doing (the job or task), what they are doing it with (the tools), and where they are doing it (the environment). The JHA lists all of the steps involved in the task and evaluates these four components in order to identify any hazards that exist.

The goal is to then find ways to mitigate those hazards in order to make the job safer for the employee. Ways to mitigate work hazards typically fall into one of these three categories:

- Engineering Controls – when possible, the facility manager should engineer controls into a job that make it physically impossible for the worker to be harmed by the hazard. Examples of engineering controls include guards on moving machinery parts, physical barriers preventing employees from entering dangerous areas, etc. This type of control is something that is engineered into the facility itself and not something that the employee must remember.

- Administrative Controls – when implementing an engineering control is not possible, FMs should implement administrative controls to protect employees. These are processes or procedures that must be followed by all employees when undertaking a job or task. LOTO is an example of an administrative control.

- Personal Protective Equipment (PPE) – PPE is the third layer of protection and the last control to consider. PPE can be gloves, masks, hearing protection, suits, etc. It is anything that the employee uses or wears that protects them from an identified hazard. Examples include wearing earplugs in a noisy environment or hearing and eye protection when using a loud piece of equipment that could throw projectiles.

Additionally, organizations must have written plans specific to their facilities. Think of these as general administrative controls covering the entire organization. These plans include an emergency action plan, hazard communication, LOTO, PPE, bloodborne pathogens, use of respirators, confined space entry, etc.

When an injury does occur, there is a good chance that it must be recorded and reported. OSHA Form 300 is a log of work-related injuries and illnesses used to classify injuries, their extent, and severity. Records must be maintained for five years and be posted every February through April on OSHA Form 300A. Rules and time limits on recordkeeping can be found at **www.osha.gov**. The full regulation is 29 CFR 1904. In addition, an organization should investigate injuries and determine if one of the above mitigation controls can be used to make the workplace safer. It is good practice to find out who in your organization is responsible for record keeping and investigations since a large part of your job as an FM is centered on safety.

Finally, facilities must maintain and update safety data sheets (SDS). Every chemical in your facility must have an SDS on file, which will provide information about that chemical, including substance identification, safe handling and storage, use, what to do if a worker comes in contact with the chemical, etc. You should know where these are kept and who is responsible for updating the records.

Emergency Management

Emergency management is the proactive planning and management of unscheduled events or natural disasters that can impact occupants, operations, or the facilities you manage. The goal of emergency management is to reduce the facility's vulnerability to hazards and increase its ability to cope with disaster. Emergency management will never eliminate all threats, but it will increase disaster response effectiveness. Potential emergency threats include fire, natural disasters (earthquakes, flood, tornadoes, hurricanes, etc.), active shooters, sabotage, terrorism, industrial accidents, etc.

Similar to managing safety and risk (discussed in the project management section), the first step in emergency management is to identify the potential emergencies that could occur and impact your facilities directly. I do not have a plan to react to a hurricane in Oklahoma, but I definitely have a plan for tornadoes.

Next, the facility uses this information to create an emergency action plan (EAP). An EAP is a document required by OSHA standards and is written in 29 CFR 1910.38(a). The purpose of the EAP is to outline what employer and employee responsibilities are during workplace emergencies. According to OSHA, *putting together a comprehensive emergency action plan that deals with those issues specific to your worksite is not difficult. It involves taking what was learned from your workplace evaluation and describing how employees will respond to different types of emergencies, taking into account your specific worksite layout, structural features, and emergency systems.*[10]

At a minimum, OSHA mandates that the EAP must include the following:

- *Means of reporting fires and other emergencies*

- *Evacuation procedures and emergency escape route assignments*
- *Procedures for employees who remain to operate critical plant operations before they evacuate*
- *Accounting for all employees after an emergency evacuation has been completed*
- *Rescue and medical duties for employees performing them*
- *Names or job titles of persons who can be contacted*[11]

You should ensure that any other facility-specific details are included in the EAP as required. An example of this might be the location of shut-offs to utilities that might be required in the event of an emergency. You also could consider including alarm panel locations and instructions needed by someone who responds to that panel. Our facility's EAP has building diagrams with egress routes to employee gathering locations where attendance can be taken by their direct supervisors and reported up to management. Make copies and don't store them all in the same location. A digital backup of the EAP is also recommended.

Section Summary

By failing to prepare, you are preparing to fail.

~ Benjamin Franklin

This section has presented an overview of the operations and maintenance basics, how to manage its activities, and the most common hard and soft services that a new facility manager can expect to either directly control or at least be a part of to some extent. O&M is vital to the health of the organization. As a facility manager, your job is to tailor your O&M strategy to the needs of your organization and ensure that all of the facility assets are meeting their intended purpose.

I look forward to hearing how you have taken the massive task of planning your O&M strategy and applied it to your specific needs. And I would love to know what new processes and tools you are using to make your FM department more efficient in terms of operations and budget.

In the next section, we will tackle a very large subject that you will most certainly need to understand as a growing facility manager: project management.

Section 4: Project Management

Of all the things I've done, the most vital is coordinating the talents of those who work for us and pointing them toward a certain goal.

~ Walt Disney

My family has a huge problem (my wife and I maybe even more so than our two children). We drank the proverbial Disney Kool-Aid and now scramble frantically each year to find various ways to hand over as much money as we can afford to the House of Mouse to share the "magic." I tried to resist. I told Leslie before our first trip to Walt Disney World it would be our last. I told her to plan everything she wanted to do because there was no way we would spend that much money on a vacation ever again. I have never been more wrong.

How is it that a man with a dream overcame such adversity to build, in my opinion, the greatest experience in hospitality in existence today? I have great respect for what Walt Disney was able to create. If he said the most vital thing he did was coordinating efforts to achieve certain goals, there is something to it. That's the entire crux of project management.

As an FM professional, learning to be a successful project manager (PM) will be invaluable. The reason project management is its own profession rests in the value of the process and the results it will yield. It is a specialized skillset that must be practiced once it is learned because knowing how to successfully manage projects brings great value to your organization. I absolutely love puzzles -- and project management is really just solving puzzles. That's why it is one of my favorite parts of the job.

As a facility manager, you can expect to constantly be involved in projects in one of three roles. First, you might very well be the PM on any number of projects for your facility. Second, you might be the owner's representative during a project and deal directly with the PM of an outside organization such as a general construction contractor. Third, you might be part of a project management team within your organization. In any case, I highly recommend learning the fundamentals of project management. Then you can lead, direct or be a valuable contributor.

This section will give you the fundamentals of project management. To really develop these skills, you should research the subject through the Project Management Institute (PMI®) at **www.pmi.org** and become familiar with their processes to manage projects. PMI®, a not-for-profit organization founded in 1969, is the leading membership association for project management professionals.[12] The organization maintains and sells "A Guide to the Project Management Body of Knowledge" (PMBOK® Guide), commonly referred to as the PMBOK® (pronounced "pim-bok"). The PMBOK® is an incredibly thorough textbook that details everything you would ever need to know about the technical processes of project management. It is a thick book and a great place to get a lot of details. Once you gain experience in the field, I recommend looking into earning your Project Management Professional (PMP®) credential. Credentials in the FM community add credibility to your experience, plus you learn a great deal going through the process.

Chapter 1: An Introduction to Project Management

According to PMI®, *a project is a temporary endeavor undertaken to create a unique product, service or result. Project management, then, is the application of knowledge, skills, tools, and techniques to project activities to meet the project requirements.*[13] So, let's take that one step further in our understanding of what constitutes a project, because this is commonly misunderstood.

Two things in this definition stand out to me. The first is that a project is ***temporary***. To go through all phases of project management, you have to have a beginning, middle, and end. You can define a project in other terms, but the intent is the same. It will be impossible to define a project accurately without a beginning, middle, and end. To me, this is the easiest way to understand the many complex requirements of project management and this is how I will explain it here.

The second major stand-out in the definition above is that a project creates something ***unique***. As an FM professional, you'll be able to define a beginning, middle, and end to a lot of routine tasks you do or assign to others. That said, a routine task does not yield a unique result and thus, is not by definition a project.

Moving forward in this section, I will explain project management in terms of three major phases (beginning, middle, and end) that encompass different sub-phases. Each sub-phase will in turn have steps within them. Before defining them, let's look at the different attributes of projects.

Attributes of a Project

No matter whose definition you use, a project is a workflow with many sequential activities. Phases within the work flow will likely have inputs and outputs, where the inputs of one phase are in fact the outputs of a previous phase. Likewise, the outputs of a particular phase become the inputs of a subsequent phase. To illustrate this point, Figure 2 below shows a basic project workflow I created to explain the process to one of my committee members before embarking on a large Design-Bid-Build (DBB) Project. Each box in Figure 2 represents milestones in this particular project's workflow that committee members needed to know.

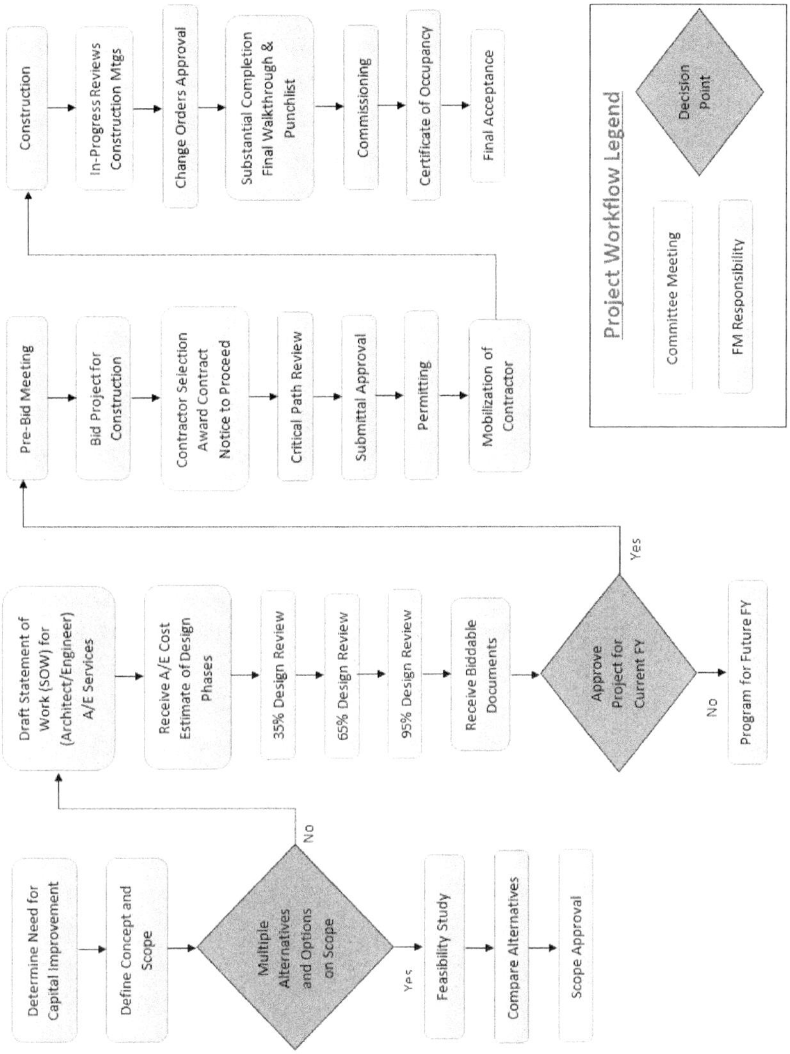

Figure 2

In this workflow, the input to the "Receive A/E Cost Estimate" step is the Statement of Work (SOW). The SOW is the output from the previous step. The cost estimate for design services is the output of the "Receive A/E Cost Estimate" step and is then approved, renegotiated, or declined prior to moving into the design phase.

If you are new to project management, you probably are unaware that I cut a lot of processes out of Figure 2 prior to showing it to the committee member. As you can probably imagine, there can be a lot that goes into "Define Concept and Scope." I write this to illustrate a very important point. Project management is extremely detailed and not every stakeholder wants or needs to know every detail. As a PM, it is important to understand project processes and apply them to situations as required. The simpler you can explain the process to stakeholders, the easier your job will be during the project life cycle.

The flip side of this point is that many people believe project management is easy. It isn't. In fact, many times it feels like organized chaos -- and sometimes finishing a project on time comes down to sheer luck.

If we go back to the definition of a project and remember it provides a unique result, then we understand the project life cycle itself will be unique. It must be tailored to the desired result. This means as a PM, you are applying a standardized process, but tailoring it to the situation.

Projects often require you to "think outside the box." Try the following exercise. Look at the nine dots in Figure 3. Attempt to connect all nine dots, using four straight lines -- without removing your pen from the page. See Figure 4 on the following page for the solution.

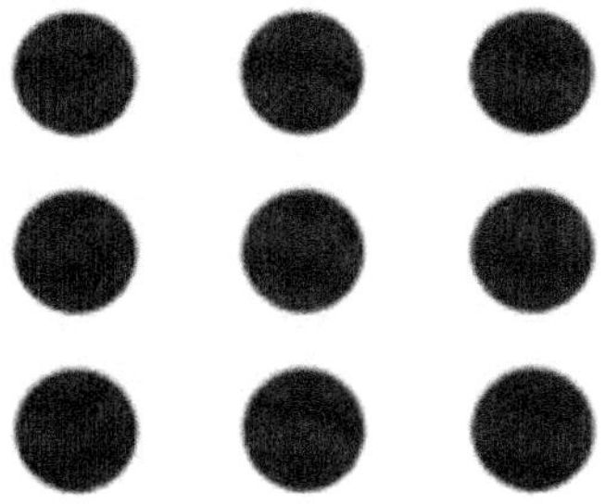

Figure 3

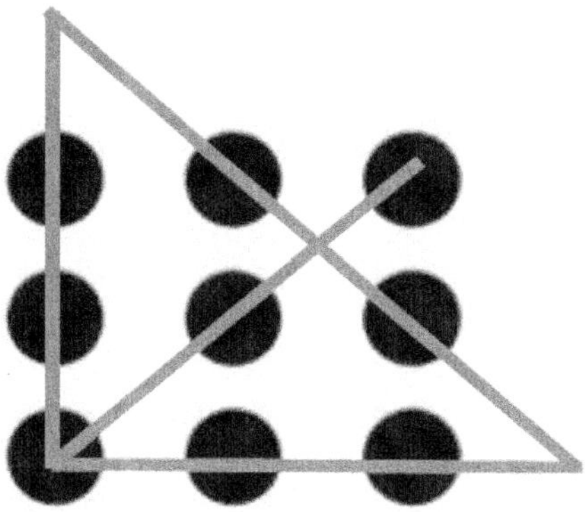

Figure 4

This exercise illustrates a literal way of thinking outside the box, but the point is the same. Many times, the solution to the problem is not right in front of you. It is our job as PMs to manage problems and solutions with all necessary stakeholders to determine the best path forward. Here is where your puzzle-solving skills will come into great use.

> In projects, flexibility is key. There is a military adage commonly attributed to 19th Century Prussian General Helmuth von Moltke. He said no battle plan survives contact with the enemy. One reason I believe the United States Army is so successful is because flexibility is a tenet of operations. Detailed instructions exist for every job in the Army. Everything Soldiers are expected to do, from cleaning weapons to complex tactical maneuvers, is spelled out in regulations. Army staffs spend countless hours using those regulations to plan operations in fine detail, but then retain the flexibility to completely throw the regulations and plans out the window when they don't work. My point is that you can plan every aspect of a project, but it will never go exactly as you anticipate once you begin to execute. So have the flexibility to adapt and change accordingly.

Projects involve risk. As the PM, one of your many jobs will be to identify and manage risk. I have yet to see a project that does not involve some type of risk. We will discuss different ways to mitigate risks, but you should understand the need for a risk management strategy.

Projects do not exist in a vacuum. Projects involve multiple stakeholders and will almost certainly require input from outside the facilities management team. For example, our last major renovation involved four separate departments of employees, representation from end users of the building (members of the club), architects, engineers, general contractors, subcontractors, the local health department, the local planning and development office, the local fire marshal, and numerous suppliers. Decisions made without considering the impact for every stakeholder inevitably will result in a negative impact to other aspects of the project. At best, these negative impacts cause minor delays. At worst, they can lead to budget overruns and deliverables that don't satisfy the requirement.

Projects require you to start at the end. What I mean by this is that in order to plan how to get somewhere, you have to know where you're going. We will discuss this in more depth, but know that to effectively manage a project, you have to first define the success criteria. That means, you have to know what result, deliverable, or outcome you want to achieve upon completion. This is also helpful because it clearly explains the end of the project.

Projects can have different project management frameworks based on circumstances. Using one framework over another will not necessarily doom your project to failure, but this is where flexibility comes in. Your organization might dictate using slightly different phases than I will describe below and that's okay because what I describe here is a way, not the way. The framework that follows in this book is how I digest and understand project management. I have both studied and been actively involved in project management with multiple organizations for more than 15 years. As scary as it is, the framework described here mirrors how I think. That said, I welcome input to any of these ideas. We can all improve how we approach our projects and if you have any suggestions, please visit **www.LearningFM.com** and get in touch with me. I will absolutely consider them for future editions of this guide.

The Framework

The basic project management framework consists of the following:

1. Beginning
    - Initiation
    - Planning
2. Middle
    - Execution
    - Supervision and Control

3. End
    - Closure

As previously stated, different organizations have slight variations of the framework, but the basic ideology remains. Let's dive into these five sub-phases in more detail to get a general understanding of what each one entails.

Initiation – Initiation is the process of getting the project started. Initiation activities include defining the problem that the project will address, obtaining approval for the project, and identifying the stakeholders who will have input or be affected.

Planning – Planning is the process of establishing how all facets of the project will the executed. Planning activities include defining the project scope and required deliverables, developing the project schedule, developing the project budget, determining how to manage quality, determining how the team will be assembled, identifying communications requirements, risk analysis and mitigation, planning procurements, and determining how to manage stakeholders.

Execution – Execution encompasses any activities required to complete the plans.

Supervision and Control – Supervision and control refers to the process of overseeing, reviewing, and modifying work through all phases of the project. This also encompasses managing the change order process.

Closure – Closure is the process of finalizing activities and archiving all records from the project. It formalizes the end of the project.

It's important to keep in mind that while these sub-phases follow a sequential project life-cycle where one typically happens before another, overlap definitely occurs. For instance, a PM will absolutely engage in supervision and control during all sub-phases to ensure adherence to quality standards. It wouldn't make sense to not control the planning process at all and wait until the project is executed before thinking about this. Adapt the activities in the life-cycle to your project. Not the other way around.

The next sections will go into each of the five sub-phases in more detail. To put everything into context, I want to incorporate a real-world example. I will use the following case study to illustrate each point throughout:

When I began work as the Facility Manager at Camp Gruber Training Center (CGTC), it took some time to learn all of the job requirements. The installation consists of 33,027 acres and more than 100 buildings of various size and age. Two of the older buildings on post were used as a consolidated post headquarters (HQ). While these two HQ buildings were close in proximity, they were not connected and not built at the same time. The older of the pair was built during WWII. Needing additional space, the Army constructed the second five decades later. These two buildings were no longer meeting the needs of the tenants and were highly inefficient.

I originally began looking at this project as a simple renovation of both buildings to update finishes, replace inefficient equipment, and add insulation to the concrete masonry unit (CMU) walls. However, after speaking with all stakeholders, I quickly realized we needed more office space and a simple renovation was not going to work. I walked the project site with the architect and we came to the conclusion that the outcome we needed was to renovate both buildings, while constructing a third building to connect the older two. The result would be a single HQ building with the additional office space we needed.

Chapter 2: Initiation

Define the Problem

Answering a clearly defined problem is the easiest way to determine what the desired results of the project should be. One tool is to create a problem statement written in the form of a question that begins with "How can we…" However you choose to do this, you must first define the problem, then identify the solution (what the end result looks like), and then move forward to solve it.

> We had to first define the problem with the two headquarters buildings before we could attempt to solve it. The problem statement went something like this, "How do we expand and renovate the two buildings to meet the needs of all tenants and increase energy efficiency, without exceeding budgetary thresholds, given that we must displace all tenants during construction?" This led us to a pretty clear desired result of a single headquarters building with more office space, larger restrooms, and added energy efficiencies.

Obtain Approval for the Project

A common term for a document used to approve a project's existence and authorize the PM to expend resources is the project charter. The project charter is the major output of initiation, but you need a summary of what the project will accomplish to get the project charter signed. Therefore, an input to this step will be the project statement of work (SOW).
The SOW is a narrative explaining the reason for the project (business case), what the end result will be (scope of product), and how the project aligns with the overall strategic direction of the organization. Your organization may or may not use the terms project charter or SOW, but the bottom line is to ensure that proper approvals are in place before expending any organizational resources on the project. This approval officially initiates the project.

One of the first classes I took while in my graduate program was on leadership. Part of the curriculum included a group project, which I was never really a fan of, but didn't have a choice. The professor assigned the groups a couple weeks into class and distributed the assignment to spark collaboration. I have no memory of the assignment's details, but I vividly remember that one of my newly assigned teammates came up with a seven-page project charter form letter that was partially filled out. He was adamant that all of us sign this document or the group project could not begin. Needless to say, we quickly dismissed him and he was not elected as group leader. Fair warning – use common sense when applying these principles.

> In the National Guard, we do not use a project charter. Projects are both requested and approved on a form called an NGB Form 420-R. For the HQ project, I filled out the 420-R, which included a brief overview of what it was we wanted to accomplish, the scope of what the consolidated HQ building would be, a justification for the project, an approximation of what the cost would be, and a few other details as required.
>
> When filling out the business case and scope of product, I always took care to explain the value of the finished deliverable to the organization. For me, I would spell out the problem and exactly how the project would solve it. After several meetings with key stakeholders, the state facility manager approved the project and I became the project manager.

Identify Stakeholders

This is a vital step in the Initiation sub-phase. A stakeholder is anyone who is affected by or can affect the project. Stakeholders can be individuals, groups, or organizations. Be sure to really analyze who this project could affect. You can always cross a stakeholder off your list, but it is hard to go back at a later date and ask for input from someone you left out of the process. As the PM, you want to make sure you list all stakeholders, their level of influence, potential impact, and any pertinent information about them (for instance contact information). Key stakeholders are typically those who have decision-making authority and could significantly influence your project. Record this information in a format you can easily access, but be careful not to let it become public knowledge. You might not want your personal assessment of which stakeholders have more influence than others getting out.

Stakeholders for the CGTC headquarters project were fairly straightforward. At one end, there were the tenants for whom I had to find a new home during six months of construction, my boss (the full-time operations manager) who controlled allocation of space, and his boss (the part-time post commander) who had an idea of the finish and feel of what he wanted it to look like. At the other end, there was the facility manager of all military facilities in the state (he controlled the money), the A/E designing the project, the contractor (who had not been chosen yet), and the state contracting agency. The key stakeholders were the operations manager, post commander, and state facility manager. Because the state facility manager controlled the money, he had the most influence. That said, he didn't really care about finish details like the post commander did because he was not stationed at CGTC -- so there wasn't much conflict there.

Chapter 3: Planning

There are two types of project triangles I have come to learn and appreciate over the years. Figure 5 shows the first, and it is something I've reminded my current boss of several times.

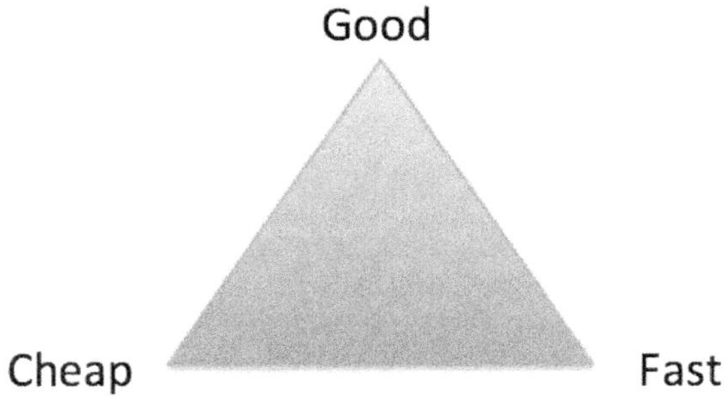

Figure 5

You can pick two of the three points in Figure 5 within your project, but you may not have all three. To get your results done well and fast, it will cost substantially more than if you are willing to wait. If budget is your primary concern, you can choose quality or speed. Every so often you may luck out and get all three, but that is the exception and you would be wise to not plan on it.

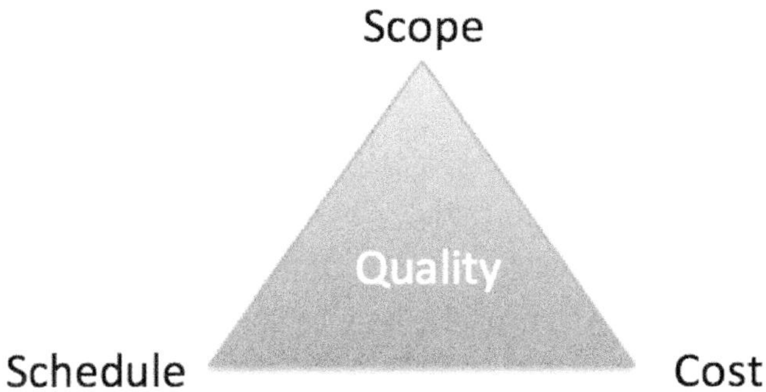

Figure 6

Figure 6 shows another project triangle. This triangle is the more universally accepted version of the project triangle; because Figure 5, while true, is a bit tongue-in-cheek. The quality triangle in Figure 6 is an equilateral triangle, meaning that all sides are equal in length. This is symbolic of the equal importance of the three cornerstones of planning: scope, schedule, and cost. As a PM undertakes the project, equal emphasis must be placed on all three aspects. If just one leg starts to waiver (i.e., the schedule starts to slip or cost overruns begin to occur), the triangle is no longer equilateral and quality suffers. The only way to ensure that stakeholders' expectations are met at the end of the project is to manage all three of these cornerstones during the entire project life cycle.

The first thing to plan is how the project will be managed. This is typically captured in an overarching plan called the project management plan. This plan should be tailored to your specific project and team. It will define how the project is executed, supervised and controlled. It can be a high-level summary or a very detailed document that encompasses sub-plans for each knowledge area (e.g., communications management plan, human resources management plan, stakeholder management plan, etc.). Here is a list of all knowledge area sub-plans that can be included when determining how comprehensive your project management plan will be:

- Scope management plan – details how changes in scope will be managed

- Schedule management plan – specifies the scheduling method and tool, in addition to formalizing how the schedule will be supervised and controlled

- Cost management plan – includes how the project will be funded, the schedule showing when costs will be incurred, and the scope statement for cost estimation

- Quality management plan – details how quality will be addressed throughout the project

- Process improvement management plan – describes how processes will be evaluated and improved throughout the project

- Human resources management plan – details reporting requirements, personnel management, and how responsibilities are assigned

- Communications management plan – specifies who will communicate information about the project, how they will do this, and when

- Risk management plan – details how risk management will be conducted throughout the project

- Procurements or contracts management plan – details how the organization will get the necessary materials or services to complete the project

- Change management plan – details how the change order process is managed and what documents are needed for changes

- Stakeholder management plan – identifies key stakeholders, their needs, and how they will be engaged throughout the project

- Configuration management plan – identifies configurable deliverables and outlines how this is done. Configuration is used in complex systems, such as IT and military weaponry

- Requirements management plan – details how project requirements are managed. This includes how to collect, analyze, and document any project requirements, in addition to product requirements

In addition to any subsidiary plans, the PM should include the scope baseline, schedule baseline, and cost baseline as part of the project management plan. A baseline is the planned value or metric that all future project performance is measured against. This plan is then developed over time, formally approved, periodically updated, and referenced throughout the project.

In the rest of the planning chapter, I will cover the steps you must go through in every project. I will cover them in the order that I do them, but understand that all planning is cyclical and plans can be adjusted at any time. Here are the steps we will cover throughout the remainder of the chapter:

- Define the project scope

- Develop the project schedule
    - Scheduling techniques
    - Scheduling tools
- Develop the project budget
- Plan quality management
- Plan communications
- Plan risk management
- Plan procurements and contracts

Define the Project Scope

The outcome of this step will be a scope statement. The scope statement includes several things, but the first is the scope itself. This is a description of work to be accomplished and desired outcomes. The statement also includes deliverables required and acceptance criteria that must be met. Statements about any exclusions that will not be covered in the project can be included here. Finally, assumptions and constraints are listed to aid in the planning process.

The CGTC headquarters scope statement included the following:

- Connecting the two buildings and creating offices in the newly enclosed space

- Renovating four small bathrooms to create two larger bathrooms that were more functional and met Americans with Disabilities Act (ADA) requirements

- Creating a museum space out of an unused waiting area

- Covering the entire façade with an exterior insulation finishing system (EIFS) for energy efficiency

- Delivering the completed building according to the A/E specifications (acceptance criteria)

- Noting that the IT room was the only room in the buildings not included in the project (exclusion)

- Completing the project in 180 days from beginning construction (constraint)

The scope statement, along with the work breakdown structure (explained next) and the WBS dictionary, form the scope baseline for your project.

Develop the Project Schedule

On the surface, developing a project schedule sounds fairly straightforward. However, the first time you put one together, you will understand how complex it can become. To build a schedule from the ground-up, you must first dissect or "decompose" the entire project into smaller, more manageable pieces. The first thing is creating a work breakdown structure (WBS).

The WBS is nothing more than a hierarchy where the top level is the entire project and it is broken down into tasks, subtasks, and finally work packages (the lowest level of the WBS). The purpose is to break down an entire project into these work packages, which can each be estimated and managed for schedule and budget. You should also include a WBS dictionary, with detailed information about each WBS component (e.g., description, milestones, person responsible, cost estimates, etc.)

The next step in the scheduling process is to create an activity list by further breaking down all work packages and identifying individual activities in each of them. Figure 7 shows the hierarchical structure of this decomposition.

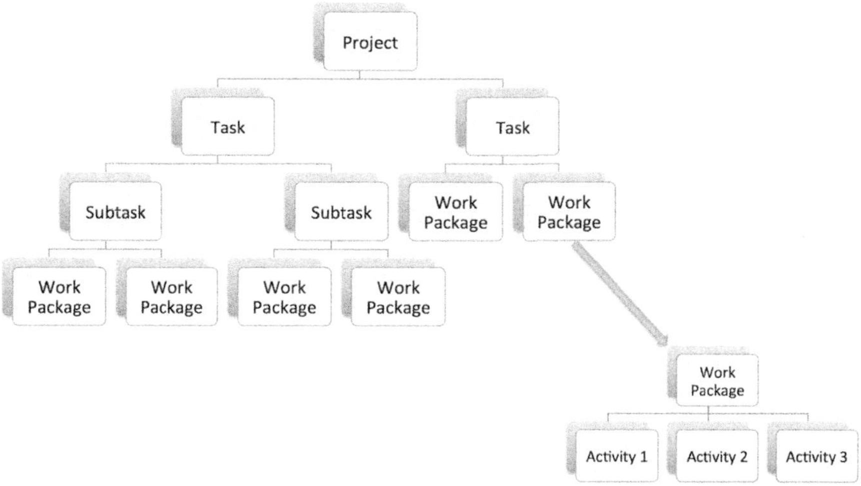

Figure 7

Once you have all activities listed, you have to do three things. First, you sequence the activities to create an initial order in which to accomplish them. Second, you estimate how long each activity will take to complete (duration). This is important because if Activity 1 has to be complete before Activity 2 can start, you won't be able to put Activity 2 on the schedule until you know Activity 1's duration. Third, estimate what you need to complete each activity (resources required). This is important because you not only have to schedule how long the activities take to accomplish, but you have to schedule lead-time for obtaining the necessary resources (e.g., building materials, permits, etc.) required to begin that activity. Once you have all this information, you can finally put together your schedule.

> At CGTC, we used a general contractor to renovate the HQ. In this case, it was his responsibility to develop the project schedule and present it to me as the PM for approval. The project was clearly defined in the scope and he began to decompose it into the tasks, subtasks, and work packages.
>
> To illustrate this point, one of the tasks he identified was the construction of the building between the two existing facilities that would connect them, creating one cohesive HQ. Several of the subtasks within this task were the foundation, framing (walls, roof), and roofing (standing seam metal roof). From there, he further broke down each subtask. As an example, he decomposed the foundation subtask into the following work

packages, to be accomplished in this sequence: construct building pad, dig footing, construct slab.

The footing work package was further decomposed into the following activities, to be accomplished in this sequence: dig footing trench, install rebar, pass footing inspection, pour footing concrete. The duration and resources to complete each of these activities were then easily defined and could be placed into the overall project schedule.

Schedule Techniques

There are several project scheduling techniques. The most straightforward is called forward pass scheduling. To use forward pass, the PM simply sequences activities in order from a given start date, to determine what the completion date will be. Backward pass scheduling is when the PM begins at a set completion date and works backward in the project, sequencing activities in order to arrive at what the start date should be.

The last one I will cover here is the most widely accepted, the Critical Path Method (CPM). This technique uses critical path analysis (discussed in the next section) to determine dependencies between activities. Then, CPM arrives at the shortest possible total completion time for the project. This sequence of dependent activities that form the shortest time to completion is referred to as the critical path. If any one of these activities is delayed, the entire project is delayed.

In all project scheduling techniques, activities that can be performed concurrently should be scheduled as such.

Schedule Tools

Critical Path Analysis – This tool combines activities and their durations into a flow chart based on their dependencies. The flow chart is commonly referred to as a precedence diagram or activity-on-node (AON).

Think of each activity node as its own icon in the overall flow chart. Within each node, the PM writes all information about the activity's schedule, including the name, duration, early start (ES), late start (LS), early finish (EF), late finish (LF), and total float (TF). All information other than the name is numerical representing a period of time (typically days). Before putting each activity into the flow chart, the PM assigns durations and identifies the icon with the specific name of the activity or task. Figure 8 below shows what a node looks like:

Early Start	Duration	Early Finish
	Activity Name	
Late Start	Total Float	Late Finish

Figure 8

To determine the early start, early finish, late start, and late finish, the PM must sequence the activities and put them in the flow chart. However, to do this the PM must know their dependencies. Dependencies are relationships between activities that affect when they can be scheduled. There are four types of dependencies between activities you must be aware of:

- Finish-to-start (this is the most common; example is that a house must be framed before shingles can be installed)
- Finish-to-finish (example is that appliances can be installed in a house at the same time as the entire electrical system is being finished, but the electrical system must be finished before the appliance installation is complete)
- Start-to-finish (example is that second shift police officers must start before the first shift ends because there has to be overlapping coverage protecting a municipality)
- Start-to-start (example is that one member of a painting crew has to start taping off trim before a second member can start

caulking the trim – the point is the tape does not have to be completed before the caulk can begin; both activities can occur simultaneously after the taping is started).

Because certain activities will be completely independent of others, the flow chart can have many branches.

For instance, in the CGTC HQ example, pouring the concrete in the footing trench was dependent upon passing the footing inspection. Passing the footing inspection was dependent upon installing the rebar in the trench. Therefore, pouring the footing had to occur after passing the inspection, which had to occur after installing the rebar (finish-to-start dependencies).

However, none of these three activities (concrete, inspection, or rebar) was dependent on any part of the task of renovating the restrooms inside the existing buildings. Restrooms were completely separate from the new construction aspect of the HQ building. The activities contained in the restroom renovation task could be accomplished independently of the activities within the task of constructing the new part of the HQ building. This means, each task and all associated activities were on their own branch of the flow chart. Figure 9 illustrates what these activities sequenced in the HQ flow chart looked like with three of the restroom activities included (tile floor, tile wall, and install vanities):

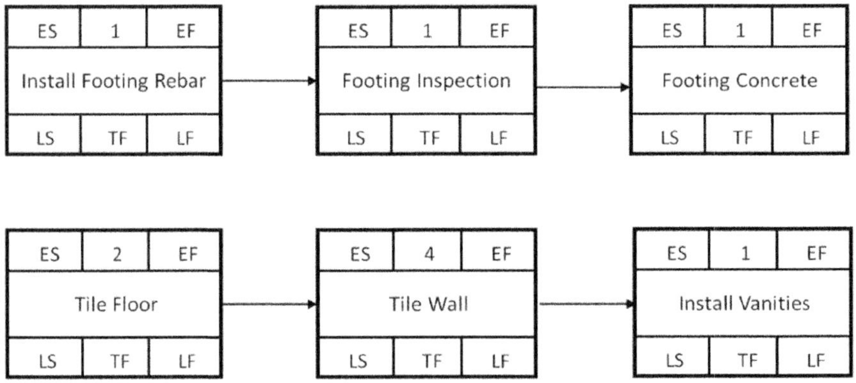

Figure 9

Notice in Figure 9 that the arrows in each branch show dependency. The arrow pointing to "Install Vanities" shows that it is dependent upon the "Tile Wall" activity being finished, because that is where the arrow originates.

The PM then uses forward pass to assign early start and early finish dates to each activity. Forward pass is where you start at the beginning and proceed to the end. The PM will then use backward pass to assign late finish and late start dates to each activity. With backward pass, you start at the end and proceed to the beginning of each activity branch.

> Going back to our example, we will assume that both activity branches will start on day 1. We already know the durations. So, here are the equations for ES and EF:
>
> ES of activity = EF of predecessor activity + 1
>
> EF of activity = Activity duration + ES – 1
>
> For me, calculating the ES makes sense. You take when the preceding activity finished and you're going to start the following activity the next day. That's why you add one day. The EF is taking the day you start, adding the number of days it takes to complete the activity (duration) and subtracting one day. You subtract the day because you started on the ES (not the day after). Here's what it looks like in our example:

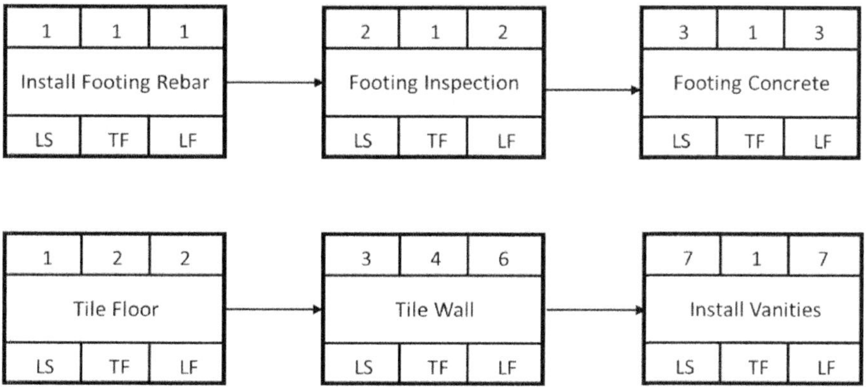

Figure 10

Looking at Figure 10, we see that both branches can start on day 1. The rebar will take one day, so it ends on day 1. That allows the footing inspection to start as early as day 2. It will take one day to get the inspection, which means the earliest it can finish is on day 2. The concrete follows this same logic. Since there are three activities in the first branch and each one lasts one day in duration, the earliest all three will be complete is at the end of day 3.

The three restroom activities are a little different, because they each have different durations. Again, the earliest the tile floor can start is day 1 and it will last two days. This means its EF is at the end of day 2. The earliest the tile wall could start would be the very next day (day 3) and it lasts four days. This means the earliest the tile wall can finish is the end of day 6. This is the logic the PM uses for all activities in forward pass.

Next, the PM uses backward pass to calculate the late finish and late start. Here are the equations for those:

LF of activity = LS of successor activity – 1

LS of activity = LF of current activity – duration + 1

For our example, we will assume that these are the only six activities in the entire project. Thus, the entire project would end on day 7 when the vanities are installed. We know this because the three footing activities should all be complete at the end of day 3. Therefore, the late finish for the last activity in either branch would be day 7, because anything that finished past that would delay the project. Understanding that, Figure 11 is what our example looks like now:

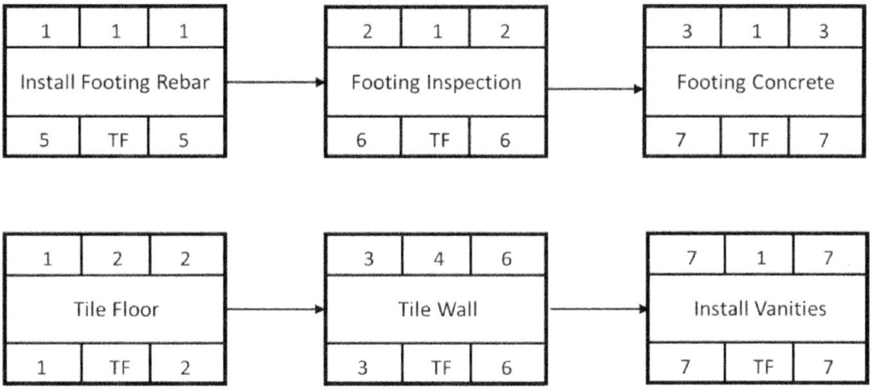

Figure 11

The path of dependent activities that creates the longest duration across the flow chart is the critical path. It took me a little while to understand that, but if you think about it, it makes sense. The longest path duration is actually the shortest possible length of time that the entire project can take. Thus, in our example, the tile floor – tile wall – install vanities path is the critical path of the overall project. If any one of these three activities were delayed, the entire project duration would be extended past day 7. That's why it is critical to the project.

Another characteristic of the critical path is that activities on it typically have no float (another way of looking at this is the ES/EF times are the same as the LS/LF times). There are two types of float, total and free. Total float is the amount of time an activity can be delayed without pushing the completion date of the project back. Free float is the amount of time an activity can be delayed without delaying any successor activities. Here are the equations for each:

TF = LS – ES

Free Float = ES of the next activity – EF of current activity – 1

Total float is what we will focus on here. It is commonly referred to as "float" or "slack" in project management.

Going back to our example, Figure 12 shows what our flow chart looks like with TF calculated for all activities. Again, notice that the critical path shows zero total float on every activity.

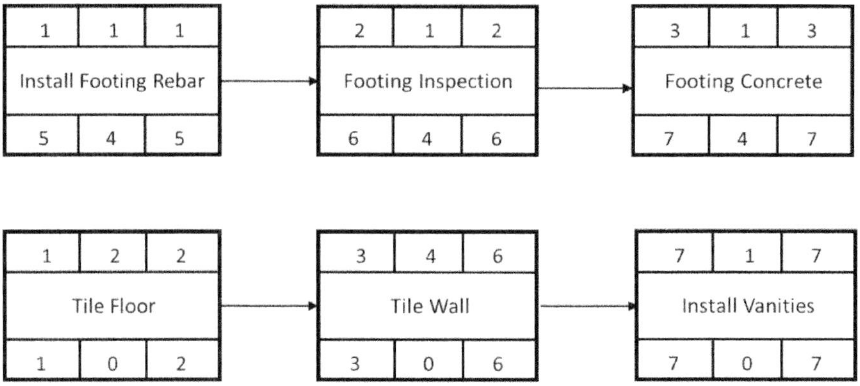

Figure 12

> Notice each activity along the footing path has a TF of 4 days. That makes sense because all three activities can be delayed up to four days before it will affect the end date (day 7) of this project.

The concept of float gets much more complex with larger projects with multiple activities and different dependencies between them. Imagine if you have an activity that has multiple predecessor activities that must be finished before it can be started. If you are interested in CPM and would like to get more in-depth with it, there are many resources online that have examples and practice questions. This is a concept to definitely become familiar with if you're interested in obtaining your PMP® certification. Here is another example of float using a different part of the Camp Gruber project:

> For the Post HQ project, the EIFS task was divided into two subtasks, the EIFS around the existing buildings and the EIFS around the newly constructed building connection. Because all activities under the EIFS tasks occur on the outside of the building, it could begin as soon as the exterior walls were finished, but had to be complete before the final grade occurred prior to laying sod and project completion. Therefore, the EIFS on the existing buildings could theoretically begin on day 1, but the EIFS on the new construction could not begin until the exterior walls of that portion of the building were complete. This meant there was more total float with installing EIFS on the existing buildings. The contractor could have started that part of the EIFS on day 1, day 15, or anywhere in between and would not affect the project completion date.

Schedule Compression – This tool is a way for project managers to decrease the total duration of a project by shortening the time it takes to accomplish individual activities. There are two ways to compress a schedule, crashing and fast-tracking, each with its own drawback. Crashing is simply adding resources to decrease activity duration. For instance, if I can frame a house in seven days with five framers, I might be able to do it in five days with eight framers. I save two days, but incur added labor cost for three additional framers over the entire five-day period. Fast-tracking, on the other hand, is taking activities that were planned to be performed in sequence and doing them concurrently. Be careful with this one. While you might not be adding resources to the project, this does increase your risk exposure.

Graphical Analysis – Models and charts can make relatively easy graphical representations of the project schedule that all stakeholders can understand. The most common is the Gantt chart. The Gantt chart, typically created with a project management software, is a bar chart that depicts the project schedule, dependent relationships, milestones, critical path, and activity list in one overview. Another model is the program evaluation and review technique (PERT), which was developed by the Navy in the 1950s and is very similar to the civilian critical path model. Personally, I prefer the Gantt chart because it is easier for me to explain to key stakeholders who do not routinely engage in project management.

Developing the project schedule takes practice. It is one thing to understand the concepts of the CPM, but another to create one successfully. I highly suggest learning more about the subject and practicing with example problems to gain experience in the skill.

Develop Project Budget

The first step in creating a project budget is to generate cost estimates. We will discuss the different ways to do that, but first we need to have a common understanding of various costs that must be considered in any project.

Types of Costs

Fixed and Variable Costs – A fixed cost is an expense that is not dependent on the amount of goods being produced. An example of this is the rent an organization pays to maintain a business office. Whether that office is managing one project or 10, the rent stays the same. In contrast to this is a variable cost. This is an expense that has a dependent relationship with the deliverables being produced. An example of a variable cost is the raw materials used to make a product. The more products an organization makes, the more materials it needs to meet increasing production demand.

Direct and Indirect Costs – A direct cost is an expense directly related to the goods or services of an organization. An example is the hourly wage of a manufacturing employee who is producing a component of an end product. In contrast, an indirect cost cannot be directly tied to a particular good or service. An example of an indirect cost is a utility cost for the building that the manufacturing employee works in, which houses many employees producing many different products.

Cost Estimates

There are different methods of estimating costs and different reasons you would use each of the following methods. When deciding which to use, choose the method that yields the most accurate cost estimate based on the information you have at the time.

Also, identify the types of costs during your estimation and account for them accordingly when circumstances change. For instance, if your project's product scope remains the same but quantity increases, your variable costs will increase along with it.

Historical Estimating – Also known as analogous estimating, historical estimating takes the known costs from a similar project that has been performed in the past and adjusts them accordingly (i.e., for inflation) to generate an estimate for the current project. While this method is typically quick and does not require many resources to complete, it is also the least accurate method and should be used only when information is limited -- such as in the early stages of a project.

> I used historical estimating a lot in residential construction. An example would be when I knew approximately what a new home would cost to construct, based on what a similar home cost three months earlier. This type of estimation was very helpful before I had finalized drawings that I could use to obtain exact bids from subcontractors.

Parametric Estimating – This method uses rate relationships between cost and variable in order to derive an estimate from simple calculations. For example, let's say I know a certain type of space costs an average of $250 per square foot to construct and I am constructing that type of space. I take my new project's square footage and multiply it by $250 to estimate total cost. This can be applied to the entire project or project components in conjunction with other methods of estimation. This typically yields a more reliable estimate than historical methodology.

Bottom-up Estimating – This method is the most accurate. However, it is also the most time consuming and should be used as information and time allow. Bottom-up estimating is simply taking the lowest level of work known at the time (activity or work package), generating the cost estimate for each, and adding up the costs to the highest level in order to get an overall project cost estimate. Because you can get more accurate costs by pricing activities individually, this method provides the most reliable estimate.

The Budget

The next step is to compile all cost estimates and add contingency reserves to create the cost baseline. This baseline is used during the execution phase to measure, supervise, and control actual costs of the project. The only thing the baseline does not contain is management reserves. The cost baseline plus management reserves make up the total project budget. We will discuss what these reserves are and when to use them.

Contingency Reserves – these funds are set aside as an allowance to mitigate risk. They are amounts determined by either a percentage of the cost estimate or an actual number calculated through some form of quantitative analysis (i.e., you identify a risk and calculate what it would cost if the risk occurred and include that amount in your contingency reserves).

Contingency reserves are included when there is a known risk. This means that the likelihood of a negative impact to the project has been forecasted and accepted. An example of this is identifying rock in a given area that must be excavated, but not knowing how much will be encountered. The PM's cost estimate would include all known costs associated with the excavation and a contingency to mitigate the risk of encountering additional rock formations, causing increased time and labor.

Management Reserves – these funds are set aside to mitigate unidentified risk. They are controlled by management and can be used as they see fit. Because management reserves are for unknown risks and out of the control of the PM, they are not included in the cost baseline.

Once again, the total project budget consists of all cost estimates, contingency reserves, and management reserves. However, the cost baseline the PM uses to supervise and control the project budget does not include management reserves.

Planning Quality Management

Quality management really has two parts in terms of project management. The first part is that of quality assurance. Quality assurance is the process of auditing operations to ensure the project is using the quality standards developed in the quality management plan. The second part is quality control, which is the process of measuring the quality of the deliverables themselves. Inspections, testing, examining, etc., are used in quality control. The quality management plan outlines quality requirements and how the project will comply with them. We will discuss both of these concepts in more detail in the supervision and control chapter.

Before we move forward, two terms that commonly get confused are quality and grade.

Quality is not the same thing as grade. Quality refers to how well the characteristics of the deliverable meet project requirements. Poor quality is never a good thing. Grade refers to categories of products with the same functional use but different technical attributes. Infiniti is a higher grade than Nissan, but both have the same functional use. Low grade is not necessarily bad. A low-grade Nissan made with high quality is perfectly acceptable in terms of a project deliverable.

Plan, Do, Check, Act

The Plan, Do, Check, Act model (also known as Plan-Do-Study-Act, Deming Wheel, or Deming Cycle) was first introduced by Walter Shewart and later modified by his protégé, Dr. W. Edwards Deming. This cycle is commonly used in quality management as a model for continual improvement. First, in the "plan" step, a purpose is identified and success is defined. Second, in the "do" step, you execute the project. Third, in the "check" or "study" step, results are tested for validity and areas for improvement are identified. Fourth, in the "act" step, what has been learned throughout the cycle is applied to improve the process as applicable.[14] The cycle then repeats. This model is the basis for quality improvement and should be considered when building the quality management plan.

In addition to identifying the specific quality standards and requirements for the project, the PM must consider organizational policies with regards to quality. Also, the International Organization for Standardization (ISO) issues quality standards that are recognized internationally. Specifically, ISO 10006:2003 establishes guidelines for quality management in projects.

Cost of Quality

Management is going to want to consider the cost of quality (COQ), which analyzes and compares costs of conformance versus those of non-conformance. This is commonly referred to as "prevention over inspection," which states that it is cheaper to prevent mistakes than correct them once they happen. Think of this as a way to prove that it will save the organization money to prevent errors at the front-end as opposed to conducting inspections, testing, and fixing those errors later.

The two categories in COQ are the cost of conformance and the cost of nonconformance. The cost of conformance includes prevention costs (such as training) and appraisal costs (such as testing). Cost of conformance is essentially building quality into the processes of the project. The cost of nonconformance includes internal failure costs (failures found before the deliverables are distributed) and external failure costs (such as warranty work and the cost of losing business due to poor product quality). Cost of nonconformance is what the organization will pay as a result for failure to conform to quality requirements.

Finally, the quality management plan will identify how quality assurance and control activities will be documented. Quality metrics should be identified to explain how specific aspects of quality will be measured. An example of this is failure rate. Quality checklists are also used to ensure all process-required tasks are accomplished.

Planning Communications

Managing communications is vital to the success of the project. As the PM, you must ensure that all stakeholders receive the right amount of project information, at the right time, and in an appropriate format. So how do we do this?

First, you need to understand what each stakeholder needs to know. In my current position, it took me a little bit to understand what the various stakeholders need to know versus what they want to know. Sometimes they are the same thing and sometimes they can be completely different. If you're not convinced already, there is a lot of information and action that goes into facility management and it's easy to provide too much information to key stakeholders.

As the PM, you need to get through the unnecessary details that might mean the world of difference to you (for instance technical characteristics that a layman wouldn't understand or care about), and get to what is important to that particular stakeholder. Know all of the extra information and save it for when they ask. If you don't, you will risk losing their interest, or worst case, losing credibility.

Second, you need to determine the amount of information and feedback required for each stakeholder. As an FM, I've always managed internal projects. Because I knew most of them pretty well before the project started, I already understood my stakeholders. However, if this is not the case for you, one tool to keep up with stakeholder communications (and project team roles) is a RACI chart.

RACI Chart

RACI stands for responsible, accountable, consult, and inform. This is simply a matrix where across the top you list the names of all stakeholders and down the side you list all activities you need to track. You then assign who will be responsible to complete the task, accountable to make the decisions or act on the task, who should be consulted in regard to decisions/tasks, and who should be informed of decisions/tasks about the project. It will look something like Figure 13.

RACI Matrix	Lisa	Steve	Carl	Matthew	Mary	Cynthia
Activity 1	I	R	I	A	I	C
Activity 2	I	I	A	R	C	C
Activity 3	R	R	A	I	I	C
Activity 4	I	I	I	R/A	R	C

Figure 13

Third, determine how and when to disseminate pertinent information to stakeholders. This will be different for many organizations. Knowing that, I will typically ask stakeholders what they prefer and I do my best to meet those expectations.

Types of Communication:

There are four types of communication at your disposal. These are:

Formal written – think of this as anything you would take an actual pen and physically sign your name to, such as a contract or official memorandum.

Informal written – this encompasses all other forms of written communication, such as emails, notes, etc.

Formal verbal – these are anything you would prepare to present to a group. Every month I put together a presentation full of pictures and pertinent details of the major project accomplishments for my board meeting.

Informal verbal – think of these more as two-way communication paths (although that rule is not firm). Examples include conversations or daily update meetings sitting in an office.

Finally, you must determine what formal meetings you will conduct. A group meeting is an invaluable tool to use in order to ensure everyone is on the same page with the same information. This can be very useful in helping everyone obtain a shared understanding of project requirements. At a minimum, projects typically include the following meeting types to disseminate information:

Kickoff meeting – this can be at the beginning of the project or each time a new member joins the team. Your organization may or may not use the term "kickoff meeting," but there has to be one point in time where all stakeholders get on the same page. This meeting should address pertinent information about the project, answer any questions, provide details on future meetings, and explain how information will be communicated.

Preconstruction meeting – this is similar to a kickoff meeting, but includes necessary project team personnel, any key customer representatives, the general contractor, and any major subcontractors. This meeting goes into more detail about project specifics and how the interaction between all four parties will occur (e.g., the change order approval process, inspections, and payments).

Project update meetings – these are scheduled at regular intervals and can include anyone who needs to be involved, but should always include the project team and the contractor.

> At Camp Gruber, kickoff meetings were typically conducted in two settings. Because the state facility manager was more than two hours away, I would conduct a teleconference with him, his staff, and my team to go over project specifics. I would then conduct a meeting at Camp Gruber with the stakeholders there. That meeting and all follow-on project update meetings transpired in conjunction with our weekly staff meetings. The preconstruction meeting consisted of the general contractor, several of his major sub-contractors, me as the PM, my construction manager on staff, the state contracting representative, and the A-E. Formal communication was only necessary for official government documents such as state contracting forms and military project approval/closeout forms.
>
> I put together a weekly project update brief that I used (when time allowed) in the staff meetings for stakeholders at CGTC and sent out to stakeholders who were not full-time employees at the installation (such as the part-time commander and the state facilities manager). The format was of my own creation, but it was a combination of pictures and key points. I always addressed deviations from the cost baseline or schedule. Figure 14 is from one of my old project update briefs and shows a couple of pictures of the new construction connecting the two HQ buildings mid-way through the project.

HQ Buildings Addition (S Side)

HQ Buildings Addition (N Side)

Figure 14

Planning Risk Management

The term "risk" carries negative connotations. And while most people think negatively when they hear the term, risk is actually defined as the potential of an unforeseen event that could have a *positive or negative effect* on the project. Positive risks are referred to as opportunities and negative risks are identified as threats. Risk is always a future event because by definition the event has not yet occurred.

Risk Identification

The first step in managing risk is to identify any risks that could have a potential impact on the project. Since risk is unforeseen, this is typically accomplished by brainstorming through possible scenarios such as inaccurate cost estimates, turnover, weather delays, material cost increases, etc. When looking at future scenarios, it is always beneficial to look at the organization's current strengths and weaknesses and see how those could lead to future opportunities and threats. This is accomplished through a SWOT (strengths, weakness, opportunities, threats) analysis. Figure 15 shows a SWOT diagram, which will help explain how the terms are related.

SWOT Diagram	Present	Future (Risks)
Positive	Strengths	Opportunities
Negative	Weaknesses	Threats

Figure 15

Having done this a number of times, I was asked to lead a SWOT analysis with the managers of my organization several years ago. We gathered all department heads, managers, and assistants in a large room and I stood in front of them with a blank canvas and marker. I used pre-determined questions to prompt them into a group discussion and debate on what they do well and where they think they could improve. Examples of questions included:

- What makes us better than our competition?
- What is great about our culture?
- Where do we lack knowledge or expertise?
- What are common complaints from guests?

It was a valuable brainstorming session that went through all aspects of the services we provide. The managers listed all of the present strengths and weaknesses within their departments first. From there, they brainstormed potential future opportunities that their strengths might allow them to capitalize on. Then, they identified potential future threats that they could mitigate now and hopefully avoid.

Each risk had someone who would own it. The risk owner became accountable for coordinating and implementing any mitigation efforts and reported back to the group at the next meeting. While this example illustrates a method for risk identification at an organization's strategic level, it can be adapted quite well to an individual project.

Once risks are identified, it is important to document them in a risk register and rate the probability (likelihood of occurrence) and the severity (how much of an impact to the project it will have once it does occur). Analytical risk planners can use more in-depth tools when doing this for ranking risks through quantitative analysis such as probability and impact matrices and tornado diagrams, but we will not get into those in this guide.

Risk Response

When planning negative risk response, the PM has four options:

Avoid – the first option is to simply change the project activity to eliminate the risk potential.

Accept – the second option is to document the risk and do nothing. This would typically be appropriate if the risk is low and there is a high cost to respond to it.

Transfer – the third option is to transfer risk responsibility to someone else. An example of this is to buy insurance that would cover the risk, so the third-party insurer bears responsibility if the risk occurs. This can obviously only be applied in certain circumstances.

Mitigate – the fourth option is to reduce the probability or severity by applying preventative measures to identified risks. An example of this would be to include a contingency reserve in the project budget.

When planning positive risk response, there are also four options available to the PM:

Exploit – the first option is to change the project activity to ensure that the risk occurs.

Accept – the second option is to not actively pursue the opportunity.

Share – the third option is to share the risk with a third party. This is what happens in a teaming agreement.

Enhance – the fourth option is to increase the probability or the positive impact the risk will have on the project.

After determining what the risk response will be, the project team must consider two additional possibilities. First, there could be the potential for residual risk. This is any risk that remains after the response has been carried out. Second, the risk response itself could cause a completely new risk. This is known as spin-off or secondary risk. Should either of these occur, the team would document the new risk in the risk register, analyze potential strategies, and carry out new risk response as appropriate.

Planning Procurements and Contracting

Procurement management is the process of purchasing materials or professional services to complete the project. Every organization should have a standardized process for procurement. Depending on how in-depth that process is, you might not have to think too much about planning this process and most of your time will be spent executing it. That said, there are several important principles related to procurement.

Contracting

As an FM professional, you will almost certainly be involved in contracting procedures on a routine basis. The need for contracts comes from facility or project requirements that cannot be met with full-time staff. From individual project contracts to ongoing service agreements, knowing what exactly is expected of you when it comes to contracting will be key to successful financial management. Let's start with the basics.

According to Merriam-Webster, a contract is *an agreement between two or more persons or parties that is legally binding; a business arrangement for the supply of goods or services.*[15] It is important to understand that for a contract to be legally binding, it must be made by parties with the required capacity, meaning they are of legal age and are mentally sound. The contract must also be lawful, meaning a contract to commit a crime is not legally binding. The contract must have consideration. Consideration is an exchange of something of value for something else of value (cash for services). There must also be some avenue for parties to remedy a breach of contract and the contract must be agreed to (usually by signatures in a formal contract) by all parties. Finally, contracts can be written or oral, but you must be able to prove they exist to enforce them.

Contract Differences

- Express vs. Implied – express contracts specifically state (either orally or written) the terms under the agreement. Implied contracts are inferred from circumstances and through facts surrounding the case and by the actions of the parties to the contract.

- Bilateral vs. Unilateral – bilateral contracts are agreed upon by both parties. This comes from an exchange of promises that are mutually agreed to. Unilateral contracts, on the other hand, involve a promise from only one party. You're probably familiar with bilateral contracts, but an example of a unilateral contract is a reward poster where one party promises to pay a set amount of money for the performance by another party (such as turning in a criminal or returning a lost dog).

- Prescriptive vs. Performance – prescriptive contracts detail all specifications that must be completed under the agreement. Conversely, performance-based contracts detail the results desired under the agreement, but leave flexibility to the service provider on how they achieve those results.

Things to Remember

Watch what you say – even after you sign a contract, you can alter it with the words you use. If you tell a contractor that you would like to have a certain change to the contract and he construes that to mean you authorized the change, that could be a legally binding change order. This is true regardless of what you actually meant.

There is fraud in contracting – be aware that contractors who bid on projects might not always be upfront and honest in their bidding. Bid rigging is when contractors get together to agree who will submit the lowest bid and everyone else submits higher bids. This effectively guarantees that one particular contractor will be awarded the project. Price fixing is when contractors agree to all have set prices, which reduces competition and violates antitrust laws.

Check your specifications and plans before agreeing to a contract – do this in detail because you can be sure the contractor will. I have seen contractors find omissions in specifications, but not question them during the bidding process. Then, they intentionally submit a low bid, knowing that change orders will have to be issued from which they can make more profit. Make sure your plans and specs are correct.

> As the facility manager at CGTC, all procurement went through a purchasing office and most were accomplished through the use of federal and state contracts. As the FM at my current organization, we utilize AIA (American Institute of Architects) forms to engage in contracts on larger projects and individual subcontractor agreements to conduct minor purchasing activities (such as when we purchase windows or interior design services). Regardless of where your contract templates originate, there are three basic types that the most commonly used contracts will fall under: fixed price, cost-reimbursable, and time and materials.

Contract Types

Fixed Price Contracts – these have a clear statement of work and the buyer accepts a seller's price for it. In this type of contract, the seller bears the risk. An example of this is a purchase order. It will establish the price, quantity, and date for the deliverable. There are several types of fixed price contracts:

- Firm Fixed Price (FFP) – the most common. A price is set from the outset and will not change unless there is a change in scope.

- Fixed Price Incentive Fee (FPIF) – this is a contract where buyer and seller share some risk and can both benefit from the seller out-performing agreed-upon metrics. In this type of contract a ceiling price is established (the maximum amount the buyer will pay). Then both parties agree upon a target cost (FP) and the target incentive fee (IF). Both added together become the target price. Finally, each agrees to a share ratio of cost overruns or underruns. The share ratio then is used to calculate the point of total assumption (PTA), where the buyer stops contributing to cost overruns and all additional costs incurred come from the seller's profit. I know that's confusing, so let's consider this example:

Let's assume I want to purchase a custom piece of equipment that a contractor will make. We agree that I will pay no more than $125,000 for this piece of equipment and that it should cost the contractor $100,000 to make. We agree that if he can make the equipment for that, he deserves a $10,000 incentive fee, which means I would pay the price of $110,000. It looks like this:

Target Cost - $100,000

Target Profit - $10,000

Target Price - $110,000 (target cost + target profit)

Ceiling Price - $125,000

Next, we agree to an 80/20 share ratio. That means that if the contractor is able to make the equipment for less than $100,000, his profit goes up by $.20 for every dollar he saves. Alternatively, any costs beyond $110,000 will be paid 80% by me and 20% by the contractor, which eats into his profit. It looks like this:

Share Ratio – 80% buyer, 20% seller

At some point, because I'm not paying any more than $125,000 total, the share ratio goes to 100% contractor and 0% me. This is the PTA and is calculated like this:

PTA – ((ceiling price – target price)/buyer's share ratio) + target cost

PTA = (($125,000- $110,000) / 0.8) + $100,000

PTA = $18,750 + $100,000

PTA = $118,750

Therefore, once costs go above $118,750, the contractor incurs 100% of them. The contractor can still make a profit (up until the cost reaches $125,000), but each additional cost eats into it.

- Fixed Price with Economic Price Adjustment (FP-EPA) – this is a third type of fixed price contract and is used for contracts that span multiple years.

<u>Cost-Reimbursable Contracts</u> – these contracts first reimburse the seller for all actual costs incurred and then add a fee for the seller's profit. In this type of contract, the majority of the risk falls on the buyer and is less desirable because of it. These types of contracts are more appropriate if there is not a clear statement of work in the beginning of the project during the negotiation process or when there are risks present too high for the seller to accept in a fixed price. There are several types of cost-reimbursable contracts:

- Cost Plus Percentage of Cost (CPPC) – in this type of contract, the seller bears zero risk and the buyer accepts it all. This is the least desirable cost-reimbursement contract for the buyer since all costs incurred by the seller are reimbursed plus a percentage of them. An unethical seller might be tempted to not control costs, as they should, since their profit increases as the cost increases.

- Cost Plus Fixed Fee (CPFF) – here, the buyer still bears all risk, but the seller's profit does not increase as costs increase. The profit is set at the beginning of the project (typically a percentage of the estimated costs) and does not change unless the scope changes, regardless of seller's performance.

- Cost Plus Award Fee (CPAF) – this contract shares the risk a little more with the seller. In the CPAF, the buyer reimburses the seller for the actual costs and then awards a fee based on the buyer's satisfaction of performance standards outlined in the contract.

- Cost Plus Incentive Fee (CPIF) – this contract shares the most risk between buyer and seller of the cost-reimbursable contracts. In the CPIF, the buyer reimburses the seller for actual costs and then pays an incentive fee that is predetermined and outlined in the contract based upon the seller achieving certain objectives.

<u>Time and Materials Contracts</u> – T&M contracts are a hybrid of both fixed price and cost-reimbursable and are used when a clear statement of work cannot be generated. An example of this is using set professional hourly rates (for instance attorney fees) when the scope (number of hours the buyer will need) is unclear. It is always a good idea to establish a ceiling or a not-to-exceed (NTE) price in this type of contract to avoid massive cost overruns.

Other types of contracts do exist and it will benefit you to become familiar with your particular organization's contracting procedures and options available to you. For instance, at CGTC we had an IDIQ (indefinite delivery/indefinite quantity) contract with a number of A-Es. This type of contract is a parent contract that comes up for renewal upon expiration at set intervals (e.g., annually or biannually). Underneath the contract, we would issue task orders to engage in A-E services for the design of certain projects. This method allowed the organization to get routine services ordered in a much quicker manner than going through an entire contracting process each time we needed this service. Issuing a task order was much faster because all of the governing terms and conditions were set in the IDIQ. All that had to be specified was the scope of the individual task order.

Bidding Contracts

So now that we've gone through the contract types, how does a buyer even get to the point in procurement where contracts are signed? From the project scope, a procurement statement of work will be developed that describes the item or service in enough detail that a seller can determine whether or not they can meet the buyer's demand. Next, the buyer will solicit information or bids from potential sellers. Options for solicitation include the following:

- Request for Information (RFI) – a formal request for preliminary information from the seller. The term RFI will also be used during project execution for a formal request for information from the seller to the buyer. An example of this would be to clarify a specification or preference.

- Invitation for Bid (IFB) – also referred to as a request for quote (RFQ), is a request for a bid on the procurement statement of work. This is a request for a price, not for the seller to come up with any conceptual details.

- Request for Proposal (RFP) – in contrast to the IFB or RFQ, the buyer informs the seller of a need and this request seeks a proposal of how the seller will meet the buyer's demand.

Since there is a high probability of being part of a project management team for construction, FMs need to understand certain contracting models and terms specific to this industry.

- Design-bid-build – this model separates the design contract from the construction contract. The owner contracts first with an A-E, who completes the design. Once the design is complete, plans and specifications are sent out for bid to general contractors and a contract is awarded after selection. This model ensures that a fixed price contract can be awarded on a large project, however it is more time consuming because the entire design must be completed prior to bidding construction activities.

- Design-build – this model combines design and construction into a single contract. The owner contracts with an organization that offers both design and construction services. The benefit to this method is that some construction activities can occur before the entire design is complete, which can result in a quicker completion time.

- Construction management – the owner contracts directly with a construction manager who then coordinates contracts with an A-E and general contractor.

- Multiple prime – the owner contracts directly with sub-contractors and issues contracts to them.

- PM or CM at-risk – the owner contracts with a project management firm or construction management firm that agrees to oversee the project and complete it with a maximum ceiling price, regardless of cost overruns. While this sounds like beneficial risk avoidance, it can also lead to the PM/CM using cheaper materials. Care should be taken to guard against this in the contract.

I tend to be a bit of a control freak, so I prefer D-B-B or multiple prime models. When time allows, I like knowing exactly what the scope is before moving forward. I'm interested to hear what your thoughts are and why you prefer them.

Best Value vs. Low Bid

When multiple contractors bid on a project, there has to be a method for determining which one gets the award. Two of the most popular methods are best value and low bid. Best value is becoming more and more preferred because it looks at other metrics such as past performance and safety history in addition to the bid amount.

This is in contrast to the low bid method where the lowest bidder is given the contract. Contracting is no different than any other type of procurement, in that the cheapest price is not always the smartest way to go.

Bonds

A bond is nothing more than a certificate that acts as a promise to pay the holder of the certificate an amount of money at a future date. Bonds transfer risk from one party to another and are often required in certain types of contracts. I have seen much confusion regarding bonds, so we will cover the basic types here:

- Bid bond – this is a bond given from the bidder to the buyer when submitting a bid for consideration. It proves that the bid is given in earnest and that if the bid is accepted, the bidder has sufficient resources to fulfill all project requirements – including the issue of a performance bond upon contract award. The buyer may only exercise this bond upon failure of the winning bidder to perform under terms of the bid.

- Performance bond – also known as a surety bond, this is a bond a bank or insurance company gives to the buyer on behalf of the contractor. It ensures that the issuing party will either take over and complete the project or pay damages up to the bond limit should the contractor fail to complete the contract.

- Payment bond – this bond also is issued by a bank or insurance company to the buyer on behalf of the contractor. It guarantees that all subcontractors and suppliers will be paid as long as they complete their end of their agreements with the contractor. This ensures that the project will be free of liens should the contractor default on any payments.

Insurance

In addition to bonds, insurance is another vehicle for risk transference. A facility is still responsible for work results and any injuries that might occur, even when contracting work out to third parties. Therefore, it is always wise to require certificates of insurance from contractors to protect the organization from contractor negligence resulting in injury or property loss. Liability insurance is the primary type of insurance required. Two of the most common types are workers' compensation insurance, which insures against work-related injuries, and general liability insurance, which insures against construction defects.

Contract Terminology

Finally, project team members would benefit from understanding the following contract terms:

- Change order – a written document approving a change in scope. These could potentially result in a change in cost or schedule, but do not have to.

- Punch list – a list generated by PM, contractor, and any other pertinent individuals during a final walk-through of the project. The list identifies remaining items the contractor must complete to close the contract.

- Substantial completion – a clearly documented point in time when the building is ready for occupancy. Minor punch list items are acceptable at this point. It is important to note that this marks the beginning of the warranty period.

- Completion date – the date at which all contract work is complete (including punch list items).

- Retainage – a portion of the contract price withheld from payment to the contractor until the contract is complete to ensure the contractor satisfies contractual obligations.

- Liquidated damages – damages (specified by the contract, typically on a daily basis) charged to the contractor for days past the specified contract completion date that the project is not finished.

Chapter 4: Execution

The execution of the project is driven by the scope and statement of work, contracting documents, and all of the work put into the planning process, creating the project management plan. As the project manager, you will be responsible for managing all of the work to ensure deliverables are produced according to the contract, schedule, and budget.

You also are responsible to direct the activities of the project management team. If a contractor is responsible for completing the bulk of the work, you are responsible for conducting inspections and ensuring the contractor fulfills his requirements. Let's look at the division of labor and responsibilities of the CGTC HQ project to get a better understanding of how some of the execution processes work for construction projects.

> All construction projects at Camp Gruber have traditionally been design-bid-build projects. The federal government does use other types of project methods, but there is one key benefit to the D-B-B process. That is the cost for full design is typically 9% of the cost of construction, which can be allocated in an earlier budget cycle.
>
> This means, you can get the ball rolling on a project where the money for construction hasn't been allocated yet in order to be ready to award the contract as soon as the project is funded (this is only for smaller projects at the state level if anyone reading this has been in military construction before).
>
> With the HQ project, the military department didn't have sufficient funding to contract the project at the beginning of the fiscal year, but the state facilities manager knew once again that he could probably get it funded at the end of the fiscal year when other states couldn't execute their entire allotments. He did have 9% of the cost of construction, however, that he allocated to design. Because the design was complete well before the end of that fiscal year, the entire project was funded and a contract was awarded for construction.
>
> All of that to say, I had two external contracts. I issued a task order under an IDIQ with the A-E who designed the plans and

wrote the specifications at the beginning of the year. I then issued an FFP contract with another general contractor at the end of the fiscal year. In addition to the PM team (my internal team at Camp Gruber), the A-E, and the contractor, we used the state-contracting agency to put the contract out to bid, award the bid, and manage the contract.

To do this, the state agency advertised the contract to the public and required certain items to be returned to them before the bid opening date. These items included a sealed bid and bid bond. The sealed bids were all opened at a bid opening, which was also open to the public. From that point forward, all four parties were involved in the project.

The A-E was in the submittal approval chain, consulted on the project, and conducted inspections. The owner (my PM team) was present to ensure the government's interests were represented, manage change orders, process payments, approve submittals and conduct inspections. The state agency physically managed all aspects of the contracting process and the contractor executed the construction activities.

Manage Project Work

Submittals

Submittals are shop drawings, samples, or data on materials and products submitted by the contractor as a check and balance to verify that the correct type and quantity of products are used during the project. These are typically submitted from the contractor, through the architect or engineer, to the owner's representative. During this process, the submittal can be approved, returned for change or clarification, or rejected. If the submittal is not approved, it is incumbent on the contractor to send a new or updated submittal prior to using those products or materials. Submittals should be checked against the plans and specifications for correctness. The PM will be responsible for ensuring all submittals are addressed in a timely manner.

There are different methods for processing submittals. The easiest way, especially when all parties are not co-located on the project site, is to use an online exchange that everyone has access to. It allows submittals to be addressed much quicker than hard copies. I've used email, but things tend to get lost in inboxes. Bottom line, use what works for you.

> When I arrived at Camp Gruber, there was a state employee who worked for me as a construction manager within the FM department. He was very good at his job, but his process of reviewing submittals was cumbersome. Most of these were brought by hand to the installation (which is really in the middle of nowhere, Oklahoma) and reviewed there. The architect we commonly used maintained an office that was more than an hour's drive from the site.
>
> So, it just made sense to digitize the submittal review and approval process. The only problem with moving everything online as a solution was that it cost money, which would be another procurement process to go through. However, we realized that we could ask the contractor to provide an online submittal approval service as part of the contract. All we needed to do was add it to the statement of work when getting bids for construction. By doing this, we alleviated a lot of the headache and legwork involved and were able to get submittals turned around quickly, many times within the same day.

Request for Information

Requests for Information (RFI) are just that. What you need to know about RFIs, however, is they must follow a process or you will get lost in them. There should be a standard form used for the RFI, they should be recorded in a register, and the same person or persons should process them every time. The quicker and more accurate the information on the response, the better the outcome will be. Finally, RFIs provide a written record of clarification. This has come in handy many times when a contractor has installed an incorrect product (maybe the wrong color, or put it in the wrong location, etc.) and did not seem to recall being told otherwise. Keep copies of all RFIs and their responses.

Change requests

One major challenge you will most likely run into in every project you manage is the subject of change requests. A change request is a formal appeal to modify contract documents, deliverables, or a baseline. Once a change request is approved, that now takes the place of the original project component it modified. Change requests fall into one of four categories:

- Corrective action – changes the current activity to get the project work back on track with the project management plan.

- Preventive action – is similar to corrective action, but ensures future work aligns with the project management plan.

- Defect repair – is a change to modify a component of or the product itself that does not conform to specifications.

- Update – is a change to a project formal document to reflect updates in the project.

Conflict Resolution

Unfortunately, disagreements arise. The most desirable way to manage conflict for all parties is through direct negotiation among themselves. This method is quick and inexpensive. If the conflict can be resolved through negotiation, do it.

From there, parties can engage in a form of alternative dispute resolution (ADR). Two forms of ADR are mediation and arbitration. Mediation is the less expensive, quicker, and generally preferred option. In mediation, some neutral third-party acts as a negotiator to resolve the dispute. When I have been involved in mediation, the two parties were kept separate (with legal counsel if they chose) and the mediator walked back and forth between the two rooms bringing offers and counter-offers. The mediator's goal is to find a middle ground that both parties can agree on, but there is no binding decision issued by the mediator.

Arbitration is much more expensive and takes longer. Both parties do have legal representation and will present their case (to include evidence and witnesses) in front of the arbitrator. When I have been involved in arbitration, we were all in the same room. The arbitrator then makes a ruling after reviewing everything, which becomes a binding decision.

The last option is litigation in the court system. This is the most expensive and takes the longest. Efforts should be made to avoid litigation when at all possible.

Don't Forget the FF&E

FF&E stands for furniture, fixtures, and equipment. It refers to any movable furniture, fixtures, and equipment that do not have a permanent connection to the building (such as office furniture). FF&E may or may not be included in the scope of the contract with the general contractor but the vast majority of building projects will have some FF&E component to them. As the PM, understand who is responsible for selecting, procuring, and installing FF&E and ensure that it is accounted for and ordered early enough in the project so that you have it when you need it. There's nothing worse than having an incredible new facility with no furniture in it because the FF&E wasn't considered early enough in the project.

Manage the Project Team

Part of the execution process is managing the project team. First, however, we need to understand these three types of project management organizations:

- Functional organization – is the "standard" organizational structure in general industry you might immediately think of if you're familiar with any sort of chain of command. In a functional organization, each department is managed by a functional manager, who then reports up to senior-level management. There is no designated project team or project manager. Departments are independent and typically organized based on their function, product they produce, or specialty. When a project is started within this organization, the functional manager of the affected department typically acts as the part-time project manager. If parts of the project cross departmental boundaries, the functional manager must coordinate with other functional managers, potentially with input from senior management. Here, the project manager has little control over areas of the project falling outside their department and therefore has low project management authority.

- Project-based organization – is the complete opposite organization from the functional organization. There is still a chain of command, but the departments are organized as project teams or units and the functional manager over them is a full-time project manager. The departments are built based on project requirements. Almost all organizational resources are dedicated to project work. Here, the project manager has the most authority since he or she controls all aspects of the project under their supervision.

- Matrix organization – is a cross between the functional and project-based organizations. There are three types of matrix organizations.

    - First, the functional matrix is an organization where functional managers have the most control, because the project manager role is more of a project assistant.

    - Second, the balanced matrix organization is where the functional manager and the project manager share project authority.

    - Third, the project matrix organization is where a lead project manager is a department head just like the functional managers, but his or her team focuses on managing projects for the entire organization, while other functional managers run their departments respectively. Here, the project manager has the most control out of the matrix organizations.

Put the Team Together

Once you determine what type of organization you are in, you can determine how much authority and control over the project and team you will have. Assuming you are acting as the PM, the first thing you need to do is put together your team. Putting together the team can be challenging, but it is important for all team members to understand their responsibilities and how they contribute to the whole. One helpful tool to assist you in this is an organizational hierarchy that graphically depicts working and reporting relationships within the project team. By using a RACI chart specific to the project team members, the PM can assign responsibilities based on activity.

Consider the following when putting your team together and assigning responsibilities:

- Function – the role the individual will play within the project itself.

- Skill Level – does the individual have the necessary skills to perform all duties of the function they will be asked to perform?

- Duties – what are the specific duties of the position on the team?

- Authority – what level of authority does the individual have in their position? This is especially important when determining who will have approval authority for things like pay applications, change orders, and conflict resolution.

Staffing Management Plan

Next, you need a staffing management plan. This is a plan that outlines how the project will get human resources, when you will need those people, and how long you will need them. As you identify when the project will need team members in the various functions, these should be put into a resource calendar and checked against the project timeline. This calendar will have to be continually updated as information and requirements change throughout the duration.

Based on all of the information you have assembled, the PM must identify which team members require additional training to perform their function within the project. There might also be training required of the entire team before beginning the project. As you finalize the staffing management plan, don't forget about incentives. Those should be clearly spelled out within the plan on how the project team will be rewarded for achieving or surpassing project goals.

Manage the Team

Now it's time for the PM to manage their team. This can be a great experience if you have good members. It can also be challenging. In 1963, Bruce Tuckman proposed a model of group development. Commonly referred to as the "Tuckman Ladder," it describes these four stages that teams go through as they work together:

<u>Forming</u> – is when team members establish base-level expectations. They will typically find common ground and establish similar goals. The members begin to develop trust and rely on one another to start tasks. During this stage, team members begin to bond.

<u>Storming</u> – is when team members start to identify control issues and can experience power struggles within the group. Members react to leadership and are not afraid to express differences of opinions. Here, team members start to work independently from one another.

<u>Norming</u> – is when team members agree on functions and problem-solving methods. They being to find solutions through negotiation with one another. Decisions are easier and team members increase their creativity. In this stage, confidence increases as the purpose becomes well defined.

<u>Performing</u> – is when results are achieved. Team members implement solutions to problems and work collaboratively. Members identify with one team identity and are motivated to accomplish the tasks at hand.[16]

While these stages normally occur in this order, it is not set in stone. Teams that have worked together in the past are likely to skip a step or two. Teams can also regress to an earlier step during the project life cycle. It is important to know, as the PM, what stages your teams are likely to go through and how to effectively manage them through that process.

Chapter 5: Supervision and Control

The process of supervising and controlling the project work is absolutely one of the most important aspects of project management. This is where the project management team will monitor, review, and report the progress of all project objectives contained in the project management plan. You will use the baselines defined during the planning process and compare them against all project activity.

From there, the PM controls the project by using a number of tools to either maintain the progress of the project or change the direction. Reporting project status to stakeholders becomes an important task throughout this process as they will want regular information about deviations from scope, cost, and time. Additionally, the PM is responsible for monitoring the quality of the deliverables throughout the project as well as the effective control of communications, risk, and procurements. Finally, the PM must validate the scope, which means they must accept the deliverable as complete and in line with scope requirements.

Variance Analysis

Throughout the supervision and control sub-phase, variance analysis is used to determine the difference between the scope, cost, and schedule baselines and contractor performance. Performance measurements are used to identify the cause and degree of the variance and necessary actions, if any, to get the project back on track.

Change Requests

A change request is a formal proposal to modify an aspect of the baseline or other component of the plan. Change requests can occur in any phase of the project, but are especially important during supervision and control. As the PM engages in these activities and conducts variance analysis, change requests are not uncommon results. I listed the categories of change requests above as corrective actions, preventive actions, defect repairs, and updates. In addition to these, it is important to know that change requests might affect only the scope, schedule, or costs; but, these requests could affect all three. I've approved many "no cost change orders" that only gave the contractor additional time to complete the project due to weather delays.

The customer, contractor, project manager, or any stakeholder can originate change requests. As the PM, I have requested change orders to incorporate additional scope as determined by senior management. I have also had many contractors submit change requests based on unexpected conditions they find as the project moves forward.

I prefer to talk through any potential changes and associated options prior to going through the formal change control process so there are no surprises. Surprises result in wasted time reviewing and revising multiple change requests before finally agreeing on an approved change order. The important thing to remember is to follow the change control process for review and approval during the manage work sub-phase. The project manager has the ultimate responsibility to conduct the change control process.

Supervise and Control Scope

Fresh out of college, I got a job working as the one-man warranty service for a residential construction company. It was awful. I was the guy who dealt with all of the unhappy customers that took possession of their home too early. I define too early as prior to all of the punch list items being complete. Why were there so many unhappy customers? The PM who built the home would typically forget about the punch list because they were off to the next house. After being ignored for months, the punch list would fall in my lap. I say all of that to illustrate how grateful I was when I was handed my first home to construct as the project manager.

After a few years, I was managing around 12 residential projects at a time and felt like I had a good grasp on them. One afternoon, another project manager I worked with ran through the sales office and into the back room where the PMs had their desks. I was working at my desk and looked up to see a panic-stricken face, turning three different shades of green.

"What's wrong with you?" I asked.

"I forgot the deck…" is all he could manage to say and he pointed in the direction of the neighborhood in which we had several homes being built.

Puzzled, I said, "let's go look."

Now, no one is perfect. We all make mistakes but there was very little I wasn't able to recover from as a PM with that company. However, when he took me into the house and pointed to the plans laying on the bar in the kitchen, I knew why he was green. This PM did not just forget a deck. He forgot to tell the framer to include an upper level deck that was built into the roofline, which the customer had added during their pre-construction meeting. The deck should have connected to a finished-out bonus room above the living room downstairs. However, the house had been totally framed and roofed with no deck in sight. Apparently, the customers were out of town and weren't able to see their house until that day. This was not good.

I don't know exactly how much that mistake cost the company, but I know it wasn't cheap. The PM had to rip off the shingles and completely reframe the second story of the house. Had he been controlling his project accurately, this would not have happened.

This is an example of how important it is to constantly supervise and control the scope of your project. All I mean by this is that you need to make sure the deliverables match the scope baseline.

In addition to monitoring the scope to ensure deliverables meet the minimum requirements, the project manager must pay attention to any deliverables going above and beyond requirements. Two examples of this are scope creep and gold plating.

<u>Scope Creep</u> – is uncontrolled scope growth during a project, when no changes are made to time or cost. This can easily come into play as something small and then work its way into something big. For example, consider a customer engaging with a developer in a website project. She asks the PM if he can add one extra feature that was not called for in the project. Wanting to be nice and knowing that it should take less time to write in the few lines of code than it would take to get a change order approved, the PM agrees. Unfortunately, after the few lines of code are written, a compatibility issue comes up because of the extra feature. It

takes the developer several extra days to resolve the issue and costs a considerable sum of money in added labor that was not accounted for originally. As a PM, you must ensure you only provide the customer with the agreed-upon deliverables in the scope baseline.

Gold Plating – this is when the PM, the project team, or the contractor adds features to the deliverable that were not included as part of the scope baseline. This is done with good intentions because they think they are adding value to the customer's deliverable without charging for it. However, it is not uncommon for the customer to not want the extra features a well-intentioned PM gave them -- and will refuse the deliverable because of it. Not only is the PM out the cost of providing the extra features, he/she has to eat the cost of removing them to meet project requirements. Gold plating is sometimes done to impress supervisors within the organization or to earn favor with customers, but care should be taken to avoid it.

> Years after I left Camp Gruber as the facility manager, a contractor was working on a job to construct several buildings as part of a larger complex. When the contractor ordered the HVAC units for a certain building, he ordered an upgraded unit from what was specified because he could get it at the same cost and it was "better." The problem was that this upgraded unit required a lot of additional training beyond the on-site technician's understanding to maintain the system. Additionally, the parts would be more expensive when repairs were required. In the end, it would have cost the government more money for the "better" HVAC systems. As a result, the FM rejected the units and the contractor was forced to return them. This is a prime example of gold plating.

Throughout the process of supervising and controlling the scope, the PM will make baseline updates as needed to reflect any changes from approved change requests. The important thing to remember is to communicate the updates and approved changes to all members of the project team to ensure everyone is on the same page. An effective communication plan is vital to this process.

Supervise and Control Schedule

In order to ensure expectations are set and managed with respect to time, supervision and control of the schedule must occur from beginning to end. This process requires the PM to monitor progress of all project activities with respect to the schedule baseline and manage any changes necessary as a result. Like controlling scope, the PM utilizes variance analysis to identify deviations from the baseline and takes corrective actions to fix them or preventive actions to ensure they do not occur.

Not all deviations from the schedule will require action, however. A large delay on an activity with a lot of float may not require any corrective action on the part of the PM or the contractor. That said, a very small delay to any activity on the critical path will require immediate attention because the entire project will be delayed as a result.

PMs will analyze start and finish dates of each activity as they relate to the critical path and the overall project schedule. Again, I prefer to use a Gantt chart in my analysis. It is the easiest tool for me to digest the entire schedule in one place. The next thing for a PM to analyze is the percentage of work complete on the project as a whole. The contractor typically supplies this information, but it is important to verify that the percent complete information they report is close to the percent complete that you as the PM estimate. I have seen more than one contractor report higher percentages than are actually complete in order to avoid confrontation. It never works and is better to address a lagging schedule sooner rather than later. Finally, the PM should be analyzing the remaining duration for all incomplete activities. Any variance between estimated duration remaining and time left on schedule must be addressed immediately.

Several tools will aid the PM in their analysis. By looking at the historical trends of schedule deviation, the PM will know if the contractor's performance is improving or lagging farther behind. The PM should also compare actual performance against critical path duration estimates when analyzing start and finish dates of each activity. Finally, the PM can use earned value management (EVM). EVM combines scope, schedule, and cost measurements to form a performance measurement baseline (PMB), and is an excellent reporting tool that can easily quantify variance analysis for senior management. All of this will make sense in the next section as we cover EVM in detail.

Supervise and Control Cost

Recall that the third leg of the project triangle is cost. I wouldn't argue that it is more or less important than scope or schedule, but costs get much scrutiny in project management. Perhaps it has just been my experience; but costs continually receive the most scrutiny in the projects I have managed. Understanding how to track and report costs is vital to ensuring senior management stays informed and you are positioned to respond quickly and appropriately when costs get out of line. The most common and effective way to do this is through EVM.

Earned Value Management

Once again, earned value management (EVM) combines scope, schedule, and cost measurements to determine variances between planned and actual performance. Like controlling scope and schedule, measuring variances is necessary to know when corrective action is needed by always maintaining an understanding of what progress has been made. EVM also generates updated estimates to future performance based on actual performance. Estimates are compared to the baseline, which allows the PM to manage risk. As mentioned earlier, the performance measurement baseline (PMB) is the integration of the scope, schedule, and cost baselines and is the basis for EVM.

EVM is a series of formulas. In order to understand these formulas, we must first have a common understanding of several key terms:

- Planned Value – planned value (PV) is the authorized budget for the work. As such, PV is calculated before work is performed. PV is the value the project should have earned according to the schedule (this forms the baseline). Do not think of PV as referring only to budgeted costs. PV also refers to schedule. PV is sometimes referred to as the PMB, budget at completion or budgeted cost of work scheduled (BCWS).

- Actual Cost – actual cost (AC) is what the work completed during a specific timeframe cost. Said another way, it is the amount of money you have spent to date.

- Earned Value – earned value (EV) is the value of work performed. EV is put in budget terms so it can be measured against the PV to analyze variance. EV is different from AC. EV is the value of what has been completed. AC is what has been spent. This is an important distinction.

EV is calculated by taking the percentage of work complete and multiplying it by the planned value for the entire project. In fact, it is likely that EV and AC will be different. The difference between the two is the cost variance. Much like measuring budget performance in financial management, it is important to measure EV in both the current period (to determine progress during that period) and from the beginning of the project (to determine cumulative performance). EV is sometimes referred to as the budgeted cost of work performed (BCWP).

- Budget at Completion – budget at completion (BAC) is the cost baseline for the entire project.

Now let's get into the actual EVM formulas using these terms and understand when and why you would use them.

- Cost Variance – cost variance (CV) is the difference between EV and AC. If the CV is negative, that's a bad thing because you have spent more money than the budgeted value of the progress. In contrast, a positive CV is great, because you have earned more value that you have spent. This is the formula for CV:

  $$CV = EV - AC$$

- Schedule Variance – schedule variance (SV) is the difference between EV and PV. This is the measured amount of how ahead or behind schedule the project is at any point in time. Like cost variance, a negative SV is bad as it indicates that the project is behind schedule. A positive SV is good, because that means you are ahead of schedule. By definition, when the project is complete all planned values will have been earned. Thus, the SV is zero when the project is complete. This is the formula for SV:

  $$SV = EV - PV$$

- Cost Performance Index – cost performance index (CPI) is the ratio of EV to AC. This is commonly considered the most vital

EVM formula as it measures the cost efficiency of the project. A ratio above 1.0 means that your project is more cost efficient than planned and is good. A CPI less than 1.0 is not good. This is the formula for CPI:

$$CPI = EV \div AC$$

- Schedule Performance Index – schedule performance index (SPI) is similar to CPI. The SPI is a ratio of EV to PV, which measures the schedule efficiency of the project. Like CPI, an SPI ratio of above 1.0 is good, while an SPI below 1.0 is bad. This is the formula for SPI:

  $$SPI = EV \div PV$$

The preceding formulas are used to analyze variance between planned and actual performance ***to date***. The following formulas are used to forecast and report on ***future performance***.

- Estimate at Completion – estimate at completion (EAC) is the forecast of what the total cost of the project will be when complete. As the project progresses, the BAC may or may not be viable depending on circumstances that might have changed through the project life cycle. At the point in time when the BAC is no longer attainable, the PM must consider forecasting the EAC based on current project performance and known future variables. There are different formulas for EAC based on known information and assumptions. They are:

  - The ***AC + Bottom-up*** formula takes actual costs to-date and adds them to all projected costs in the future. It is the most accurate, but also the hardest to calculate because you have to go back and re-estimate all costs again. Essentially, you are creating an entirely new project budget from scratch, but starting at some point during the life of the project (hence, taking actual costs incurred and adding them to estimated future cost estimates). Here is this formula:

    $$EAC = AC + Bottom\text{-}up\ ETC$$

- The $AC + (BAC - EV)$ formula takes actual costs to-date and adds them to the remaining work at the budgeted rate. It assumes any past cost variances were out of the norm and all future work can be accomplished on budget. It looks more confusing than it is. All you're doing here is taking actual costs incurred and adding them to all budgeted line items that haven't been performed yet. Here is this formula:

  $$EAC = AC + (BAC - EV)$$

- The $BAC \div CPI$ formula assumes all current cost variances will continue throughout the life of the project by taking the budget at completion and dividing it by the cost performance ratio. So if you've been over-budget on everything to-date, this formula assumes you will continue to be over-budget by the same margin for the rest of the project. Here is this formula:

  $$EAC = BAC \div CPI$$

- The $AC + (BAC - EV) \div (CPI \times SPI)$ formula assumes both cost ***and*** schedule performance will continue throughout the life of the project. Here is this formula:

  $$EAC = AC + (BAC - EV) \div (CPI \times SPI)$$

- Estimate to Complete – estimate to complete (ETC) is the forecast used to determine the cost of remaining work. The formula for ETC is:

  $$ETC = EAC - AC$$

- Variance at Completion – variance at completion (VAC) is the forecast of how much cost variance the project will have when complete. The formula for VAC is:

  $$VAC = BAC - EAC$$

- To-Complete Performance Index – to-complete performance index (TCPI) is a ratio that gives the PM and senior management a measure of performance that must be accomplished to meet the specified goal. Taking the work remaining and dividing by the funds remaining calculates TCPI. There are two formulas for TCPI. They are:

- The TCPI formula immediately below assumes the original budget can still be achieved.

$$TCPI = (BAC - EV) \div (BAC - AC)$$

- In contrast, the TCPI formula below is used when the original project budget is no longer attainable. In this case, the BAC is replaced with the EAC (the new project budget) to yield the measure of performance that must be accomplished moving forward.

$$TCPI = (BAC - EV) \div (EAC - AC)$$

I realize that all of these formulas make very little sense by themselves. The following is an example of a simple project and how these formulas are used in EVM to analyze it:

Landscape Project – A project manager hires *Local Landscapes* to install five flowerbeds in five days at a rate of $20 per hour for 40 hours ($800 total project cost and five-day total project duration). The PM has an expectation of Local Landscapes working eight hours per day and completing one flowerbed per day.

Based on this scenario, we know the following information:

PV = $160 per day ($160 on Day 1, $320 on Day 2, etc.)

BAC = $800 (the total budget is the total estimated project cost)

Because no actual work has been done, there is no EV or AC value yet. Recall that the planned value (PV) is the performance measurement baseline (PMB). Graphically, Figure 16 shows what the PV looks like for the entire project:

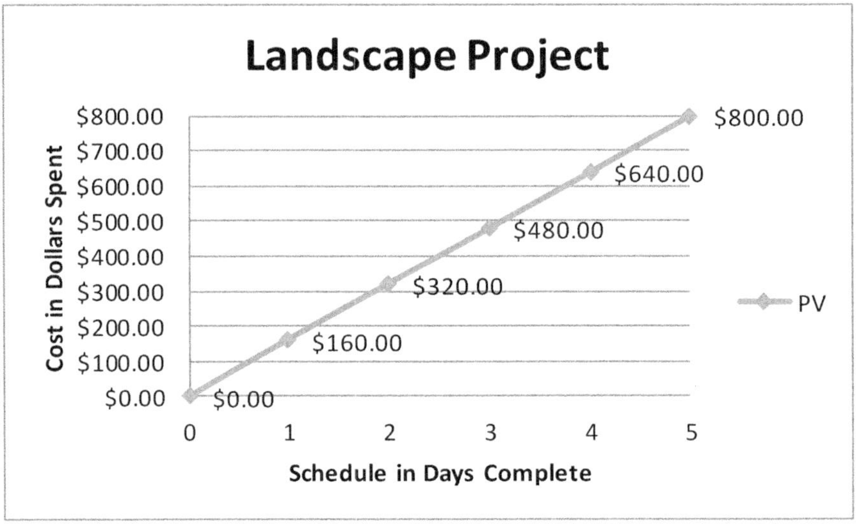

Figure 16

Now let's consider what happens in this hypothetical scenario throughout the life of the project.

At the end of Day 1, Local Landscapes worked 7 hours and finished 2 flowerbeds. Therefore:

PV = $160

BAC = $800

EV = 2 flowerbeds built x $160 = $320

AC = 7 hours worked x $20 = $140

Knowing this, we can determine the following EVM calculations:
The cost variance below means we are currently $180 under budget at the end of Day 1.

CV = EV – AC = $320 - $140 = $180

This schedule variance means we are 1 full labor-day (8 hours x $20 per hour) ahead of schedule.

SV = EV – PV = $320 - $160 = $160

Another formula below shows this CPI as a ratio of our cost performance. Remember anything above 1.00 is beating budget.

$$CPI = EV \div AC = \$320 \div \$140 = 2.29$$

This formula shows this SPI has a ratio of greater than 1.00, meaning the project is ahead of schedule.

$$SPI = EV \div PV = \$320 \div \$160 = 2.00$$

The below EAC formula assumes that for the rest of the project, the flowerbeds will be constructed right on budget. However, not knowing the specific circumstances and whether the cost and schedule variances will continue, I have included the EAC formula below. It is important to note that the results are different, depending on future variance forecasting.

$$EAC = AC + (BAC - EV) = \$140 + (\$800 - \$320) = \$620$$

The below EAC formula assumes that we can finish the project at the same efficiency as the first day. If that was the case, we could get all five flowerbeds for $350.

$$EAC = BAC \div CPI = \$800 \div 2.29 = \$350$$

The final EAC formula is one that we won't use because it is probably not realistic in this situation. That formula takes both cost and schedule into consideration when weighting estimate at completion. However, rarely will you be in a situation where you are less than half of your budget and working twice as fast as you thought you would. These formulas that have multiple options should be applied with discretion by the PM.

The ETC below forecasts remaining costs based on the new estimate at completion. For now, I will use the first EAC formula above that yielded $620 as a result, as this is probably the most likely outcome.

$$ETC = EAC - AC = \$620 - \$140 = \$480$$

Based on the new estimate at completion, the following VAC shows how much under budget the project will be at completion. A negative VAC would indicate a budget overage at completion. Because I am assuming all remaining budget items will come in on budget, the variance for the entire project is the same as the variance for the first day ($180).

VAC = BAC – EAC = $800 - $620 = $180

The TCPI below shows the ratio of performance efficiency the contractor must accomplish for the remainder of the project to bring the project in on the original budget (BAC). A ratio of 1.00 would mean that the contractor has to perform consistent to the original budget. A ratio of above 1.00 would mean the contractor would need to pick up the pace and outperform himself for the remainder of the project.

TCPI = (BAC – EV) ÷ (BAC – AC) = ($800 – $320) ÷ ($800 – $140) = 0.73

Graphically, Figure 17 illustrates what the PV, EV, and AC look like at the end of Day 1:

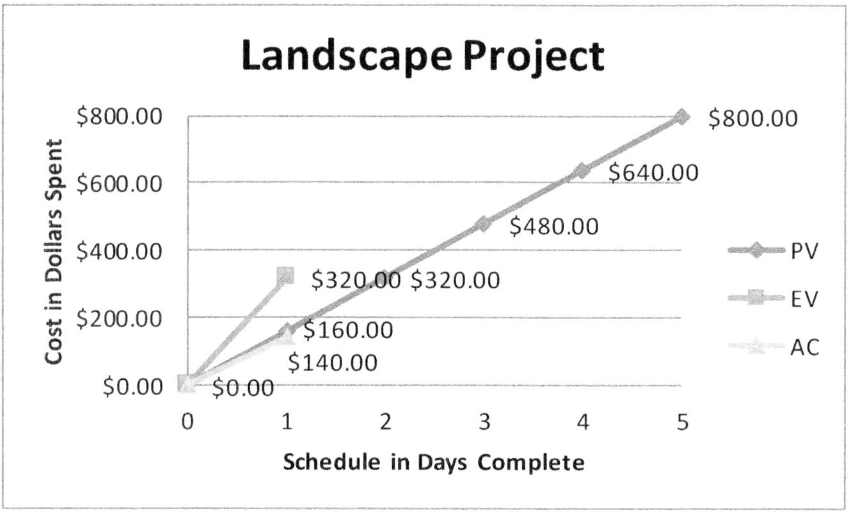

Figure 17

Thus, at the end of Day 1, the project is eight hours ahead of schedule and $180 under budget. Not bad for the first day.

These calculations can easily be continued for the remaining days. Each variable can be adjusted based on actual performance, and it's very likely each day will be different unless the contractor performs exactly the same as they did the first day.

EVM is a very useful tool that can help visually and numerically depict project performance for reporting to senior management and managing risk moving forward. The easier your project reports are to understand, the better your communication will be. My rule of thumb is that I want to present information my kids can easily understand. If I tell them to look at Figure 17 and show them the line with diamonds is where we are supposed to be and the line with squares is where we are, they will know we are doing better than we originally thought. Don't talk down to stakeholders. However, you should not assume they understand complex schedule and budget calculations either.

Supervise and Control Quality

This is when we check and act, the last two steps of the plan-do-check-act model. Once again, quality is broken down into two parts: quality assurance (QA) and quality control (QC). Other frameworks place quality assurance in the execution sub-phase because it is the process of auditing work performed during operations. However, it makes more sense for me to have both parts included here, but we do need to understand the difference in the two terms.

Think of quality assurance as process improvement. QA is often done by a separate department that audits operations as they are performed. The point of the quality audit is to objectively measure processes and how they are implemented. There are many tools for quality assurance and an in-depth review is beyond the scope of this book. However, the PMBOK® Guide lists the Seven Basic Tools of Quality as an example. If you are interested in learning more, it is a great resource for a place to begin.

Quality Control is the process of measuring deliverables against the requirements in the scope. Various tools such as inspections, examinations, etc., are used to "QC" deliverables to determine if they meet scope requirements. This is considered a validation of project deliverables. The other thing QC does is identify causes of nonconformance in the deliverable. Methods for QA and QC should be spelled out as part of the project management plan when planning quality management.

Commissioning

Once a new system is procured and installed, it should be commissioned (if that is an option). Commissioning (Cx) is the process of testing, adjusting, verifying, and documenting that the asset functions in accordance with the specifications. This process will establish the correctly functioning system as a benchmark for future operation, provide the owner with documentation (for instance O&M manuals) and provide operator training. This process is focused on quality and can be used in different building systems such as mechanical, life safety, utilities, controls, etc. If nothing else, I try to always commission large HVAC installations.

Typically, the commissioning authority (CxA) is contracted by the owner directly (not through the contractor) as a third-party consultant on the functionality and performance of the new system. Although this is not always the case due to the increase in cost to the project, it is the best way to ensure the system is properly commissioned. The CxA needs to be involved early in the project during initiation, so that they can help identify potential issues during design before becoming major issues during and after execution. Completion of the commissioning process typically marks the transition from the project to O&M.

One additional thing to note about Cx. Recommissioning is another quality process that goes back after the asset or system has been installed and functioning (long after the project is complete). This is not a repair activity. Recommissioning is performed with a certain goal in mind such as increasing the performance or the energy efficiency of a system.

The supervision and control sub-phase does not stop there. Supervision is a continual process, the result of which is control of all aspects included within the project management plan. Care must be taken to properly supervise all other sub-plans that might be included as required. Once again, the PMBOK® Guide goes into great detail on how to set up the additional sub-plans, should you need them. I suggest getting a copy of this book and referencing it as a project manager if you need additional technical assistance with specific steps within your projects.

Chapter 6: Closure

Project closure is really the step we all strive to get to. Being able to hand off a successful project to the end user gives me great satisfaction, especially when we have brought it in on-time and under-budget. It sometimes takes a herculean effort to complete projects. Once the major work is done, all we want to do is pass it off as soon as possible. However, we can't rush through properly closing out a project. There are three things we absolutely must do to close out a project: final inspection, close out contracts, and release of the team.

Final Inspection

Hopefully, you are used to conducting periodic walkthroughs and routine inspections of the progress of project work up to this point. You have controlled the work, managed change requests, and supervised scope, schedule, and cost. At this time, there should not be any surprises in quality or contract performance. The final inspection should be quite simple and quick. What you are doing is conducting a validation that all contract specifications and change orders have been accomplished and all punch list items are complete. Therefore, two things must be done prior to final inspection. First, you must create a punch list in a final walk-through. Second, you must agree upon a substantial completion date.

Punch List

Various project frameworks explain this slightly different than I do, but this is how I make the most sense out of project closure. I conduct a final walk-through with all necessary stakeholders for the specific purpose of creating a punch list. I do this far enough in advance of the final inspection that I give the contractor enough time to complete the punch list prior to inspection. This means I can conduct the final inspection alone with the contractor and validate that all items are complete. Waiting until the final inspection to create a punch list is not fun. When choosing necessary stakeholders for the final walk-through, ensure the following people are there with you:

- Contractor

- Major sub-contractors that have work yet to complete (this will ensure the message is conveyed directly to them and does not need to go through the contractor first)
- End-user representative (make sure this is the manager or managers over the end users of the space who agreed to the scope – you do not want every last worker trying to make new suggestions at project closure)
- Contracting personnel (the person responsible for signing that the contract is complete – this might be you, a contracting officer, an architect, a senior executive, etc.)
- Architect-Engineer (anyone directly responsible for interpreting the specifications – this should be who has been reviewing and approving submittals throughout the project)

Throughout the walk-through, you are going over all aspects of the project and itemizing anything that needs to be done or repaired as a result of work performance. This can be anything from materials yet to be installed to touch-up paint. The party responsible for executing everything on the punch list (typically the general contractor's project superintendent or project manager) should be creating the list. Ideally, the list would be copied and distributed to all parties. This is the list you will use during your final inspection to validate satisfactory completion.

Substantial Completion

The second thing you need to do before the final inspection is to determine when you will accept substantial completion, which means take responsibility for the deliverable (i.e., move into the space after a renovation). This is the point when the majority of the project is done and only minor things are left outstanding. Ideally, everything would be finished before accepting substantial completion, but that is not often the case. This happens pretty frequently in construction projects where one or two finish materials might be back-ordered, but it doesn't affect the usability of the space. Something to remember, however, with substantial completion. It allows you to start using the deliverable, but it also starts the clock on the contractor's warranty (typically a year). To be clear, it is entirely possible that you accept substantial completion prior to all items on the punch list being finished, which means this could occur prior to final inspection.

Close Out Contracts

This one may seem obvious, but don't overlook it. Once you have accepted substantial completion, it's easy to move on to the next project and forget about the lingering details of the current one. Make sure, once everything is done and the final inspection has been passed, to close out any open contracts. This should consist of formally signing a document stating that the contract is closed and approving final payment to the contractor.

One important step in contract closeout is to file away all pertinent project documents (including O&M manuals, warranty information, product information, correspondence, contracts, as-builts, etc.) into a historical archive that can be accessed at any point in the future. Too many times, I try to research past projects and come up empty handed. I also want to stress the importance of as-builts. As-builts are approved drawings that have been changed to reflect any modifications that happened in the field during execution. There are often changes from the approved drawings and it is important to capture these for your records. You should request as-builts from your contractor and keep them for future reference.

Release the Team

The final step in closure is to release the team. You should make this a formal process and recognize outstanding efforts of individuals and the success of the entire project team. This does a couple of things. First, it serves to motivate the team members. Projects are huge undertakings and can be very stressful. Take the time to recognize your team members and the next project they engage in will benefit from your diligence. Second, it formally ends their ties to the project. Have you ever been a part of a team where you thought everything was complete, but nothing ever really signified the end of the work? It's confusing.

Section Summary

All things are created twice; first mentally; then physically. The key to creativity is to begin with the end in mind, with a vision and a blue print of the desired result.

~ Stephen Covey

As with everything you want to achieve, project management requires that you begin at the end. To do this, you must determine the desired result and then make a plan for how to get there. This project management section covered many concepts and tools on how to successfully tackle any project you might face. Like you, I am continually learning. If you disagree with anything I have said or if you have anything to add, please visit me at **www.LearningFM.com** and let me know your thoughts. I would love to get your feedback and include those in future versions of this book. In the next section, we will cover another valuable pillar of facility management: business finance.

> The Camp Gruber HQ project ended with little fanfare. We did, however, have our problems along the way. In fact, the contractor had to completely remove and re-pour the slab for the new construction portion of the project due to cold temperatures. We also had a number of change orders along the way. One of these changes was to turn a small waiting area into a museum, showcasing Camp Gruber artifacts from WWII. That was the Post Commander's idea and it was my favorite part of the project.
>
> In the end, we handed the end users at the installation one consolidated HQ building that was more energy efficient, larger, and completely renovated. The project was a success and I couldn't thank our PM team members at Camp Gruber enough. Whenever you think you're alone as the project manager, remember you have a support system in place. Rely on those people. They want to succeed as much as you do.

Section 5: Finance

As a kid growing up in Tennessee, we were not a wealthy family -- at all. My idea of finance was counting the number of weeks it would take me to purchase a Nintendo Entertainment System® while making the staggering income of $1 per week allowance. Here's a hint….it took a while.

I remember the day I got my first raise. I went from $1 to $2 per week. It was a glorious moment because, while it doesn't sound like much, I doubled my income! Any day you get a 100% raise is a good day in my book. Both dollars from then on went straight into savings (which was an empty crayon box) and stayed there until I found something worth blowing my entire life savings on. Since the money was usually burning a hole in my pocket, I could make it two or three weeks before finding a comic or baseball card to buy. Life was so simple.

Then, I turned 16 and got my first job at the local movie theater. I was less than pleased with that first paycheck when I found out who FICA was. Alas, I had a nine-year-old Honda that I had to keep insured and put gas in, so I kept shoveling the popcorn, wearing my pink plastic bowtie (I am not exaggerating). I kept a written record in my checkbook of everything I spent and saved. I felt like I had a pretty good handle on things.

Then I graduated college. Ugh. I got my first real job, an apartment, a fiancé, and a CPA in tax season to keep track of everything. As it turns out, I was able to figure the financial management aspects of life just fine and even learned to do my own taxes for a while. I enjoyed learning more and more about economics and money management from articles, websites, and talk radio. I enjoyed it so much that I went back to school and earned my MBA in finance.

After all of that, it didn't take long to figure out I didn't know enough. I had to reapply the principles of finance in the varying contexts my different employers used. If you don't think a privately owned smaller company manages money differently than a larger, publicly traded company, you would be mistaken.

And don't even get me started on the federal government…

Hopefully, this illustrates how everyone needs finance in order to be successful in life; but not everyone needs to use it at the same skill level. This holds true for FM professionals at different levels. If you're new to a facility team, you might not have authority to obligate money on behalf of your organization, but you still need to understand your department's budget and financial goals.

As a facility manager, you will almost definitely be expected to create and maintain facility-related budgets, be involved to some degree in procurement, and recommend facility strategies to senior management in financial terms (e.g., payback from energy reduction projects). Even if you are not required to recommend initiatives at the strategic level, it will greatly benefit you to understand your organization's financial statements. This lets you know the financial health and strategic direction of the organization.

There can be varying consequences associated with failing to understand the basic concepts of finance. At the very least, you won't be as effective at your job as you could be. In fact, it's so important that one of the first things I was required to do as the FM of Camp Gruber was attend a two-day course on fiscal law. This was immediately followed by a three-day course on cooperative agreements (an agreement between the federal government and the state that outlines what each will pay). Needless to say, the federal government takes financial management very seriously.

As a facility manager, you are entrusted with your organization's largest assets (real estate, buildings, fixed equipment, etc.). That is a huge responsibility. While FMs operate in the background much of the time, we manage a large percentage of our company's worth.

This section on finance will cover what is arguably one of the most important and valuable knowledge domains a facility manager can possess. The good news is, it does not have to be overly difficult to learn. So, if you've ever been intimidated by accounting principles or financial terms, read this section.

Chapter 1: The Fundamentals

To begin, we need to have a common understanding of accounting basics, terminology, and application. These tools will then lead us into more advanced principles. Accounting is record keeping that gives management financial control and enables them to report on the financial condition and operational results of the organization.

All of the requirements that go into this record-keeping system occur in an annual cycle called a fiscal year. Fiscal years can coincide with calendar years (January 1 – December 31), but do not have to. The State of Oklahoma's fiscal year begins on July 1 and ends June 30. The federal government's fiscal year begins October 1 and ends September 30. It is important to understand when your organization's fiscal year begins and ends in order to understand the budgeting cycle and process.

There are two types of accounting to be aware of:

Financial accounting – If you've ever heard your CFO refer to the balance sheet or income statement, this is the type of accounting he is referring to. Accountants use financial accounting records to generate financial statements for the company that will be viewed by external organizations (auditors, investors, etc.). To see examples of these, go to an investment or market research website. Look up a publicly traded firm and download their historical financial statements. The information contained within these statements must adhere to standards prescribed by governing bodies, which is highly regulated.

Managerial accounting – In contrast, managers within the organization primarily use this type of accounting, which is not regulated and not required to adhere to standards. Managerial accounting is specific only to the part of the organization the manager is responsible for (unlike financial accounting that reports on the organization as a whole). This type of accounting will contain financial information, but also can contain other information that will help managers make informed decisions about the future of their department.

In the United States, companies (public and private), not-for-profit organizations, and governments must use standards in financial accounting as a basis to prepare financial statements. These statements include the balance sheet, income statement, statement of cash flows, and statement of shareholders' equity. Financial statements are used for numerous reasons from making financing decisions to holding public officials accountable for their actions. *Established in 1972, the Financial Accounting Foundation (FAF) is the independent, private sector, not-for-profit organization responsible for the oversight, administration, financing, and appointment of the Financial Accounting Standards Board (FASB) and the Governmental Accounting Standards Board (GASB). The FASB is responsible for standards for public and private companies and not-for-profit organizations. The GASB is responsible for standards for state and local governments.*[17]

The accounting standards developed by the FASB and the GASB are collectively known as Generally Accepted Accounting Principles (GAAP). GAAP standards seek to ensure that financial statements are relevant, comparable to other organizations, verifiable/auditable, and understood by stakeholders.

Accounting

Every organization must have a way to keep track of all of the information that goes into financial statements. This is typically done with accounting software. This software ranges from fairly simple to incredibly complex to use, depending on the needs of the organization. That said, the basics remain the same.

Chart of Accounts

The chart of accounts is a numerical listing of all the accounts in the organization's general ledger. An account is where accounting transactions will be summarized and recorded. It is how all pieces of information are organized and aggregated into the financial statements by the accounting software. These are the five basic account types and are typically listed in this order of appearance on financial statements:

- Assets – are what the organization owns. An asset has lasting value to the organization and can be tangible or intangible. Examples of assets would be cash, buildings, and machinery. Typical assets include:
    - Cash

- Accounts Receivable (money owed to the organization)
- Securities
- Inventory
- Prepaid Expenses (future expenses paid in advance)
- Fixed Assets (long term assets – property, plant, and equipment (PP&E))
- Accumulated Depreciation (how much the organization has depreciated an asset – purchase price minus accumulated depreciation equals the book value of an asset)

• Liabilities – are what the organization owes. There are current (come due in one-year or less) and long-term liabilities (don't come due within the year). Examples of liabilities include loans, taxes, and wages owed. Typical liabilities include:

  - Accounts Payable (money the organization owes)
  - Accrued Liabilities (expenses incurred but not yet paid)
  - Notes Payable
  - Wages Payable
  - Taxes Payable

• Stockholder's Equity – sometimes referred to as owner's equity, net assets or net equity, is the difference between the assets and liabilities, since liabilities lay a claim to the organization's assets. An example is a worker who has put in 40 hours, and is due the wage for time worked. This liability will come from the company's cash assets and lays a claim to the amount of money the worker is owed. The equation is:

  - Assets – Liabilities = Owner's Equity

  Typical Stockholder's Equity includes:

  - Common Stock (a security that represents ownership in a company – the number of shares of stock multiplied by their value equals the capital of the company)

  - Retained Earnings (earnings not paid as dividends – could be used to reinvest in the company or for debt service)

- Revenue – is the sale of services, goods, and products. Also included are earnings from interest, dividends, etc. This is the organization's income during this period.

- Expenses – are the organization's outflow or money spent. There can be many expenses, but typical expenses include:

  - Cost of Goods Sold (COGS) – direct costs of producing goods sold by a company during this period
  - Depreciation Expense – the portion of a fixed asset that has been consumed during this period, according to accounting
  - Rent
  - Supplies
  - Utilities
  - Wages

You might apply the chart of accounts in your organization to various things (such as invoices, or income sources) before you turn them into accounting for input into the accounting software. Let's say we work for a company that uses a four-digit chart of accounts. Here is a simple example of a chart of accounts showing the relationship between the number and the account:

Assets:
1000 Cash
1020 Checking
1040 Savings
1200 Accounts Receivable
1220 Prepaid Expenses
1300 Inventory of Products for Sale
1400 Inventory of Buildings
1500 Other Assets
    1510 Vehicles
    1520 Tools

Liabilities
2000 Accounts Payable
    2010 Taxes
    2020 Payroll
2100 Short-term Debt
    2110 Loan A
    2120 Loan B

2200 Long-term Debt
    2210 Loan A
    2220 Loan B

Owner's Equity
3000 Contributions by Owner
3100 Distributions to Owner
3200 Retained Earnings

Revenue
4000 Sales of Products
4100 Sales of Services

Expenses
5000 Cost of Goods Sold
5100 Depreciation
5200 Rent
7000 Maintenance Department
    7010 Wages
        7011 Salary
        7012 Hourly
    7020 Supplies
    7030 Repair & Replacement

You can see in this example that the four-digit numbers denote the type of account and ensure subaccounts fall in the correct place. In this example, the first two digits classify the major account type and the last two digits specify the subaccount. If I received an invoice for a repair on a building asset from a subcontractor, I would code it to 7030, Repair and Replacement. There are many methods on putting together a chart of accounts, but this example illustrates the principle of keeping different accounting items consolidated and separate from other types. Determine which method your organization uses and become comfortable with it.

Ledgers and Journals

A ledger organizes a company's financial information by account. The chart of accounts becomes the organization's table of contents for their general ledger (all of their financial information by account type). A Journal, or book of original entry, is a record that keeps financial transactions as they occur in chronological order. When a transaction is entered, it is called a journal entry.

Journal entries are typically done using the double-entry method. Double-entry bookkeeping means that there is an exchange between two accounts. The way this happens is by entering the journal entry in two places, a debit to one account and a credit to a different account. Each journal entry has a date, an explanation, and the accounts and amounts debited and credited. Figure 18 shows an example of what that looks like:

Date 2017	Account	Reference	Amount	
			Debit	Credit
March 1	Cash	1000	35,000	
	Notes Payable (Took loan for $35,000)			35,000
March 2	Equipment		10,000	
	Cash (Purchase of equipment from Company B)			10,000
March 3	Building A		100,000	
	Cash			20,000
	Mortgage Payable			80,000

Figure 18

The whole purpose of the double-entry system is to balance this equation:

Assets = Owner's Equity + Liabilities

Credits are opposites of debits. Debits are recorded on the left and credits are recorded on the right. For asset accounts, debits increase the account balance and credits reduce it. For liability accounts, debits decrease the account balance and credits increase it (i.e., you borrowed more). This can be confusing, so Figure 19 will help you keep track of that:

Journal Entries – Debits vs. Credits		
Account Type	**Debits**	**Credits**
Income	Decrease	Increase
Expense	Increase	Decrease
Equity	Decrease	Increase
Asset	Increase	Decrease
Liability	Decrease	Increase

Figure 19

For assets and expenses, debits increase the account and credits decrease the account.

For liabilities and revenues, debits decrease the account and credits increase the account.

So let's take another look at Figure 18 above. In this example, on March 1 the company increased its cash (asset account) balance by $35,000 from taking out a loan. This was then also recorded as an increase to the notes payable account (liability account), as part of the double-entry system.

The next day, they bought $10,000 worth of equipment (asset account) by paying cash for it. This decreased the cash account (asset account). Notice again, this $10,000 transaction is coded twice with the double-entry system.

The third day, they bought a building for $100,000, which increased the Building A account (asset account). They did this by doing two things, paying $20,000 in cash and taking out a mortgage for $80,000. Here, there are three entries, but the equation still balances. The assets go up $100,000 and the cash goes down $20,000 while the mortgage payable account goes up $80,000. Here's what that equation looks like:

Assets = Owner's Equity + Liabilities

Building A + Cash = Owner's Equity + Mortgage Payable

$100,000 + (-$20,000) = $80,000

$80,000 = $80,000

The reference column in Figure 18 is present in both journals and ledgers and is a way to cross-reference the two. In the journal, it references to which account the entry was posted in the general ledger. In the above example, the $35,000 was posted to account number 1000 (Cash in the general ledger). In a ledger, the reference indicates in which journal the entry was made (if the organization used more than one) and sometimes on which page.

Facility managers won't be the ones expected to make journal entries in the accounting software, but we should have a basic understanding of accounting. Accounting is cyclical with journal entries being posted, adjusted, and reviewed prior to the reporting of financial statements during a given period.

Financial Statements

Have you ever looked at an official financial statement from a publicly traded company you were thinking of investing in? Did it make sense to you? I have taken multiple classes in finance, but I am still not an accountant and neither are you. These things can get confusing for a few reasons. First, there is no standardized mold that all organizations use for all of their accounts. This means you're going to see financial jargon that you won't necessarily recognize because it won't fit into a model of the "normal" company's financial statement you might have seen previously. Second is the fact that you must have context to understand financial statements. Management decisions, the economy, changes in technology, etc., all affect what you see on financial statements. Third, people create these documents and those people are fallible. This is not an exact science. My goal here is for FMs to have a basic, but solid, understanding of what financial statements are, what information you can obtain from them, and why that might be useful to you.

Financial statements can be found in the organization's annual report. There are three main types that you should be familiar with as a facility manager: ***the income statement, the balance sheet, and the statement of cash flows.***

Income Statement

Commonly referred to as the P&L (profit and loss report) or earnings statement, the income statement reports an organization's income, expenses, and profits during the reporting period. This statement shows income when it accrues, meaning when the transaction actually occurs. This is sometimes different than when the cash actually changes hands. The overall basic format for the income statement reports on revenues (sales), subtracts operating expenses from it, and shows the resulting net profit (or net loss if the company didn't do so well). Keep in mind, the income statement shows the business results for a specific period. Figure 20 shows an example of a generic income statement:

Company A USD in Millions		
	2017	**2016**
Total Revenue	$10,000	$8,000
Expenses		
Selling Expenses	2,000	1,000
Research and Development Expenses	1,000	500
Interest Expense	500	500
Income Before Taxes	6,500	6,000
Income Tax Expense	2,000	1,800
Net Income	$4,500	$4,200

Figure 20

The income statement serves management as a tool to understand the financial state of their organization. It is compared to historical periods to show how well the company did during the same period in a previous month, quarter or year. Sometimes a variance column is included to show the dollar amount or percentage difference between the current period and the historical comparison. Using the above example, the variance of net income between 2017 and 2016 is $4,500 - $4,200 = $300. The percent difference is calculated by taking the percent change divided by the base period for comparison. In this case, that is $300 / $4,200 = 0.0714 = 7.14%.

Income statements are valuable in trend analysis. By comparing historical financial data to current period data, management can make decisions about operations based on trends they see.

Balance Sheet

Referred to as a statement of financial position (SOFP) in not-for-profits, the balance sheet is a snapshot of a company's financial position at one moment in time. The balance sheet includes assets, liabilities, and equity, which again balances this equation:

Assets = Liabilities + Owner's Equity

Generally, the assets are listed first in one section and the liabilities and equity follow in a second section, like the two sides of the equation. Assets are listed in order of liquidity (how quickly they can be turned into cash). Liabilities are listed in order of when they will be paid off. Equity is the difference between the assets and the liabilities. It is the net worth of the organization.

Think about it in terms of your home or car. The asset is the home. The liability is the mortgage. And the difference in the two is your equity in the home. If you didn't own or owe anything else, that would be your net worth. Figure 21 shows an example of a generic balance sheet:

Company A December 31, 2017 USD in Millions		
Assets	**2017**	**2016**
Current Assets		
Cash and Cash Equivalents	$100,000	$90,000
Accounts Receivable	20,000	15,000
Inventory	30,000	15,000
Total Current Assets	150,000	120,000
Plant, Property, and Equipment	500,000	450,000
Other Assets	100,000	100,000
Total Assets	$750,000	$670,000
Liabilities and Owner's Equity		
Current Liabilities		
Accounts Payable	$10,000	$11,000
Income Tax Payable	20,000	15,000
Short-term Debt	0	1,000
Long-term Liabilities		
Mortgage Payable	90,000	100,000
Total Liabilities	120,000	127,000
Owner's Equity		
Common Stock	500,000	500,000
Retained Earnings	130,000	43,000
Total Owner's Equity	630,000	543,000
Total Liabilities and Owner's Equity	$750,000	$670,000

Figure 21

Notice that in each year, the total of liabilities plus equity equals the total of all assets. Thus, the equation balances. The date in the heading of the balance sheet tells you when the snapshot was taken. Similar to the income statement, additional columns can be added for variances between the time periods to aid in trend analysis.

The balance sheet can give management, employees and investors a lot of information about the financial health of the organization. It is a direct reflection on how efficient the organization is at managing its liabilities and using its assets. You can determine how much of the assets come from creditors (these are liabilities on the balance sheet) and from owners (equity). An organization should use leverage wisely. Leverage is using debt (borrowed money) to acquire assets. Companies that use a lot of debt compared to equity are "highly leveraged." Using leverage can be smart because the organization frees up cash in order to grow the business at the same time. However, too much debt can indicate financial problems.

Statement of Cash Flows

The statement of cash flows shows the levels of cash across a reporting time period. This information is used to determine if the organization can pay liabilities when they are due. This statement is a merger of the income statement and the balance sheet by reconciling the information in operating (cash from regular business revenue), investing (cash from buying and selling assets), and financing activities (cash from debt and equity). This statement will also include any dividends paid or cash spent to repurchase stock. Figure 22 shows an example of what a statement of cash flows might look like:

Company A December 31, 2017 USD in Millions		
	2017	**2016**
Operating Activities		
Net Income	$1,000,000	$950,000
Depreciation	200,000	75,000
Non-cash Items	100,000	75,000
Changes in Working Capital	50,000	30,000
Cash from Operating Activities	1,350,000	1,130,000
Investing Activities		
Capital Expenditures	(380,000)	(400,000)
Sale of Equipment	20,000	0
Cash from Investing Activities	(360,000)	(400,000)
Financing Activities		
Financing Cash Flow Items	0	0
Payment of Dividends	(400,000)	(300,000)
Cash from Financing Activities	(400,000)	200,000
Net Change in Cash	$585,000	$930,000

Figure 22

In this example of Company A's statement of cash flows, I did not use numbers from the previous income statement and balance sheet for simplicity. However, I want to point out that cash inflows appear as positive numbers and cash outflows appear as negative numbers (in parentheses).

When it comes to daily facility management duties, you will not utilize cash flows in your decision-making. However, you should be familiar with the subject.

Financial statements typically have notes associated with them to provide a more complete picture of the reporting period beyond just numbers. To evaluate the financial health of an organization, you need to understand the notes, which provide meaning to the numbers.

Analyzing Financial Statements

Now that you know what the basic financial statements are and what they are used for, it is helpful to know how to use them in your financial analysis in determining what the numbers mean. While you won't use this on a day-to-day basis as a facility manager, these tools are great for looking at the financial health of your organization, future employer, or future business partner. Additionally, a basic understanding of these tools will help you understand senior management decisions and terminology used in making and explaining the strategic direction of the company.

The tools we will use in this section are financial ratios. These ratios have been developed to make sense of financial statements using quantitative analysis. Essentially, this is making the numbers mean something. This quantitative analysis is not a full picture of the overall health of the organization, but it will help anyone who understands them compare relative strengths and weaknesses of companies. One thing I want to emphasize is that it is more beneficial to analyze trends over time in ratios than it ever is to analyze one ratio in a single point in time. Also, if comparing different companies, it is important to keep in mind that ratios vary when you make comparisons across industries. What I mean is, comparing ratios from companies in different industries is like comparing apples and oranges. They don't operate the same, carry the same level of debt, have similar inventory turnovers, have assets with the same liquidity, etc. Bottom line, compare ratios of companies within the same industry.

Ratios are nothing more than comparing figures for analysis. Here we are just doing it with financial statements. For our purposes, we will classify the following ratios into four distinct categories: ***liquidity, activity, solvency, and profitability***.

- Liquidity – these ratios are very widely used and are important to creditors because they illustrate the organization's ability to pay short-term debt. Again, the need for cash varies across industries. For example, an organization that has a high level of inventory turnover will need higher levels of cash to purchase additional inventory than a law firm would need. Here are the liquidity ratios:

- Current Ratio – this is a measurement of current assets against current liabilities. It essentially answers the question if the organization would be able to pay off short-term liabilities by using current assets (this would be accomplished through liquidating assets and using on-hand cash). The higher the current ratio, the stronger the indication of liquidity. For instance, if a company has a current ratio of .80, that means that if all assets were liquidated, they could only cover 80% of their current liabilities. Extremely high current ratios could be negative as it can be an indication of carrying too much inventory. Here is the equation for current ratio:

  Current Ratio = Current Assets ÷ Current Liabilities

- Quick Ratio – also known as the acid-test ratio, is a measure of immediate liquidity. Unlike the current ratio that incorporates all assets, the quick ratio only takes into consideration an organization's cash, short-term securities, and accounts receivables to measure against current liabilities. The reasoning behind this is simple. This tells the analyst what assets the organization can reasonably convert to cash quickly in order to service short-term debt. For instance, it completely eliminates inventory from the liquidity ratio because that can't necessarily be converted to cash easily and quickly for the full value of the inventory the company is carrying in its accounting books. If it could, the company would just sell the inventory anyway as part of their operations. Here is the equation for quick ratio:

  Quick Ratio = (Cash + Cash Equivalents + Accounts Receivables) ÷ Current Liabilities

- Cash Ratio – is the most conservative of the liquidity ratios. As you might have guessed, it is only cash and short-term securities measured against current liabilities. In the cash ratio, it is likely that cash equivalents can be converted to cash quickly and for their book value. The equation for cash ratio is this:

Cash Ratio = (Cash + Cash Equivalents) ÷ Current Liabilities

- Activity – these ratios provide analysts with a gauge of operational performance of the organization as they measure the efficiency of its use of assets to generate income. This is done by measuring how quickly the organization turns over assets and liabilities. Here are two frequently used activity ratios:

  - Inventory Turnover – shows how many times an organization's inventory is turned over (sold and replaced) in a period of time. This ratio is better analyzed when compared to other companies within the same industry. Inventory turnover is a measure of business performance because organizations that can sell their inventory quickly are operationally better. The formula for inventory turnover is:

    Inventory Turnover = Sales ÷ Average Inventory

  - Receivables Turnover – measures how quickly an organization collects on their outstanding bills. Since this translates directly into cash, organizations that have higher receivable turnover ratios are typically more efficient. That said, ratios that are too high can indicate an organization is missing out on some sales due to very strict credit policies. Here is the ratio for receivables turnover:

    Receivables Turnover = Net Revenue in Credit Sales ÷ Average Receivables

- Solvency – measures an organization's ability to pay long-term obligations. This will tell analysts how much financial leverage the organization is using and information on the company's capital structure. Again, financial leverage is the use of debt to acquire assets. Too much debt is a bad thing, but too little debt could be bad as well. It can be a signal that the organization is not operating to its full potential and not capitalizing on opportunities in the marketplace. When looking at solvency ratios, it can be helpful to compare companies in the same industry to determine industry average. Here are two of the more commonly used solvency ratios:

- Debt-to-asset Ratio – measures the percentage of assets financed by debt. High numbers indicate the organization is accepting more financial risk by using more debt to acquire additional assets. Here is the formula for the debt-to-asset ratio:

  Debt-to-asset Ratio = Total Liabilities ÷ Total Assets

- Debt-to-equity Ratio – measures how much debt the organization uses to finance assets compared to the value of the shareholders' equity. This ratio is another tool to determine the amount of financial risk the organization is accepting in order to leverage operations and grow the business. The formula for the debt-to-equity ratio is:

  Debt-to-equity Ratio = Total Liabilities ÷ Shareholders' Equity

- Profitability – these are the most widely used ratios in financial statement analysis. Profitability ratios measure an organization's ability to earn a profit in its operation. Profitability margins vary greatly by industry, so it is important to measure trends within the same company and measure those against companies within the same industry. Here are some of the most common profitability ratios:

  - Gross Profit Margin – measures the proportion of revenue remaining after the organization pays for cost of goods sold (COGS). Gross profit is defined as revenue minus COGS. Gross profit margin then measures how effective an organization is at making a product or selling a service. Low gross profit margins could indicate the company will not be able to pay operating costs out of gross profit. The formula for gross profit margin is:

    Gross Profit Margin = Gross Profit ÷ Net Sales

- Operating Profit Margin – takes gross profit margin one step further. Operating profit margin measures the proportion of revenue remaining after the organization pays for COGS and operating expenses. Operating profit is defined as revenue minus COGS, general (not attributable to a single product) and administrative expenses. The formula for operating profit margin is:

  Operating Profit Margin = Operating Profit ÷ Net Sales

- Net Profit Margin – takes operating profit margin one step further. Net profit margin measures the proportion of revenue remaining (net income) and compares that to net revenue. Net income is defined as gross profit minus operating expenses, taxes, and interest taken out. It is what is left over after all costs have been accounted for. The formula for net profit margin is:

  Net Profit Margin = Net Income ÷ Net Sales

- Return on Assets (ROA) – is a measure of the efficiency of an organization's use of assets by comparing profit to assets. ROA shows how a company utilizes assets to generate revenue. The formula for ROA is:

  ROA = Net Income ÷ Total Assets

- Return on Equity (ROE) – is a measure of profitability compared to money shareholders have invested. The formula for ROE is:

  ROE = Net Income ÷ Shareholders' Equity

While you won't need to use these formulas on a daily basis, they will come in useful to conduct your own financial analysis from time to time. I've also found that understanding these concepts helps to engage with the accounting department and understand senior management decision-making from a financial standpoint.

Key Concepts

Accounting can be a confusing subject. It's no surprise that becoming a Certified Public Accountant (CPA) is one of the hardest processes for professionals to accomplish. My goal throughout this section is not to make you an accounting expert. I'm far from an accounting expert myself, so that would be a considerable challenge. That said, there are a few key concepts facility managers need to understand to talk intelligently with the accounting staff at their organization. Even if you don't need to routinely deal with the accountants, it is likely that you will hear these concepts during daily operations and want to form an understanding of them. The first concept will be important to understand when we discuss budgets and how to use them: the difference between capital and operating expense.

Capital Procurement vs. Operating Expense

Accountants and managers alike must differentiate between a capital procurement and an operating expense. The main differences are due to life of the asset and organizational cost thresholds. Both require cash, but capital procurement generally refers to assets with a useful life longer than one year. Once an asset is capitalized, it gets recorded as a fixed asset and is depreciated over its useful life (discussed next). If an asset has a useful life of less than a year, there is no point to depreciate it. Organizational policies might also mandate that an asset or service be capitalized if its cost exceeds a certain threshold. For example, replacing a roof membrane could be considered a repair expense, but it might have a useful life of 30 years and could easily exceed a cost threshold. A new roof would typically be capitalized.

Depreciation

Depreciation is a non-cash deduction (expense) used by accountants to spread the cost of a physical asset over its useful life. You will most commonly see it and hear about it when referred to property, plant, and equipment. For most PP&E, the value of the asset goes down over time as it ages and is used. Depreciation is a way to show reduced value of the asset year after year. So why do accountants depreciate assets? There are two reasons: ***accounting and taxes***.

- Accounting – to put it simply, accounting principles require organizations to recognize (or record) revenues and expenses when they occur. This is known as the realization principle (or recognition principle). For instance, when you sell a product you would record the sale when it happens, not when the customer actually pays the invoice a month later. If we apply this to capital assets, however, the process can get a little confusing. Consider a huge construction project that spans multiple years. If the end result is a single building, how do you record that revenue when it accrues? You can't wait until the end of the third year to record the entire sale. An extension of the realization principle is the matching principle. This principle states that you record expenses incurred in producing a product at the same time you record the sale of the product. For instance, if you produce a machine and sell it on credit, you record the revenue the day the sale is made (not when the cash exchanges hands) along with all costs associated with the sale of the product. This is why we depreciate assets. We want to recognize the portion of the asset's value that contributed to the company's operation during the same period of operation. An example is if you have a machine that is expected to last five years, you might depreciate 20% of its value every year for the next five years until it's residual value is zero.

- Taxes – the second reason to depreciate assets is to gain a tax advantage. Because the depreciation expense has consequences on cash flow, it will influence the tax bill. The organization might be able to take advantage of tax laws and be better positioned financially utilizing depreciation.

What does this really look like? Let's assume Company A purchases the machine worth $5,000 and uses the most straightforward depreciation method, straight-line depreciation. The straight-line method means that the same amount is depreciated every year. Assume that the useful life is five years and the machine will be written down to zero (have no residual value at the end of the five years). The cash outflow would occur immediately when Company A buys the machine, but instead of deducting $5,000 as an expense, the accountant would depreciate the asset by recording a $1,000 expense every year for five years. Keep in mind that the $1,000 expense has nothing to do with cash exchanging hands. That already happened when Company A purchased the $5,000 machine in the beginning. The $1,000 is just an accounting number used as an application of the matching principle discussed above.

We are going to discuss the three primary means of depreciation. The first is straight-line depreciation mentioned above. This method depends on time and is based off of this formula:

Straight-line depreciation per year = Depreciable Amount ÷ Useful Life of Asset

In the above example, the depreciable amount is the entire $5,000 because it is being written down to zero and the useful life is the five years. Thus, the formula calls for the asset to be depreciated $1,000 per year for five years.

The second method of depreciation is the activity method. This method does not depend on time. It depends on actual productivity versus expected productivity of the asset in a given period.

The third method of depreciation is the accelerated cost recovery system (ACRS). The ACRS, instituted in 1981, allows for an accelerated write-off of property depending on various classifications. In the Tax Reform Act of 1986, the ACRS was modified to the MACRS (Modified ACRS), which establishes different classes for asset type that govern useful life (tax life). Once an asset is assigned a class, its cost is multiplied by a fixed percentage to obtain the depreciation amount per year. Examples of the classes are industrial equipment (seven years) and automobiles (five years).

It is important to understand depreciation because, as a facility manager, you might be required to budget depreciation expenses assigned to the assets you manage. You will most certainly manage many assets that will be depreciated; but, the methods different organizations use in their accounting varies.

Funding Depreciation

I want to cover the concept of funding depreciation. This is one of the more overlooked concepts that I consider important to the future financial health of the organization. If you haven't already wondered what happens when the asset reaches the end of its useful life, you were bound to. In many cases the organization really has no plan how to deal with these assets and instead limps along with a repair budget, only replacing them out of the capital budget when they just can't be fixed any more. This is not the best way to plan asset replacements.

Funding depreciation means the organization invests an amount of money every year into a depreciation account equal to the amount of the depreciation expense that year. So if Company A wrote off the $5,000 machine at $1,000 per year over five years, they would then turn around and invest $1,000 per year over five years into an account (or certificate of deposit, money market account, etc.). The result is that Company A would have $5,000 available to buy a replacement machine at the end of its useful life. Company A could then decide when to replace the machine or could automatically replace it as part of a life-cycle replacement program (replacing the asset at the end of its useful life).

The problem, however, is that many organizations need the cash they would use to fund depreciation for other operating expenses and it never ends up happening. Another issue is that only funding depreciable assets won't be enough to maintain operations. Consider a building that requires repainting. Paint is not depreciable, but you will most assuredly need to repaint prior to the end of the building's useful life. Finally, if companies use debt to purchase the asset, there ends up being two cash outlays during its useful life: the debt-service payment and the funding of depreciation. That can make it very hard on the company's bottom line.

Chapter 2: Foundations in Finance

The Time Value of Money

Bear with me. Many financial books find the most confusing possible way to explain what should be an easy concept. I'm going to attempt the easy route.

The time value of money means that one dollar today is worth more than one dollar in the future.

But why? Because money has earning potential. So, if I got \$1 today and stuck it in an account bearing 5% interest, I would have \$1.05 in one year. That means that \$1 today is actually worth \$1.05 one year from now. Thus, \$1 today is worth more than \$1 a year from now because \$1.05 > \$1.

Future Value

In this example, the \$1.05 is considered the future value (FV) of the \$1 today, one year from now. FV is simply the value an amount of money will grow to over a period of time while earning a given rate of interest. Thus, the formula for future value in a single period is this:

$$FV = Investment \times (1 + r)$$

In this formula, r is the interest rate in decimal form.

Assume that we have \$100 and a simple interest rate of 10%. The equation looks like this:

$$FV = \$100 \times (1 + .10)$$

$$FV = \$100 \times (1.10)$$

$$FV = \$110$$

However, what happens if we leave it invested for two years? Is the future value $120? No, it's not that simple (pun intended). The concept of compound interest means that you not only earn interest on your initial investment, but you earn interest on the interest itself because both are reinvested. In this example, the first year we earned 10% on the $100, which was $10. Added to the initial investment, the FV was $110. The second year, however, we would earn 10% on the entire $110. 10% of $110 is $11, not $10. Thus, after the second year, we would have $121. The equation for FV assuming compound interest is this:

$$FV = Investment \times (1 + r)^t$$

In this formula, *t* is the number of compounding periods of investment. Thus, our formula for our example looks like this:

$$FV = \$100 \times (1 + .10)^2$$

$$FV = \$100 \times (1.21)$$

$$FV = \$121$$

If you want to determine the future value of the $100 invested for five years at 10% interest compounded annually, the formula looks like this:

$$FV = \$100 \times (1 + .10)^5$$

$$FV = \$100 \times (1.6105)$$

$$FV = \$161.05$$

Now you can determine future values with multiple cash flows. What happens, for instance, when you invest an additional $100 per year into the same account making 10% interest?

Present Value and Discounting

When determining future value, we want to know what our investment will be worth someday. Really, the future value can be used for anything that is going to grow at a constant rate. However, in financial management a question that is asked often is future value in reverse. This question will be phrased more like, if I need to have $100 five years from now and I can earn 10% per year on my investment, how much money do I need to invest now? This question answers the Present Value (PV). Since PV is really the reverse of FV, another way to say this is that we *are discounting the future value back to the present.* By rearranging the formula for future value, present value looks like this:

$$PV = FV \times [\,1 \div (1 + r)^{t}\,]$$

So, let's put the $100 in five years with 10% interest scenario into the equation:

$$PV = \$100 \times [1 \div (1 + .10)^{5}]$$

$$PV = \$100 \times [1 \div 1.6105]$$

$$PV = \$100 \times .6209$$

$$PV = \$62.09$$

So, to have $100 five years from now, we would need to put $62.09 in an account returning 10% interest compounded annually. The rate used in the PV calculation is referred to as the discount rate.

Net Present Value

It is the goal of senior management to bring value to shareholders through their decision-making. These decisions are not made in a vacuum, however, as financial tools are necessary to make the most informed decisions that have the greatest chance of creating the most value. Net present value (NPV) is the difference between the cost of an investment and its market value, subtracting the cash outflows from the inflows. It can be very useful in these decisions because if a manager can determine that the market value of an investment is greater than the cost of the investment, it would make sense to pursue it. However, if the investment costs more than it will be worth, then the manager would not pursue it because there is no value there.

Let's use an example to illustrate this point.

> When I managed residential construction projects, we would sell completely finished custom homes on lots that we purchased. Consider a lot that costs $50,000 and a home that costs $150,000 in labor and materials to construct. With another $25,000 in

overhead, the total investment of the home would be $225,000. If the home took four months to construct and sold for $250,000, it would have a market value of $250,000. Subtract the investment costs from the market value and you have a NPV of $25,000. If you could determine the NPV at the beginning of the project before you purchased the lot, then you could make a pretty easy decision to build the house since the market value would be $25,000 higher than the investment costs. Making this decision to build would be bringing value to shareholders.

The formula for PV is rearranged to create the formula for NPV and looks like this:

$$NPV = -C_0 + \Sigma[C_i \div (1 + r)^i]$$

Where:

C_0 = ***Initial Investment***

C = ***Cash Flow***

Σ = ***Sum of all Cash Flows Received from Project***

i = ***Time Period.***

Another way to write this formula would be:

$C_0 = C_1 \div (1 + r)^1 + C_2 \div (1 + r)^2 + C_3 \div (1 + r)^3 + \ldots$ ***(and so on for each cash flow period)***

This formula definitely makes more sense when used in an example. Consider this:

We are starting a new business that will cost $100,000 to get going. We are going to operate the business for 6 years until we close it down to retire and live the good life in Florida. Assuming all goes as planned, the business will generate $80,000 in revenue each year, but cost $50,000 per year in operating expenses. We estimate the residual value of the equipment will be $5,000 when we close the business and we need a required rate of return of 15%. Is this a good investment?

To determine this, we take the difference between the initial cost of $100,000 and the present value of cash inflows (what we will make over the 6 years once operating expenses are deducted) To show the steps a little more clearly, I am solving for FV first (solving for multiple cash flows with a slightly more complex FV formula derived from the base formula above), then PV second, and finally NPV third. Here is what the formulas look like:

PV = PV of yearly profits + PV of equipment sold

$PV = FV \times [\, 1 - (1 \div (1 + r)^{t}) \div r \,] + [\, \textit{PV of equipment sold} \,]$

$PV = FV \times [\, 1 - (1 \div (1 + r)^{t}) \div r \,] + [\, FV \times [\, 1 \div (1 + r)^{t} \,]\,]$

$PV = FV \times [\, 1 - (1 \div (1 + .15)^{6}) \div .15 \,] + (\$5{,}000/1.15^{6})$

$PV = (\$80{,}000 - \$50{,}000) \times [\, 1 - (1 \div 2.3131) \div .15] + \$2{,}161.64$

$PV = \$30{,}000 \times [\, 1 - (0.4323) \div .15] + \$2{,}161.64$

$PV = \$30{,}000 \times [\, 0.5677 \div .15] + \$2{,}161.64$

$PV = (\$30{,}000 \times 3.7847) + \$2{,}161.64$

$PV = \$113{,}541 + \$2{,}161.64$

$PV = \$115{,}702.64$

$NPV = -\$100{,}000 + \$115{,}702.64$

$NPV = \$15{,}702.64$

If you solve the formula and get a close but slightly different answer, it is probably due to rounding. Now, if this were the only decision to make, it would be only slightly complicated. However, as a decision-maker in the residential construction company, I would look at the cost of constructing different house plans on that lot and on other lots worth more and less than the $50,000 lot in the above paragraph. Location would make a difference in ultimate market value and the length of construction time would make a difference in how quickly we would realize the profits. Some house plans might take longer to sell than others on average. All of this information would generate options and the majority of them might lead to a positive NPV, with the market value ending higher than the investment costs. If, however, we could only build one house at a time, we would probably choose the options that yielded the highest NPV.

The basic rule when using NPV in management decisions is to reject investments with negative NPVs and accept the ones with positive NPVs.

Payback Period

Another tool used by financial managers to make decisions is determining payback. Payback is the amount of time it will take to recoup the organization's initial investment. In one of my current facilities, I recently used this in determining whether or not to invest in a light conversion from LED (light emitting diode) to metal-halide. LED lights are considerably more energy efficient and would therefore pay the investment back over time in the form of lower energy costs.

The initial investment was $68,000 to complete the conversion. After calculating the savings at $23,000 per year, I determined the payback period was three years. This is easy to do by dividing the initial investment by the amount of return during the given period. Since we determined that a payback of anything less than five years would mean we approved the conversion, I signed the contract and the LEDs were installed the next month. It turned out to be a great decision. Payback is a simple, but good tool FMs can use to convince senior management to take on projects when they are hesitant at first.

That said, because it is so simple, the payback rule does not give a complete picture because of a few shortcomings. First, it completely ignores the time value of money because there is no discounting of cash flows involved in the calculation (this can be solved by discounting the cash flows, but is not a part of the basic payback period calculation). Second, risk is not taken into consideration. Finally, since the acceptable length of payback time is somewhat arbitrary based on internal preference, there are other factors that might sway senior management more or less than payback period. For instance, with the LED conversion, the quality of light was a bigger factor than the length of time before the initial investment was repaid. For smaller decisions not requiring detailed analysis, however, the payback rule is very useful in daily operating decisions.

Internal Rate of Return

The internal rate of return (IRR) is another extremely useful tool in financial decision-making and is closely linked to the NPV. The IRR finds the one rate of return that summarizes the outcome of the project. The rate is internal to the project because it does not take into consideration any alternatives offered outside the project. The IRR is then compared to a required rate of return (the rate of return necessary to approve the project) pre-determined by management. If the IRR exceeds the required rate of return, the project is accepted. Otherwise, it is rejected.

I say it is closely linked to the NPV because you use the NPV formula where the unknown quantity is the rate, so you are solving for "r". When you plug in the variables, the IRR is the rate that makes the NPV equal to zero. For better understanding, let's go back to our simpler example to illustrate this. Consider we have $100 and want to get $110 in one year. We already know that the rate is 10%. This is the IRR. When solving for an NPV equal to zero, it looks like this:

$$PV = FV \times [1 \div (1 + r)^{t}]$$

$$\$100 = \$110 \times [1 \div (1 + r)]$$

$$0 = -\$100 + [\$110 \div (1 + r)]$$

Because we want the rate that makes the NPV zero, it looks like this:

$$NPV = 0 = -\$100 + [\$110 \div (1 + r)]$$

$$NPV = -\$100 + [\$110 \div (1 + r)]$$

$$\$100 = \$110 \div (1 + r)$$

$$\$100 \times (1 + r) = \$110$$

$1 + r = \$110 \div \$100$

$1 + r = 1.1$

$r = 1.1 - 1$

$r = 0.1$

Thus, when the NPV is equal to zero:

IRR = 10%

These examples get more complex as you add variables, but they are the building blocks to begin to understand finance and how it leads to management decisions. Should you approve a certain project? Is it better to invest cash or use it for another purpose? Should you leverage debt to promote growth? Can you articulate why? These are examples of questions you will face -- knowing how to answer them brings value.

Chapter 3: Financial Management

Budgets

Budgets are essential to operate in business, and especially the facility management world. Understanding the budgeting process and your role in it will set you up for success and ensure you are ahead of the power curve in your organization. I know several high-level leaders and managers who have never understood budgets and they still manage to make a living. However, they have come nowhere close to truly realizing the potential they could have if they had only understood this subject in depth. Similar to the Oklahoma Army National Guard's FM that understood how to use the budgeting process to his advantage, you will recognize opportunities in both operating and capital budgets that can make you very successful.

At the very least, forming the best understanding of how your organization budgets and executes money will make you stand out among your peers. Still in today's climate, there are too many managers who only care to understand tasks immediately in front of them and don't care to study strategic level goals and how they add value in getting their organization to achieve them. This is how you build value for yourself. Understanding finance is key.

Many managers consider building and managing their budget a waste of time because they would be better utilized engaging in day-to-day management tasks like direct employee supervision. I'm here to tell you that this is not an uncommon belief, but it is a horribly dangerous one to hold. In the Army we have combat multipliers, which are tools to enhance the relative combat power of the number of Soldiers actually available to fight. For example, field artillery is a combat multiplier to infantry Soldiers because a small group of field artillerymen firing rockets has much more destructive power than the same size group of infantry Soldiers who only have small-caliber rifles. Understanding budgets is a combat multiplier. If I spend three hours creating a budget and formulating a plan to save the organization tens of thousands of dollars, I have been considerably more effective than if I was directly overseeing a few maintenance technicians conducting repair activities for those three hours.

To understand finance, we first need a common definition of a budget. A budget is a formal financial plan of how assets will be used during a set operating period. Most people understand that a personal budget is how much money you should spend during the month based on how much money you make during that same time period. In theory, you shouldn't spend more than you have or can repay on a debt schedule. Many people either don't bother creating personal budgets or don't stick to them afterward. Reasons may vary from lack of interest to external factors such as a job loss or unforeseen expenses like medical bills or car repairs. Whatever the reasons, this is the formula for personal financial trouble. At the very least it can cause financial stress; but in the worst cases will lead to bankruptcy or desperate financial situations. However, people who create and stick to a budget often find financial peace and prosperity. Those who can create a plan and stick to it have a much better chance in accomplishing the plan's goals in the end. So, why would business be any different?

For companies and individuals alike, budgets serve two purposes. The first is that they lay out a plan for the future for how the organization or individual will perform financially. The second is that they serve as a benchmark to measure performance throughout the budget period. If you are within your budget and meeting non-financial performance expectations, you are doing well. If you're outside of the budget, there is room for improvement whether or not you are meeting other performance measures. Possible areas for improvement in this case might be that you are not managing appropriately, you did not budget effectively for unforeseen circumstances, or you simply did not budget correctly for known expenses.

Budget Approaches

These are the three different approaches to budget creation:

Top-down Budgeting – also known as authoritative, this budget approach involves senior management dictating budgets to lower levels of management. The benefit to this approach is that the organization's strategic direction is incorporated into the budgeting process. Sometimes middle management is not fully read-in on the long-term plans of the organization and they cannot strategically budget because they do not have the necessary information.

Top-down budgeting is the approach the Army uses. Our

budgets were directed and we had absolutely no say as to the amounts that went into them. They were largely dictated by members of the organization at the highest levels, Congress, and historical data. If it took $100,000 to keep the power on last year at Camp Gruber, then you obviously need $100,000 this year to keep the power on. This is definitely not the most accurate and efficient way to budget.

To begin with, managers at the lowest level had zero ownership of the budget. So, when you were handed a ridiculous budget with no basis in reality, you felt little pressure to meet that budget. Also, there was no common sense applied to setting budget amounts apart from historical data. For instance, if the reason it only cost $100,000 to keep the power on at Camp Gruber was because the training levels were low due to a large majority of the units in the state being on deployment, no one at the national level took that into consideration. Finally, there was no reward for meeting or beating your budget.

In fact, there was only a negative consequence. If you were able to out-perform your budget and keep the power on for $95,000 during that period instead of the $100,000, you didn't get a bonus. All you got was a reduced budget the next year of $95,000, because apparently, that's all it ever takes. It was frustrating, to say the least.

Bottom-up Budgeting – also known as participative, this budget approach involves managers at the lowest levels putting the budgets together for approval by senior management. The benefit to this approach is that first-line managers have the expertise needed to effectively budget for day-to-day operations. This leads to greater buy-in and ownership at all levels of management since all are involved in the process. However, if the lowest levels of management do not understand the strategic direction of the organization, this type of budgeting could end up being a waste of time because it would be greatly subject to change by senior management throughout the budget period.

Bottom-up budgeting can lead to another, unintended problem. Because the majority of the ownership is at lower management levels, there can be a tendency for these managers to pad their budget numbers. By this, I mean they determine what each budget activity is likely to cost and then add a percentage to it as a cushion, enabling them to easily complete the activity under budget. This makes them look good the first time. What they fail to understand is that doing this over and over again is not good. Senior management will easily see through what they are doing and will not trust their budget numbers, which leads to worse problems than top-down budgets have. Care must be taken when engaging in this budget approach.

Combined Budgeting – this budget approach is the best of both worlds. Senior management communicates strategic goals of the organization and operational managers use them to create their budgets for senior management approval. This builds ownership at all levels of management and tends to lead to tighter controls.

An added benefit is that all managers not only own their budgets, but also feel ownership in all departments as they can see how their budgets contribute to the overall strategic plan. My organization currently budgets this way. To add to this, organizations can tie bonuses to both performance objectives and whether or not budgets were beat, met, or exceeded at the various levels of management throughout the budget period.

Budget Types

There are two types of budgets that facility managers must become familiar with to be effective in their role. These two types are operating and capital budgets.

Operating Budgets – are short-term in nature and are typically created and managed in one-year cycles. Being cyclical, these financial plans encompass all routine expenditures necessary for the day-to-day operations to be carried out successfully and as efficiently as possible. For other departments, these budgets will have both income and expenses throughout the budget period. Many FM budgets will only have expenses, as we typically don't manage revenue-generating activities.

The operating budget will be broken down into monthly projections of what daily operations will cost and these monthly costs will be further broken down into accounts that match up in the general ledger (GL). For example, my current budget has one GL account for all utility costs incurred by the organization. Any electric, gas, water, or transportation invoices I receive get coded to that GL for the month the service is incurred. Examples of operating budget accounts can include:

- Salaries and Hourly Wages
- Insurance
- Taxes
- Administrative Costs
- Repair Activities
- Utilities
- Training
- Automobile Expenses (gas, tires, etc.)
- Office Supplies
- Refuse
- Pest Control
- Monitoring Contracts (security, fire, etc.)
- Uniforms

Operating budgets are compared to actual expenses on a routine basis (typically monthly on an annual operating budget cycle) for managers at all levels to check how they are performing financially as it relates to operations. This is important because it affords them the chance to change methods of operating before the end of the fiscal year, if they are not meeting budget projections during the month.

The key to success in creating and maintaining FM operating budgets is the ability to read trends through historical data and apply them logically along with assumptions about future events. We do this to accurately predict costs you will incur during the upcoming budget cycle to create next year's budget submission.

> For example, looking at electric consumption costs for the building we upgraded from metal halide to LED lighting, I was able to determine that I would save an average of 66% on my electric utility invoices for that building based on an average cost paid per kWh. I then adjusted my budget for the following year to account for the savings and give senior management an accurate depiction of what their utility costs would be. To be fair, it is still an educated guess because you can't predict exactly what the usage will be for the building or if energy costs will increase. But, the key is to be able to articulate why you included the amounts you did for each line item in the proposed operating

budget.

Capital Budgets – are long-term in nature and created for non-routine expenditures that only occur during that budget cycle. Capital asset procurement is carried out using capital budgets. As previously discussed, these assets are depreciable and have a useful life of longer than the budget cycle. Capital budgets typically require significant investments on behalf of the organization and therefore necessitate longer forecasting. It is not uncommon for organizations to set a capital procurement strategy 10-20 years in the future.

It is your job as a facility manager to inform senior management of the capital assets that will need to be replaced within the timeframe of your organization's long-term capital plan. For instance, if part of the organization's strategic plan is an expansion, you must advise the planners on the PP&E and FF&E associated with those expansion projects.

> Each organization will have its own methodical process to capital budgeting and it is up to you to navigate your way through that. In my current organization, we have two separate capital procurement accounts. The first is funded at the same level every year, requiring department heads to recommend a procurement strategy every year by taking their capital plan and prioritizing what needs to be accomplished. Senior management will then approve the highest priority items across the organization based on the overall strategy. The second account is dictated by the board of governors and funded through various means such as long-term debt. This account is what funds major renovation and expansion projects that encompass multiple departments or the entire organization at once.

Additionally, you are likely to find different approval thresholds for capital expenditures based on cost. For instance, some organizations give mid-level managers approval authority up to a certain dollar amount. Past that, the procurement would need to be approved by the person or entity with a higher approval limit. To be clear, don't exceed your authority.

Budget Methods

So, how do you create a budget? Many managers will simply look at what was spent last year, change the dates to match the next year, and call it good. This should raise red flags right off the bat. The first problem here is that there is no actual basis for why the manager is recommending what they are budgeting. "Because it was done like this before," is not a method. It is a recipe for disaster. I've been asked before during a budget review with a previous manager why I was asking for certain amounts in the next budget cycle and I haven't had a great answer. That's not a fun position to be in, which leads to my second point. The problem with this method is that the manager has no clue what "right" looks like when he executes the budget. Here's an example:

> We currently have one 50' flag pole at our main facility. That flag pole has a large American flag with a smaller state flag underneath it. I budget for three replacements of these flags per year. The budget for these three replacements falls within an overall repair account in the facility management operating budget umbrella. If I didn't know that I had three replacements in the budget, I almost certainly would either not replace the flags often enough or replace them too often. This would result in either a substandard presentation of the flags to anyone passing by or an overage for the repair account within my budget. To be effective, you must know how each budget number is calculated and why.

For our purposes, I will cover two budget methods: incremental and zero-based.

<u>Incremental Budgeting</u> – is the simpler of these two budget methods. Here, the manager takes the current period's budget compared to the actual performance to date and adds incremental amounts to each item as appropriate. Typical increments will be added to account for inflation, cost of living increases in wages, or planned increases in costs of materials. The major benefit of incremental budgeting is that it is easy to do and can be done rather quickly. It is also easy to explain in terms of justifications for requesting increases to the current period's budget. Looking at it from a senior manager's perspective, this budget method can be easy to justify to mid-level managers by saying all departments will receive a set increase (alleviating any conflict between department heads who think their department is not receiving its fair share).

The negatives of incremental budgeting, however, out-weigh the positives in several ways. First, it is based on the assumption that all activities being performed are necessary to the success of the organization at current levels. Second, there is no detailed planning required by managers to determine more efficient ways of operating and opportunities to reduce costs. Finally, managers are not challenged to excel in their performance, because the only metric for success is repetition of the current period's budget with a slight increase.

Zero-based Budgeting (ZBB) – is just that. In this method, there is no reference to the current period's budget because all activities begin at zero dollars as the budget basis (essentially you start with a blank page). Then, all department activities undergo a detailed review, are analyzed for necessity and efficiency, and receive allocations based on requirements of the department and organization as a whole. The major benefit of zero-based budgeting is that it forces managers to justify all activities for the budget period. Because it requires this level of detail, ZBB is also better suited to a bottom-up or combined budgeting approach, which involves management at all levels.

The negatives of ZBB do sometimes prevent organizations from engaging in this method. First, it is time-consuming. I always use ZBB for my budgets and it takes several days to more than a week to put them together every year. That is a huge contrast to simply taking this years' budget and adding 3% to all activities. Second, not all managers possess the skills to start from scratch and put together an entire budget that is sufficient for the next operating period. It isn't the easiest thing in the world to do and if you don't have any experience with it, can be very frustrating. Finally, because all activities within the organization are reviewed, they are all competing for priority and funding. Ranking activities among different departments can be challenging due to the vast differences that exist between different parts of an organization.

Even though it is more difficult and time-consuming, zero-based budgeting is the preferred method. That said, some organizations will only use ZBB every few years to check their budgets and then use incremental budgeting for the years in-between. The organization you work for will determine which method you use, but it is important to understand the differences in the two in order to know what is expected of you when it comes time to submit your budget request.

Closing out the Fiscal Year

As you approach the end of your fiscal year, the organization will need to conduct activities to close the year out. This will require you to close out your budget. Closing the budget could require formal requests or it could be as simple as a date that marks the last day you can allocate funds from the current fiscal year.

> In the military, closing the budget is fairly complex and the money tends to dry up toward the end of the fiscal year due to senior staff officers forecasting what they believe you will be able to execute. This process gets rather frustrating at times. Of course, if you are able to execute more than your current year's allocation, they might plus up your budget at the end of the fiscal year if there is money left over from other states. It's a complicated system and I wouldn't wish it on anyone.
>
> My current organization relies on the department heads to close their own budgets and it works rather well. We are held accountable for execution and expected to operate efficiently while staying within our budgets. At the end of every month, we submit variance reports explaining significant variances from our monthly budgets. Then, at the end of the year, we submit an annual variance report closing out the budget in order for accounting to close out the accounts and prepare for the annual audit.

Regardless of how your organization closes out the fiscal year, be assured you will need to review your budget and close it out in some way before you begin the next budget period. This is easier for some departments than it is for others because based on what their operations are, they might be able to fully close one budget and open another before executing any funds. However, with facility management, you never really know when it will be absolutely necessary to spend money to fix something that is broken. Needless to say, planning is key to budget execution and closeout. You must always make sure you have the means to maintain and repair facilities regardless of your organization's current fiscal process.

Financial Management Tools

Cost-Benefit Analysis

After learning about financial tools used in decision-making such as IRR and payback period, you probably understand that financial decisions require a fair amount of analysis and justification in some form or fashion. Large capital projects will require much more justification and higher-level approvals than small, routine expenses. To be sure, FMs must prove to senior management the value of proposed projects. The most common way to do this is through a cost-benefit analysis (CBA). Facilities management, along with any departments that add expenses and do not contribute to revenue generation, can be an easy target for cost-cutting measures. It will be to your benefit to learn how to effectively communicate and market your ideas to the decision-makers of your organization. The CBA is one tool that can help you do that.

The CBA is a systematic process to measure strengths and weaknesses of proposals, put in terms of costs and benefits. This process describes costs and benefits in monetary values and considers the time value of money throughout the life of the proposal. Therefore, the NPV calculation would also be useful in conducting a cost-benefit analysis.

The CBA has two primary goals. First, it is a tool to measure whether or not benefits of the proposal outweigh costs. This gives management an idea if the proposal is worth considering for inclusion in the budgeting process. Second, the CBA yields a common basis for comparison between proposals of a similar nature. For instance, a CBA on buying a new building instead of leasing might show greater benefits than costs associated with the purchase. From there, it would be logical to create CBAs for different building purchase options and compare them to each other. While buying is more beneficial than leasing in this example, buying Building A might have a greater cost-benefit than buying Building B or Building C. This could be due to different factors from price to location or maybe Building A is more conducive to the operations of the company and will be more efficient in the long run.

For any proposal, the CBA will consider a minimum of two options: the proposed initiative and the status quo. Status quo is simply not changing anything and conducting business as it has been conducted. There can be as many alternatives as management deems appropriate, but all CBAs must consider the costs and benefits of no change. There are variations in different methods, but these are the basic individual steps for conducting a cost-benefit analysis:

- List Benefits – once you have a proposal to evaluate, the first step is to make a comprehensive list of all associated benefits. First, list the tangible benefits such as revenues that will be realized by implementing the project. Second, list the intangible benefits such as increased employee morale or better safety procedures.

- List Costs – the next step is to identify all direct and indirect costs of implementing the proposal. Consider these costs from two perspectives. First, list all front-end costs, which must be paid immediately upon approval. Second, list all on-going costs that will be incurred over the life of the project. Front-end direct costs could be things like the actual cost of purchasing the building, increased training for new employees, and design fees. Examples of on-going costs could be higher utility bills or insurance premiums and additional property taxes.

- Identify the Life of the Project – every proposal has a finite life. If you don't know the exact life of the proposal (from implementation through retirement or disposal), use an educated guess based on industry data and experience (such as an estimated useful life table).

- Quantify Costs and Benefits – the benefit of the CBA is that all metrics are quantified by a common monetary basis. So, all costs and benefits must be given a monetary measurement for comparison. Take care not to let personal bias influence estimated costs or benefits. This process should be as impartial as possible.

- Aggregate and Compare – all costs and benefits are aggregated and then compared. If the benefits outweigh the costs, it is a proposal that should move forward. If not, the logical choice would be to abandon the project and either consider an alternative or stay with the status quo.

The CBA does have its limitations. This type of analysis can easily help you argue whether a proposal should or should not be done when it comes to minor capital purchases or projects. However, when it comes to major projects that have lasting effects (both costs and benefits) over many years, the CBA becomes much more difficult to complete effectively. You must consider the time value of money, cost of debt, and internal rate of return. You must also consider the cost of lost business from other revenue streams.

> For example, consider a hotel restaurant manager arguing for a renovation to a dining area for the purpose of attracting more business with packaged wine dinners. This manager has done his own CBA with basic information and shows a 4-year payback period based on the following:
>
> Cost of Renovation: $40,000
>
> Revenues Generated per Year: $20,000 (based off of selling 10 packaged wine dinners at a cost of $2,000 each per year)
>
> Net Income Received: $10,000 (based off of 50% projected net income per dinner)
>
> On the surface, this makes sense. However, the manager must make sure he has considered the cost of lost business from other sources. Would the people paying for these dinners already be patrons of the organization even without the renovation? If so, the manager would have to list the cost of losing their business in another dining room (where they eat if there was no renovation) as part of the CBA.

Obviously, the above CBA is also missing other elements such as inflation, cost of labor increases, NPV, etc. But this is a fairly typical analysis that can be used to show whether the benefits of this project outweigh the costs associated with it.

Finally, there is one other element you must not consider when conducting a CBA. This is the sunk cost. Sunk costs are costs that have already been incurred and cannot be recovered, regardless of what the decision is. These costs should be ignored from future business decisions because they won't change as a result of any decision, for or against the project.

Business Impact Analysis

The business impact analysis (BIA) is a tool used to forecast the consequences of a disruption in business operations due to any number of reasons such as an interruption of supply chain activities. Facility managers should use the BIA specifically to analyze the business impacts of facilities failing in whole or in part. The BIA should be used in conjunction with a risk analysis to determine impacts of natural disasters and unexpected service interruptions (e.g., power outages) and mitigate those risks by developing contingency plans that can be enacted quickly, should the need arise.

The BIA is also a very useful tool to utilize while performing the CBA for proposed projects. With any project, there is a likelihood of an impact on the current ongoing business operations. In some cases, the impact might be minor such as shutting down an area of a facility for a few hours to conduct routine maintenance. In other cases, however, the BIA might indicate a major impact to business operations such as a total renovation of a facility that is used in key revenue generation.

Much like a CBA, the BIA should begin with an identification of the operational and financial impacts that will likely occur as a result of the unexpected or planned event. When doing this, consider lost revenue, direct and indirect expenses, fines, penalties, and intangible costs such as customer dissatisfaction. One effective tool to use while conducting this analysis is to survey functional managers and let them tell you exactly how their business will be impacted.

Once the BIA is complete, you will generate a report that should list steps in contingencies for unexpected events and prioritize them according to business importance. For example, if a storm damages multiple facilities, contingency plans would make an effort to get critical building systems online first and then restore non-critical services afterward.

For planned events, make every effort to take the facility offline during non-peak times and evaluate possible mitigations prior to beginning the project. For example, if a block of offices is renovated for several months, determining where the displaced employees can work is vital to the business prior to beginning the renovation.

Key Performance Indicators

Key performance indicators (KPIs) are measurable values used to show how effectively departments and organizations are meeting goals and objectives. To be clear, these are not only used for financial performance as evidenced in my examples below. However, they do make sense when related to quantifiable metrics such as budgets and time.

KPIs for individual departments must be nested within the strategic KPIs for the organization as a whole. Facility managers will be responsible for measuring, tracking, and reporting on their KPIs, typically at pre-determined intervals (monthly, quarterly, etc.) to senior management to show how their performance during that period compares with their goals. If your organization does not have KPIs already set for facilities, you may be asked to recommend some. Here are several examples of KPIs as they relate to facilities management (there are many other possibilities):

- Operations and Maintenance
  - Response times
  - Length of time of open work orders
  - Number of work orders
  - Labor and repair costs per square foot
  - Energy costs
  - Cleaning costs
  - Utilization
  - Rework
- Projects
  - Number of open projects
  - Project cost
  - Project schedule
  - Punch list closeout timeline
- Other
  - Recordable injuries occurred
  - Overtime across departments
  - Operating and capital budget execution
  - Employee satisfaction
  - Customer satisfaction

There are several keys to building effective KPIs. First, they must be measurable. If you cannot measure desired value against actual value, the KPI is useless because there is no comparison to the benchmark. Second, the KPIs must be more than pure financial measurements. True, budget is important, but so is quality. You can easily meet your budget if you don't do anything, but it will likely result in a deteriorating facility with unhappy end users. Finally, they must be aligned with the organization's KPIs. A facility manager whose KPIs do not contribute to the strategic goals of the company is not a contributing manager.

Here are the steps in setting KPs. First, the strategic goals of the organization must be developed. Then, managers determine how their department contributes to the successful accomplishment of those strategic goals. Next, plans are put in place for the entire team and metrics are created that can be measured. Finally, the most important contributing metrics should become the KPIs.

The Dashboard

As the Operations Officer of an Army Engineer Battalion (approximately 650 Soldiers), I constantly wanted to know where our units were located, what they were doing, and how their operations were going as it related to the plan our staff had put together. For any military unit, that is a lot of information to digest, but for an Engineer Battalion with eight separate Companies (each with their own mission from medical support to horizontal construction, using earth moving equipment), it can get overwhelming. The solution was a common operating picture (COP).

In military operations, the tactical operations center (TOC) is the hub of all operations and from where command and control of all subordinate units occur. In Army TOCs, staffs use a COP as a way to easily digest complex information in one central picture that anyone can understand quickly. The COP generally consists of two or three projected images complete with a map, a description of operations, and up-to-date information on the status of all operations. This way, anytime the commander came into the operations center, he could be updated with exactly what was going on by just glancing quickly at the three screens.

In the civilian world, we use executive dashboards in a similar way. An executive dashboard is an interface (typically computer generated) that shows key decision-makers and senior management KPIs for the organization. This information must be easily understood as the dashboard will be a high-level summary of complex operations with many moving parts. You can find many examples of dashboards on the internet. There is no set format because it should be tailored to your organization and how the senior management best understands the information presented to them (for example, would they rather see colors, charts, words, graphs, etc.). Figure 23 on the following page is an example of the dashboard I use to track monthly energy consumption over the trailing three-year period:

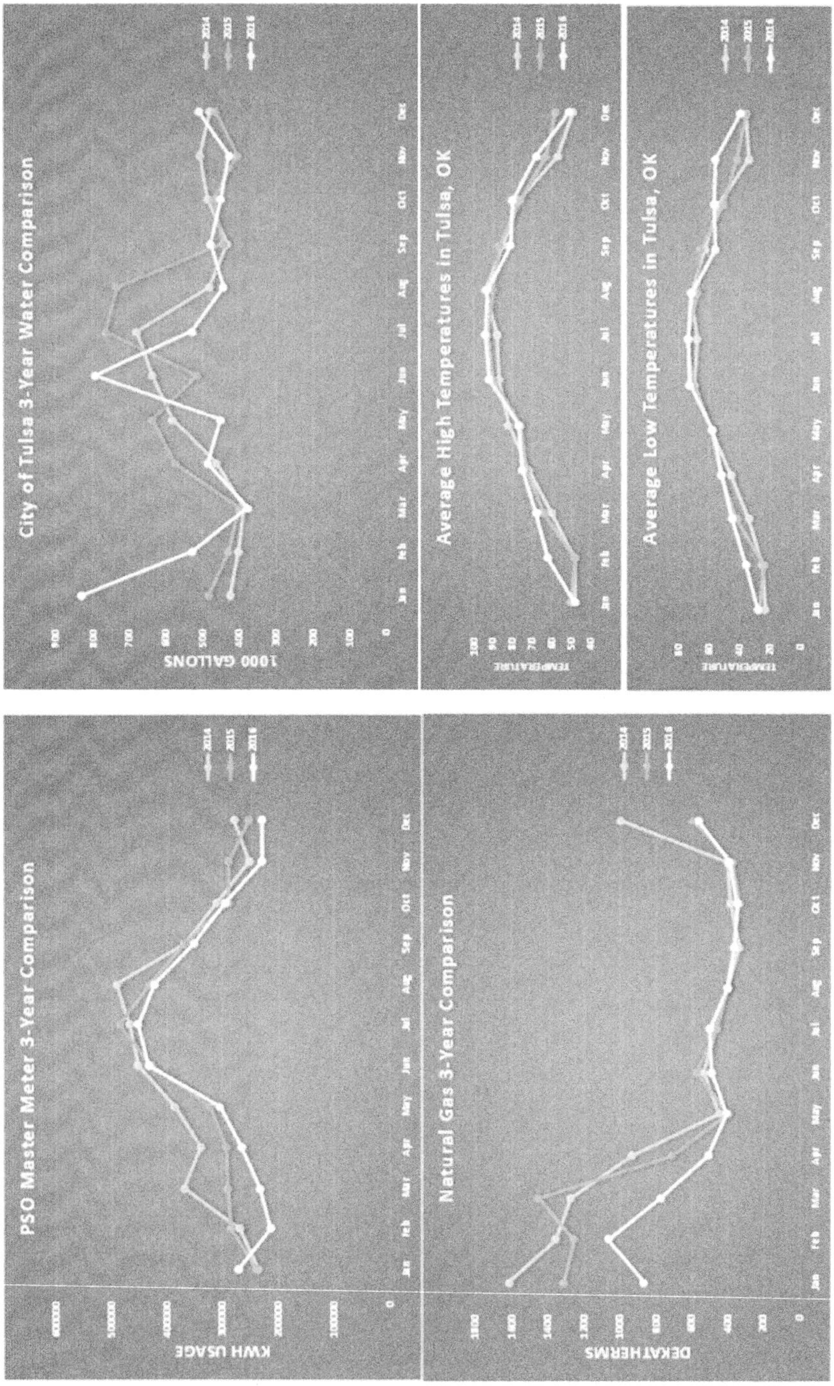
PSO Master Meter 3-Year Comparison
KWH USAGE
Natural Gas 3-Year Comparison
DEKATHERMS
City of Tulsa 3-Year Water Comparison
1000 GALLONS
Average High Temperatures in Tulsa, OK
TEMPERATURE
Average Low Temperatures in Tulsa, OK
TEMPERATURE

Figure 23

This dashboard (Figure 23) compares energy usage with average high and low temperatures. I routinely use it to explain energy expenditures and show results from any sustainability projects with the goals of reducing consumption. While I track these metrics monthly, I will typically only report them to my board quarterly.

Pro Forma Financial Statements

Pro Forma statements are financial statements (income statement, balance sheet, statement of cash flows) with variables changed representing assumptions or hypotheticals about future events. The hypothetical variables will then show management what the financial statement would look like if the variable came true. This gives management a tool to use in determining the direction the organization should take now in order to shape its future.

Pro forma statements occur at the end of budgeting and show management financial conditions for the organization at the end of a future budget period. The pro forma income statement summarizes projected revenues and expenses at the end of that future budget period. The pro forma balance sheet begins with the current balance sheet and changes variables of how the company's assets will be managed over the entire period. The pro forma cash flow projects how cash flow will look during the budgeted period. Forecasting cash flows is vital to the health of an organization because failing to do so properly could leave it with no money. That is a bad situation for everyone.

> For example, my organization routinely uses pro forma statements when we determine the size and scope of large capital projects. We have a cap on the amount of debt the shareholders are willing to accept, so taking on any amount of debt less than that is an option and can become a variable in a pro forma. We are also able to predict a range of the amount of revenue we will realize based on historical data -- and the low and high ends of the range become variables.
>
> Between the two, senior management is able to look at multiple scenarios from only using cash to only using debt to using a combination of both in several different pro forma statements. These give us a range of total dollars we will have available to take on a large capital project at some point in the future, which

leads us to the third major variable: time. Because we pay down long-term debt every month and we generate more revenue than we incur operating expenses, our borrowing potential and cash reserves go up every month. Therefore, pro forma statements five years from now will show a smaller dollar amount available for projects than pro forma statements projecting 10 years into the future.

Lease-or-Buy Decisions

Facility management is full of lease-or-buy decisions. While this literally means making an informed choice between leasing an asset or purchasing it outright, I'm using this term to refer to the many this-or-that decisions you will be faced with when choosing how you will conduct capital procurement and what information might affect your decision. These decisions might include whether to rent a building or build one. You might be faced with leasing vehicles or purchasing them. I routinely make decisions on whether to repair something in-house versus hiring an outside contractor to repair it. That goes hand-in-hand with financial decisions to hire more in-house labor or outsource contracts for various operations. The list goes on and on, but here are some of the considerations you will want to look at before making any of these decisions:

- Budget – the first thing to look at is what will the budgets allow? In my current position, we have more flexibility with our capital budget every year, but our operating budget is consistently tight. Therefore, if I need a new vehicle for the facilities personnel, I will most likely purchase it outright where I am able to accrue the cost to the capital budget. This is in contrast to leasing the vehicle, which would force me to find additional room in my operating budget that just isn't there.

- Need – what is the business need for the procurement or service you are trying to obtain? Can it feasibly be done with labor or assets that you already have? Does it really need to be done at all or is it superfluous to the organization's mission?

- Time – many this-or-that decisions will come down to time. I have very capable maintenance technicians who can fix many things, but I don't have enough to fix everything that all end-users want fixed in the timeframe they want them fixed. This means I need to outsource certain repairs.

- Accounting Benefits – in addition to having money available in an operating or capital budget, there are likely accounting considerations to think of. Is there a tax advantage to buying over leasing? Have you looked at depreciation or residual value of the asset? If you are comparing outsourcing versus in-house labor, have you looked at all financial factors, including insurance, training, and time-off?

- Intangible Benefits – sometimes the decisions will come down to simply wanting to have full control over the asset. This might mean that you end up building and owning the facility versus leasing it. Or perhaps, maybe you can't find the perfect property for your organization's needs to rent or lease and a purchase is the only suitable option for senior management.

Once you believe you have considered all of the angles, the best course of action is to create a business case for the project or procurement. The business case contains an executive summary of the proposal, the current situation or requirement, any assumptions you have made, a summary of the analysis you have done (this includes any relevant information in the bulleted items above, plus costs and payback), a risk analysis of what might happen with or without approval, and the final recommendation with what will be accomplished and when it will happen. Not all procurements will require a business case, but it is an extremely helpful tool to explain to senior management the value of your proposal and what might happen if it isn't approved.

Controlling Costs in Facility Management

I have always had a love-hate relationship with operational support and controlling costs. On one hand, it only makes sense to control costs in FM and to a certain extent, I think it is in our nature to want to do so. Just by being a facility management professional, I believe you have a proclivity toward improving efficiencies in everything you do. If you don't now, you will soon. From figuring out ways to constantly repair things with a limited budget to implementing energy management strategies, cost containment is at the forefront of our minds.

However, in the organizations where I have managed facilities, the pressure from senior management on revenue-generating departments to increase their production/sales/functions/output continually rises. If the operational output this year was X, then the expectation is that the operational output for next year will be X plus 3%, or whatever increase management feels appropriate. To be fair, this makes sense because organizations seek growth and they should. However, there is rarely a direct correlation between operational growth of other departments and the financial costs of supporting that operational growth within the FM department. Consider this example:

> I am currently a facility manager for a private country club. While the facilities belong to the members of the organization, we routinely rent facility space, with member approval, for outside organizations to hold large functions. The rental income helps to pay for not only the food, beverage, and labor for the event, but it aids in the operating expenses of the overall club and keeps member dues lower than they would be otherwise. It's only logical that increasing sales of these functions is encouraged because it leads to better financial health of the organization.
>
> However, when functions increase, my budget does not. Herein lies the hate side of my relationship with operational support and controlling costs. If you think about it, with more functions come more usage. This means there are more guests and employees utilizing the facility, which causes greater wear and tear on the facility. It also leads to higher utility bills because the facility is occupied when it would otherwise not be. The result is that my facilities team has to learn how to do more with the same budget amount that we started the year with, regardless of how many functions are booked long after the budget has been approved.

This is a great example of why controlling costs are so important in FM. You do not have the luxury of ignoring your facilities when budgets are tight. FMs are expected to maintain the facilities to certain standards with the resources they have, because it is necessary for the daily operations of the organization. As I've said before, when everything in facility management is running smoothly and nothing is broken, no one notices. That's when you know you're doing a great job. Therefore, the tighter you can control your costs, the more flexibility you will have in maintaining your facilities correctly. Unfortunately, too many times FMs are forced to cut corners due to limited budgets and the facility suffers.

Here are some of my favorite ways to control costs that have led to much success:

- FCI – explained in an earlier section, the facility condition index is a great tool to use in determining what assets should take priority in being replaced. When you couple this with an expected useful life analysis of all facility assets, you develop your life-cycle replacement capital plan and recommendations for replacements during the budgeting cycle. Because the FCI requires some qualitative analysis in addition to the formula itself, you can use the numbers to justify why an asset needs to be replaced or why it could benefit the organization to delay the replacement until a future year and utilize those budgeted funds for a higher priority need. Let me say that in a slightly different way. If an asset is at the end of its useful life but has a very low FCI, you can justify not replacing it and controlling that cost that can be used for an unexpected replacement that must be done immediately.

- Chargebacks – I haven't talked about chargebacks yet and part of that is for a reason. I'm not a big fan of chargebacks, but that's because of the positions and organizations for which I've managed facilities. That said, they do have a place and a purpose and I can imagine that they would be very helpful and effective in many organizations. So it's important to understand what they are and when they should be used. A chargeback is allocating costs of materials or services from the FM department to another department that is directly receiving and benefiting from the material or service. An example of this would be a discretionary project such as an office renovation required by an operations department that was not budgeted for in a capital improvement plan and only benefits the operations department. If approved, the cost of the renovation would go through the FM department and be charged back to the operations department. The benefit here is that it does not impact the FM budget and in this situation, I would also use a chargeback. However, what I've found is that managers can get carried away with chargebacks and this ends up becoming a nickel and dime system that results in an "us versus them" mentality. I know a lot of organizations that do use chargebacks and make it work very well. The key is to have a set system and policy (what constitutes a cost eligible for a chargeback and how that is conducted) in place and to follow it every time.

- ZBB – explained in detail earlier, zero-based budgeting is the best way to analyze all of your budget items, weed out the unnecessary costs, and find ways to control costs.

- Energy Efficiency – improving the efficiency of energy usage is vital. It is regulated by the federal government, better for the environment, and helps greatly in controlling utility costs. When I explain energy improvement projects for my board, I tell them I look at three types of projects. These projects are:

    - Behavioral Change – this is the least expensive type of improvement project as it relates to controlling energy costs. However, it is often the most complicated. Behavioral changes include things like employees turning the lights off in a room when they exit, turning the thermostat up or down when a room is unoccupied so that the HVAC doesn't run as much, and changing the set points for HVAC in rooms when they are occupied (instead of cooling to 72°F in the summer, cool the space to 74°F). These are simple in theory and cheap to put in place, but tend to be resisted internally. Even if these changes are widely accepted, it becomes difficult for everyone to remember to engage in the new behavior and not revert to old habits.

    - Space Efficiency – this type of infrastructure project is aimed at increasing the energy efficiency of the space itself. These types of projects are not always easily accomplished. I've found that incorporating these improvements into renovations help greatly, but I have had some success with doing individual projects in spaces that I can get to relatively easily. Examples of space efficiency projects include energy sealing the building, adding better insulation, and replacing inefficient windows with efficient ones. Spray foam insulation in the attic is an example I have been able to do several times as several stand-alone capital improvement projects when the budget allowed.

    - Equipment Efficiency – upgrading your facility assets to be more energy efficient is best accomplished when the need for a replacement arises. It is a much easier sell to senior management to argue the need for a more efficient HVAC system when you're already replacing it than it is to argue the need to replace a system that is still in good working condition. Examples of equipment efficiency projects include upgrading HVAC systems (higher SEER ratings, incorporating variable air volume vs. constant air volume, etc.) and upgrading inefficient incandescent lighting to LED.

- Negotiation – it is entirely possible to control costs and still maintain the same level of service from suppliers through negotiation. Sometimes, this will require the organization to agree to an extended service plan or give the service provider a larger portion of the organization's business. In any case, it is worth the conversation if you think there is room to work with a service provider you plan to use in the future.

- Reduce Staff or Hours – I personally hate this plan, but it is always an option. For me, it is my last resort because I expect my staff to be loyal to the organization and the organization should be loyal to them. That said, labor costs tend to be a huge part of the budget and it will be an option open to you. Just understand there is a price for using this option.

- SOPs – if you don't have standard operating procedures in place for routine actions, get them. If you do have them, review them for inefficiencies and update them periodically.

There are many other ways to control facility management costs. The point is -- think outside the box and explore all of your options. I once saved my organization 30% on the group cell phone plan for key managers by taking advantage of a program the phone carrier began to attract new customers. We weren't a new customer, but they gave it to us anyway to retain our business. The second part of this is to make sure senior management knows the successes you have when you are able to control FM costs. One caveat, some managers will want to take the savings back from you immediately, so have a recommendation on where to use that money that will also benefit the organization moving forward.

Section Summary

This section has taught you the fundamentals of finance and accounting, the foundations in finance you need to be successful, and the principles of financial management you will definitely need in order to be the best facility manager possible. While not often looked at as a must-have skill for FMs, business finance is truly an important knowledge domain to master. You might be able to function in the built-environment for a while without understanding finance, but you will excel with it. In the next two sections, we will talk about the last knowledge domain: Leadership.

Section 6: Leadership

Leaders don't create followers, they create more leaders.

~ Tom Peters

Leadership is what I've looked forward to writing most. It lies at the intersection of all other knowledge domains, because truly understanding leadership and how to do it will set you up for success. To be sure, you cannot manage your facilities, projects, and budgets by yourself. The people who work for you and with you will make you successful (or ultimately lead to your search for success elsewhere). Understanding how to develop as a leader and then develop other leaders is vital to this success. Thank you for giving me the opportunity to pass on what I have learned about leadership and what I continue to learn to this day.

This section will take you through a series of steps you must take to make the most out of your leadership development. First, you need to make the conscious decision to lead. The concept of a natural born leader is not one that I promote. Leadership, like many things, is an art that is learned, practiced, and improved. It is a perishable skill that will degrade over time when not practiced and is not binary in nature. What I mean by that is leading effectively is not all or nothing; but it exists on a sliding scale. You can (and most likely will) be more effective in certain leadership competencies than others. You will naturally tend to have stronger leadership attributes than others and it is up to you to improve in weaker areas.

Second, I want you to have an in-depth understanding of leadership and some of the theories behind styles of leadership and effectiveness. I've learned that being able to identify the fundamentals of leadership, attributes of great leaders, and the competencies they exhibit are really foundational to our own understanding and growth. However, this book is not just another series of short stories and quotes from specific leaders. I will describe what makes leaders successful, why, and how you can use that to develop.

Third, I will list specific tools you can use for leadership development. When you are starting out, you will use these tools on a personal level, but I want to emphasize the importance of transitioning to using them to develop your team. Developing leaders around you will not only continue your personal growth on a new level, but will pay dividends for your organizational progress and engagement.

Finally, I will give you a number of tips and techniques throughout this section that I personally follow. These might not have a direct impact on learning leadership, but absolutely enable me as a leader to be more effective. Just as a PM checklist helps your maintenance technician become more efficient, you can use any of these tips when applicable.

As I close this introduction to leadership, I want to be mindful to always be as descriptive as possible to promote practical learning. Leadership is intangible and can become a nebulous subject with no clear direction. I've read books on leadership that left me with more of a vague concept than a plan for how to improve. This is not one of those books.

Chapter 1: Why Me?

After three full days of sitting in lectures at an FM leadership symposium, I collapsed into a lounge chair across from the facility manager of a rather prestigious country club in the United States. The symposium was complete and I just wanted to unwind. Over a glass of Canada's finest beer, we began visiting about the challenges in our organizations and how to overcome them. He described to me the current situation at their club and how the previous general manager had left two years prior. That GM position remained vacant and no single leader had emerged in the meantime. The original intent behind not finding a new GM was conceived by their Board of Governors. They wanted to act as senior management for the club, but leave the daily operations to be carried out by all department heads, each with an equal amount of authority. The only problem with this strategy was that the Board of Governors only met once per month, resulting in a leadership void. Without one person leading the daily operations of the club, every department was headed in their own direction. Getting rid of one chief and making six more does not work.

As the facility manager talked through this issue, I could see how passionate he was for his club. He truly cared about the direction it was going and his role within the organization. He described how the other department heads were looking out for themselves and took every opportunity to shine in front of the board. This was great for them as individuals, but contributed little to the overall teamwork of the club. After listening for a while, I couldn't take it anymore.

I interrupted him and said, "You need to lead your club."

For me, it was so clear what had to happen. From my perspective, there was only one person with the vision of where that club should go and the passion to really see it through. He just happened to be sitting across from me. But I caught him so off guard from my comment that he didn't say a word. He sat there speechless, looking at me.

> Finally, I saw him make a definitive decision in his mind. "But, I don't want to be the general manager," he declared.
>
> I casually explained, "I didn't say anything about you being the GM. I said, 'You need to lead your club'."
>
> At that moment, I saw a light come on. At that moment, I recognized the look on his face as he thought to himself, "Why me?" And then I saw the recognition, as he understood the answer to that question.
>
> Sometime later I touched base with him again and asked if any changes were made. He said the differences within their club were amazing -- and the biggest change was his mindset. Once he made the decision to look at himself and his employees differently, he began to lead effectively, which permeated the organization.

To be clear, there is no universal answer to the question, "Why Me?" Becoming a leader is an individual choice everyone must make. The FM from the story above also began to understand that management and leadership are two completely different things. This is a concept that I will get into later; but the point I want to make now is you do not have to be the senior manager to lead your organization. You do, however, have to make the choice to lead.

This brings me to the second point I want to make and it is something I have learned after many years of studying leadership and developing leaders. Anyone can lead. There is no magic formula that every great leader is born with, which prevents anyone else from becoming a leader. While this concept seems to run contrary to many opinions and teaching on leadership, let me explain. There are traits that successful leaders share and there are skills, attributes, techniques, and methods of leading that certainly will make you stand out. However, anyone can learn any of these. The key is to make the decision to lead and then learn how. Never let anyone tell you that you are not fit to lead. And by anyone, I really mean you. You can become your own biggest obstacle. Don't allow that to happen.

Leadership Tip #1 – Anyone can lead. Make the decision to be a leader and don't look back. There is no room for second-guessing your decision.

As you seek the answer to "Why me," the final point I want to make is don't quit on yourself. We all have setbacks, but how we persevere is what will make all of the difference. Consider Abraham Lincoln, arguably one of the best presidents in United States history. His leadership kept the nation together throughout a dark time in our past. However, before Lincoln became president he had a number of failures. He lost eight elections, suffered a nervous breakdown, and failed in business more than once. Through all of it, he managed to become a very successful lawyer and politician, not to mention a great leader.

Once you make the decision to lead, believe in yourself. If you don't, no one else will.

Chapter 2: Why am I Teaching Leadership?

Each time I stand in front of a group to speak on leadership, I describe my background, education, and experience. I don't do this to brag. I do this to give credibility to the thoughts I'm about to share, because I want my audience to first listen, and know wherein my experience is rooted.

> In the military, the uniforms we wear act as resumes for entire careers. If you look at an Army officer's dress uniform, you can see their rank, name, job classification, special schools they attended, unit they deployed with, current unit affiliation, and any awards or decorations they have earned throughout their entire career. Daily, Soldiers across the world wear utility uniforms. If you look closely, you will notice they all have a patch on their left shoulder and many have a patch on their right shoulder. The left shoulder patch signifies their current unit of assignment, while their right shoulder patch signifies the unit they were assigned to when they deployed to an active combat zone.
>
> As Soldiers, one of our primary responsibilities is to train to deploy to combat zones. I have attended many schools, classes, and lectures on deploying, and the first thing I do when a new speaker stands in front of me and my Soldiers is look at their right shoulder. If they don't have a combat patch, I automatically discount what they are saying. Does not having this patch mean they don't have credible things to say? Absolutely not, but I cannot help it. If you have not had the experience of deploying to a combat zone, how can you teach me about it?

I think this logic is important to understand. Whether or not you feel the same way I do, rest assured that at least one of your direct reports does. It's for this reason that I will give you my background in leadership.

My military leadership started in 2002, when I enlisted in the Army during my senior year of college. Later that year, I went to basic training at Fort Knox, KY. Talk about a wake-up call. Learning the basics of being a Soldier was like someone hit me in the face with a 2x4! I vividly remember waiting for permission to eat, standing at the position of attention behind my meager tray of breakfast the morning after I met my Drill Sergeants. It was still dark outside and all I could do was stare through the window in front of me into the black abyss, wondering what I had gotten myself into. The Drill Sergeant's job was to break us all down and remold us into Soldiers, capable of working together as a team and following orders in combat. It was here, however, that I made the conscious choice to be a leader. I fought to learn the skills required, excel at them, and help my peers along as well. By the end of the 9-week training, I promoted to Platoon Guide, which is the basic training equivalent of the leader of our platoon of trainees (about 40 soon-to-be Soldiers). At the time, there was nothing better than marching the platoon to the Post Exchange (PX), giving them commands and singing cadence to ensure everyone remained in synchronized step.

Less than a year later, I entered Officer Candidate School (OCS) and began my formal leadership education in the military. OCS is basic training for officers. It is the job of the OCS instructors (similar to Drill Sergeants) not to make Soldiers, but to make leaders of Soldiers. Because I am in the National Guard, OCS took place one weekend per month and two-weeks each summer for 18 months (while holding a civilian job during the week). Throughout OCS, we learned small-unit tactics, leadership skills, mission planning, public speaking, and the myriad other skills the Army deems necessary to lead. After 18 months, I commissioned as a Second Lieutenant (2LT) and soon after left for five months of active-duty training at Fort Benning, GA, as an infantry officer. As a 2LT, I led a platoon (38 Soldiers) during training events for the next two years. Part of being a Platoon Leader involved mobilizing them to New Orleans, LA, during the Hurricane Katrina response in 2005. Leading armed Soldiers through American streets was something I never thought I would do and it's something I never care to do again.

After two years, I was promoted to First Lieutenant (1LT) and became the Executive Officer (second in command – if the commander was gone, I was in charge) of a company of 123 Soldiers. Here, I deployed to Baghdad, Iraq, in support of Operation Iraqi Freedom in 2007. It's ironic that for years I had been training to lead in armed combat exclusively, but my greatest leadership challenges occurred inside the relative safety of the base. It was here that Soldiers had money issues, family troubles, and personality conflicts with other Soldiers in their team. I learned many lessons in leadership in Iraq, but the most valuable ones came out of harm's way.

Upon my return, I promoted to Captain (CPT) and accepted a position teaching leadership to future officers at the same OCS program I graduated from five years earlier. It is true that the best way to learn is to teach. I learned very well all of the lessons from attending OCS years earlier as I taught them to my students. Up until then, there was nothing I had done that was as satisfying as teaching leadership lessons to Soldiers and watching them turn into leaders themselves over time. I still serve with some of those students and I still feel proud as I watch them develop today. As a CPT, I also attended my next leadership school, Career Course. There we graduated from leading small unit tactics to learning to lead larger groups of Soldiers and understanding military planning processes. The last two and a half years as a CPT, I commanded an engineer company where I mentored five to six junior officers at any given time. Commanding a company was certainly challenging, but extremely rewarding, as I was ultimately responsible for everything the Soldiers within the company accomplished or failed to do.

After five years as a CPT, I promoted to Major (MAJ) and attended my most recent formal leadership school, Intermediate Level Education (ILE). As a MAJ in ILE, we learned the basics of strategic level leadership. Leadership in the military exists at three levels. The lowest level is tactical leadership, which exists in the smallest units in tactical operations on the battlefield. The middle level is operational leadership in larger formations of thousands of Soldiers and includes planning and conducting military campaigns. The highest level of leadership is strategic that exists at the Pentagon and includes planning at the highest level of employing national power. I am currently still serving as a MAJ as the Operations Officer for an engineer battalion (over 600 Soldiers), where I am responsible for the planning and training of all operations and mentoring the officers on my staff.

Throughout my military service, I've had the privilege of serving under many excellent leaders. These leaders have garnered respect from countless subordinates they have commanded, senior politicians, and international leaders from across the globe. However, these leaders pale in comparison to the finest leader I have ever met. He was a sergeant, the lowest leadership rank in the Army, and in charge of four Soldiers. He knew his job inside and out. He knew his supervisor's job and he knew everything his four Soldiers should be doing and how to motivate them to do it. Because his entire world centered on the well-being of those four Soldiers, they respected him more than anything. They would have died for him. He was a true leader.

My civilian leadership education really began after college when I became the warranty supervisor of a residential construction company. I learned several valuable leadership lessons while supervising individual subcontractors for warranty work, which carried on to my next position as the vice-president of construction for another residential construction company. Here, I supervised both outside subcontractors, and several company employees who reported directly to me. This was my first experience as a manager in a civilian role.

After my Baghdad deployment, the residential construction market took a turn and I entered the Tulsa Police Academy. This six-month, full-time school focused quite a bit on effective leadership traits and tactics including active-listening techniques, stress management, and negotiation skills. Unfortunately, the economy hit Tulsa's sales tax revenue (which pays for police labor) and I was laid off, twice. That is when I landed my first commercial FM position at Camp Gruber, where I supervised 24 employees, including four managers. I also went back to school to earn my MBA in Finance. My current position is the Director of Facilities for Southern Hills Country Club, where I directly supervise four departments and contribute to club-wide management training on a routine basis.

Leadership Tip #2 – Develop leadership and technical abilities at the same time through formal education, informal study, training, experience, and mentorship.

Ironically, all of my formal continuing education in the civilian world (including my MBA) did not include much leadership education at all. From facilities to project management, this formal education tends to focus on practical, vocational knowledge. This is vastly different from my military education, which focuses in large part on leadership specifically. For me, an equal balance between the two makes the most sense and is where I root all lessons within this section. You will never be an effective facility manager without the knowledge described in previous sections, but you will also fall short without the ability to lead.

Chapter 3: What is a Leader?

Let's begin by defining what a leader is not. A leader is not a manager, meaning these two words are not synonymous like some people think. That said, a leader can be a manager and a manager can be a leader. A manager forecasts and controls resources, from budgets to people. Management is all about ensuring tasks get accomplished. You might commonly hear references to workers being put in "leadership positions" and maybe that's true. But that worker is not necessarily a leader just because of his or her new position. They are simply managing resources in a position of leadership. To be truly effective, you must learn how to be a leader.

The Army defines leadership as *the process of influencing people by providing purpose, direction, and motivation to accomplish the mission and improve the organization.*[18] A leader influences others to accomplish the goals of the organization. Leaders motivate and inspire the people within their sphere of influence. The distinction between management and leadership is an important one because I've seen too many managers who think they are leaders and the team suffers from it.

Leadership Tip #3 – Do not ask your employees to do anything you are not willing to do yourself.

The degree of influence one person has over another exists on a sliding scale. At one end of the spectrum lies complete commitment to a vision, fueled by an enthusiasm to accomplish the tasks at hand. At the other end of the spectrum lies obedience, where an individual will unwillingly accomplish the tasks at hand only because they are instructed to do so. Focusing on inspiration and motivation, leaders gain commitment. Focusing on controlling resources, managers gain obedience.

Bases of Social Power

In 1959, John R. P. French and Bertram Raven described five separate forms of power in social influence. Raven later revised the findings and added a sixth. French and Raven defined social influence as intentional or passive acts that have the potential to affect the beliefs, behaviors, or attitudes of someone else.[19] I have found that these bases of power in social influence relate very closely to garnering respect in any leadership position. The bases of power are coercive, reward, legitimate, referent, expert, and informational.

Coercive Power – the idea behind coercive power is that one person forces another to do something that they do not want to do. You've heard of the carrot and the stick? This is the stick. This is not an effective tool to use in leadership. First, it's not fun for anyone. No one likes to be forced to do something through threats of punishment. Second, in order for it to be effective, the person wielding coercive power must constantly keep an eye on their target to punish them when they fail to comply.

Reward Power – this is essentially the opposite of coercive power and is the carrot in the analogy. With reward power, one person gives a reward to another for compliance with their wishes. They can also withhold rewards for non-compliance. This is not too much better than coercive power because rewards lose their luster with time and your employees might focus only on the reward and lose interest in why they are there. Rewards are not inherently bad, but should be used in conjunction with other bases of power.

Legitimate Power – this is the most basic form of power and is handed to the individual simply by granting them a title. It occurs through election, selection, and appointment into a position of authority. In any organization, a manager is given legitimate power by accepting the position of manager. Society assigns this type of power to people in positions of authority. Have you ever had a boss that you did not respect, but complied with their directives anyway? They had legitimate power.

Referent Power – this is power that is ascertained from one's associations. I sometimes garner a certain amount of referent power from people who have never been in the military simply because I am an Army Officer. They have no idea if I am a good leader or not, but I have an association with a leadership organization. The spouse of a successful politician gains referent power from their proximity to the position.

Expert Power – this is power that comes from the knowledge, skills, and experience of the individual yielding it. It's important to understand that it is the perception of the expertise that gives someone this type of power. A medical doctor yields expert power based on the degree they hold, which indicates they have much more knowledge about the human body than the layperson.

Information Power – this type of power comes from someone having knowledge that others desire or need. It is how this information is used that can influence others, which leads to the base of power. Information can be shared or withheld strategically, which creates the social influence.

I have found that capitalizing on more than one base of power will proportionately extend your social influence, which directly affects your effectiveness as a leader.

> While teaching OCS, I learned how important these types of power are and when to use them to my advantage. When candidates came to OCS, they were not leaders. They were Soldiers who signed up to learn how to be leaders. Soldiers tend to be motivated by the stick and the carrot, because that is a lot of what they learn at basic training. The OCS instructors routinely used both coercive and reward power in the beginning quite frequently because that is what the candidates understood and we had not yet proven our expertise. When candidates would make mistakes, they would be punished through physical activity (i.e., doing pushups until they couldn't do any more). When they had successes, they received rewards such as more freedom between classes. As instructors, we automatically had legitimate power we earned from being put into the position of leading candidates through all stages of OCS; and we had referent power from the black hats we wore. The black hat signified an association with a special group of OCS instructors that taught and evaluated leadership (as opposed to teaching technical skills like supply-chain planning). As time went on, we earned expert power through demonstrating our experience prior to coming to OCS to teach. Finally, OCS instructors gained information power by sharing information candidates needed at the appropriate times, enabling them to learn key leadership lessons.

Leadership Styles

Different leaders use different leadership styles. Much research has been conducted on the different styles of leadership and they all vary to some degree. However, I've found that these five leadership styles encompass the traits of all different leaders. Which style describes you?

Laissez-Faire Leadership

French for "let (people) do as they choose," laissez-faire describes a hands-off approach.[20] Laissez-faire leadership will typically yield the lowest results because the leader does not directly supervise the employee. Decision-making is left to the employees with little to no guidance from leadership. Leaders will provide resources, but employees are expected to diagnose and resolve issues on their own. This can be effective in situations where employees are both motivated and capable to work on their own with minimal direction from management. This should not be used if your employees lack the knowledge or drive to accomplish tasks on their own. In this situation, it could lead to confusion, little work being accomplished, and a sense that you do not care about them. You might consider using this style of leadership in situations where a direct report knows considerably more than you do on a subject, but you should remain available for questions and to give feedback.

Autocratic Leadership

Also known as authoritarian leadership, autocratic leadership is the opposite of laissez-fair. The autocratic leader exercises total control over all decisions and allows very little input from employees. While this sounds like a recipe for disaster, this leadership style lends itself to situations where quick, decisive action is warranted and there is little time for debate. In the military, there are definitely times where a quick decision and direction coming from the leader can make the difference between life and death. That said, to adopt an autocratic style 100% of the time is not advisable. Total autocratic leaders are often disliked by their employees, which stifles creativity and can lead to high turnover rates. The key here is to understand when this type of leadership style is warranted and then avoid it at all other times.

Participative Leadership

Also known as democratic leadership, the participative approach blends laissez-faire and autocratic leadership to find a middle ground. The participative leader actively encourages participation from employees in decision-making, but then makes the final decision for the group. The benefits here are improved employee morale as they feel valued and respected; and many more creative ideas being brought to the table from all members of the team. This leadership style, however, does not work so well in those instances when decisions must be made rapidly as the participation process can take some time to sort through.

Transactional Leadership

Transactional leadership incorporates rewards and punishments in exchange for employee performance. The leader and employee will agree on goals and pre-determined standards to meet those goals. In this style, the leader provides direction and oversight and then reviews the employee's performance in meeting their goals. Employees are rewarded for meeting or exceeding the goals (e.g. with bonuses) or punished if they fail to meet their goals. This style of leadership is typically more passive and does not encourage out-of-the-box thinking.

Transformational Leadership

Transformational leaders create a vision for their employees and communicate it often. These leaders identify the need for change and then become that agent for change through inspiration and motivation. This leadership style will typically improve employee morale and promote inclusion within the group. The transformational leader is a role model for employees and strives to understand their strengths and weaknesses in order to enable them to be their best. In contrast to transactional leadership that maintains the status quo, transformational leaders inspire their employees to change to meet the strategic goals of the organization.

Leadership Tip #4 – Learn how and when to use all leadership styles for maximum effectiveness.

The most effective leaders are not married to one particular leadership style and can switch between each style depending on which is most appropriate in a given situation. That said, if I had to choose one best style, transformational leadership lends itself best to empowered and engaged employees, strategic-thinking leaders with clear visions, and open communication at all levels within the organization.

Levels of Leadership

Leadership is different based on the size and structure of the group you lead. What your followers expect of you and the responsibilities you manage both change drastically according to size and scope. What follows are the basic requirements at each level of leadership you can expect to find across many organizations.

Self-level Leadership

The smallest and most basic form of leadership is leading and preparing yourself. While most people don't think of this as true leadership, I disagree. This can sometimes be quite a challenge. How do you motivate and inspire yourself? By reading this guide, you should understand that you are preparing yourself to manage facilities and lead those around you. Continue this self-development throughout your career.

Direct-level Leadership

This is when you directly lead other people and is typically the step that follows self-leadership. Here, you learn to influence direct reports, peers, and superiors while interacting with them to accomplish the organization's mission. This level of leadership is characterized by mostly interpersonal communication and daily collaboration with those you lead.

Group-level Leadership

Leaders move from personal interaction to leading groups of people. An example of this is when you are in charge of multiple departments, each with their own manager. For your direct-report managers, you engage in direct-level leadership. However, you are really leading the entire department, even though you do not interact with each individual person on a daily basis. Here you are learning to become a leader of leaders. Not only should you continue to focus on your own self-development and developing those around you, but you should mentor the junior leaders reporting to you and guide them as they begin to transition to group-level leadership.

Functional-level Leadership

The functional-level leader has transitioned from leading groups to leading functions. In this reference, a function exists beyond anyone one person's experience. This level of leader brings together many different skills and contributors to accomplish longer-term objectives. Consider the project manager leading a diverse team to accomplish a multi-year project together. Functional leaders bring together and lead group-level leaders.

Integration-level Leadership

Moving beyond the functional level, the integration-level leader establishes a vision, learns to communicate it and focuses on organizational goals to motivate and inspire followers. More time is spent on the future than the present, including a drive to move all employees in a direction that accomplishes the strategic mission of the company. Think of these as executives over entire branches or large business units under the overall organizational umbrella.

Organizational-level Leadership

The organizational-level leadership must establish a clear vision for the entire organization that drives the strategic mission of all employees. This leader, more so than at any other level, relies heavily on their employees' experience and expertise. It is only through the efforts of their followers that organizational-level leaders will be successful. These are the CEOs of companies. At this level of leadership, you must be humble and be a visionary.

Leadership Tip #5 – Establishing a clear vision and communicating it to your employees becomes increasingly important as you move from Self to Organizational-level Leadership.

Chapter 4: Leader Attributes

Through these next two chapters, we are going to explore what makes great leaders from two different sides: attributes and competencies. An attribute is a characteristic of a person where a competency is knowledge or the ability to do something. In this chapter, as I lay out leader attributes, consider them the foundation of what you should be in order to be the most effective leader you can be. For each attribute, I will describe what it is, why it is important, and how to cultivate that characteristic in yourself and others.

Leadership Tip #6 – No leader is perfect in every attribute and competency. The great leaders understand their weaknesses and work to develop them.

Empathy

At a recent facility management conference, I attended a seminar on leadership. The speaker and I began talking about military leadership after the session had ended. Not ever being a part of the military, he was curious about the similarities and differences of certain points he made to the audience. Toward the end of our conversation he asked me what I considered to be the most important leadership trait one could possess. I told him empathy.

He looked intrigued and said, "Interesting, I've never heard that one before. How so?"

I told him, "Think about it. How can you hope to lead another person if you can't understand their point of view?"

Empathy is the ability to understand the feelings of another from their perspective. To be truly empathetic, you must share their feelings as though they are your own. This is important because you cannot hope to inspire and motivate others until you understand what it is that inspires and motivates them. If you don't truly understand what your employees are feeling, how can you possibly hope to influence those feelings? The ability to influence feelings of others is the foundation for motivating them to accomplish goals ***because they want to accomplish them***.

Ironically, how you become empathetic is easy, but many supervisors continue to resist. Too many times, I've seen managers hear one person's point of view (often their own), make a judgment based on that one-sided story, and attempt to affect change from there. Does it work? I'm sure it does occasionally, I mean even a broken clock is right twice a day. But it isn't effective.

In order to learn to be empathetic, put yourself in the other person's shoes. Approach a problem from their perspective and ask yourself how that is different from how you view something. If an employee comes in late, before immediately chastising them, ask why they are late and if you can help.

If you find yourself having trouble with practicing empathy, try these things. First, pay attention. When someone comes into your office, stop what you're doing, look them in the eye, and actively listen to what they have to say. Repeat a summary of what they said back to them to make sure you really did understand what they meant. Second, take a genuine interest in the people you want to lead. Ask them how they are feeling and link those to non-verbal clues to understand how they communicate (e.g., facial expressions, posture, general attitude). Finally, take note of how they respond to your requests and the organizational environment to better empathize with how they will potentially feel when evaluating different plans and options.

Leadership Tip #7 – Making emotional decisions based on how you feel without understanding how other parties feel is a recipe for disaster.

Character

Having a strong character is important. Leaders with character possess integrity and operate according to a code of ethics. Integrity is simply doing the right thing even when no one is watching. Ethics are a set of rules that guide moral behavior. Unethical leaders are not respected and are often talked about behind their backs. This undermines their leadership ability by eroding any hope of inspiring and motivating those around them. Individuals lacking integrity might subscribe to a code of ethics, but will look for loopholes in those ethics whenever possible.

Most professional organizations maintain a code of ethics, which is a good place to start if you are new to this. IFMA publishes their code of ethics on their website. I would suggest looking at these to incorporate along with the ethical principles of your organization. Additionally, ensure you maintain integrity. One thing I tell my junior officers when I counsel them is to assume someone is watching all the time and never do anything that you would not want your loved ones to see as a headline on the six o'clock news. It's surprising how such an easy concept can get people in so much trouble. Leadership is hard enough to develop without undermining your progress by acting without integrity.

Confidence

There are two sides of confidence a leader must develop and continually improve in, the inner and the outer. Both are complementary of each other. Let me explain.

I will refer to the inner as self-confidence and the outer as inspiring confidence. One simple definition of confidence is *full trust.*[21] Self-confidence is believing in yourself and knowing that you are capable to accomplish whatever you set your mind to do. Inspiring confidence is both instilling full trust in you from others and trusting them in return. This motivates them to achieve their own levels of self-confidence.

Inner and outer confidences build upon each other. Have you ever been around a confident leader and felt it in yourself? Confidence inspires other confidence. It's contagious. In the same vein, however, a lack of confidence erodes trust in yourself and others. If you are not confident in your own abilities, how can you expect other people to be? If this is starting to sound like a vicious cycle, you're right. So then, how do you gain and build confidence?

<u>Build your own value</u> – there is no way to get around this. To build your own self-confidence and to inspire trust from others in your abilities, you must build your own sense of value through experience and education. This is a continual process. As you gain experience and learn more, you will become more confident.

<u>Remain calm and cool</u> – everyone has stress, but confident leaders manage it well. Stress typically carries a negative connotation as we most often associate it with an overwhelming feeling of pressure caused by external

stressors such as personal problems, increasing workloads, and short deadlines. Not all stress is bad, however. Managing our response to stressors not only affects our level of confidence, but will also affect our health and well-being.

You can find many books and articles on the subject, but some great ways to effectively manage stress include the following:

- Eat well, limit caffeine and alcohol, and exercise regularly
- Manage time effectively by scheduling time for work, family, and personal enjoyment
- Delegate and learn to say no (more on this later)
- Breathe deeply in stressful situations
- Limit distractions and don't try and multi-task
- Manage personal finances like you manage professional accounts – use a budget and stay within it
- Find your emotional happiness (spirituality, companionship, etc.) Understand that learning to remain calm in emotional situations takes practice. Unfortunately, you cannot learn this skill without actual stress being present. That said, remember to not act immediately when faced with a stressful situation. Take a breath, evaluate all options, and make a rational decision. If you need more information, seek it before acting.

Dress for success – I use this phrase to encompass all aspects of your physical presence. This begins with your physical fitness. While you don't need to be running marathons to be an effective leader, your confidence will grow as you become more physically fit. You will begin to carry yourself better as well. Improving your posture is a huge boost to self-confidence and largely noticeable to those around you. Stand straight, walk purposefully, and pull your shoulders back with your head high. Leaders who carry themselves with excellent posture, exude poise. The clothes you wear are important too. You do not need to spend a fortune on them, but if you take care of the clothes you have (wear clean clothes, iron them when needed, polish shoes, etc.), it will be evident that you care about yourself and can pay attention to detail.

Speak publicly – I don't recall where I heard that one of the greatest fears held by most people is public speaking, but it seems to be true in my experience. I used to be terrified to speak publicly and I still get nervous standing up in front of a group of people to speak. This is normal. Having the ability to speak publicly is important for two reasons. First, it will add to your overall confidence level. Second, you will most likely need to do it in your role as a manager, so it would benefit you to learn how to do it effectively. The best way to learn how to speak publicly is to take a course (this can be formal or informal), practice with a mirror or a video camera, and then find venues where you can speak in front of people. Try to be conscious of using filler words like "umm" or "like" and minimize excess hand gestures and pacing back and forth. Public speaking gets easier with practice and you get better each time.

Be Decisive – a confident leader is not afraid to make decisions and understands that making mistakes is part of the package. Know that you too will make mistakes, but understand that mistakes are healthy and that is how we learn and grow. Own your mistakes and build on them. Worse than making mistakes is being indecisive, paralyzed by fear of failure. Just don't make the same mistake twice.

Competence

Competence refers to the knowledge a person possesses and what they do with that knowledge. It encompasses far more than possessing book smarts from formal education. Competence is the practical application of an individual's intellect. Let's break that down to these components:

Mental Agility – this is the ability to change and adapt to unforeseen conditions. A mentally agile leader is one who can adjust rather quickly. They are constantly looking for new ways to improve and critically reason their way through challenges.

Sound Judgment – this requires the leader to think critically and make decisions that are rational and solve the problem at hand. Sound judgment does not mean that a leader knows everything. Part of this includes knowing when to ask for help in order to choose what action to take from multiple options. The best way to improve your mental agility and your judgment is to conduct an after action review (AAR). To do this, you and your team look at the problem, what was supposed to happen, what actually happened in the course of solving it, and what could have or should have happened differently. Take this information, because hindsight is always 20/20, and then look at it through the lens of your own decision-making at the time. Ask yourself what your thought processes were when making your decisions and what you could have done differently to come up with better solutions. Then, use those lessons to change how you critically think in the future.

Innovation – this is the ability to create and to come up with new ideas, solutions, or concepts. This is important because anyone and anything can be improved upon, but it takes innovative leaders to see how to make a situation better. If you want to improve innovation, create brainstorming groups and use them in a team-building exercise. Learn how others look at problems and then use what works in your own creativity.

Interpersonal Relations – part of being a leader is having the ability to interact with other people in any situation. This starts with self-control. As a leader, you will be faced with situations that make you angry or frustrated with individuals with whom you need to work. Learning to control your emotions is important to maintaining an open line of communications, a working relationship, and a positive work environment. A good tool to do this is to learn how to recognize diversity in culture, religion, background, race, etc., in order to form a basis of understanding of your employees and co-workers. This, in turn, helps enable you to be that empathetic leader by providing context for the other person's situation.

Expertise – finally, expertise is the knowledge a leader possesses from formal and informal education, experience, and training. Without question, this leads to an overall competency in your field, but I want to emphasize that it is not enough. Improving your expertise goes back to building your own value, which aids in confidence. It is combined with the other components above to form a well-rounded, competent leader.

These leader attributes are important characteristics for any leader to develop. This is especially true with facilities management. FM can be a stressful profession by its very nature. Continually developing these attributes will help you in your growth as an FM professional throughout your career.

Chapter 5: Leader Competencies

While attributes are personal characteristics, core competencies are what leaders actually do. There are three groups of core competencies that we will study here: ***leads, fosters, and achieves***. These three groups are comprised of acts that all leaders must engage in and improve upon in order to lead successfully. Like attributes, leader competencies can be learned and should be practiced as often as possible.

Leads

At the lowest levels, leaders influence and motivate on a personal basis. From leader to follower, task and purpose are given, goals are set, and the organization conducts business. Senior leaders at the strategic level influence the entire organization through setting a vision and inspiring their employees to grow and improve.

We already know that leadership is the process of influencing others by providing purpose, direction, and motivation. To influence another, you are packaging your message and changing the way you act in a way that affects the behaviors and motivations of others. There are different ways to influence those around you. Let's examine these methods next and how they tie into the leadership styles and bases of social power.

<u>Pressure</u> – this is only used when you desire obedience over commitment. Using pressure is a way to negatively influence others by establishing consequences for non-compliance. Think of this as setting a deadline with an established punitive action for anyone that misses it. Pressure is sometimes useful in time-sensitive situations where you do not care to truly motivate your employees, but be careful. Employees tend to resent managers who rely on pressure as a method of influence. Autocratic leaders tend to use pressure and they rely on coercive power as their base.

<u>Legitimizing</u> – This is when you rely on legitimate power to influence others by simply using your position as a means of gaining compliance. This can also be a less direct form of pressure because the insinuation is that you can apply consequences for failure to comply with your requests, because of your position.

Exchange – transactional leaders use reward power to influence others with an exchange of reward for successful performance. This provides motivation, but only enough for the employee to realize the instant gratification of the reward.

Personal appeals – here the leader influences another by requesting their help. If successful, the appeal is a result of a personal relationship and the ability of the leader to strike an emotional cord with the individual.

Collaboration – this is the result of a team effort between the leader and the employee or a group of employees. Influence occurs as a result of the individual feeling part of the team and a general desire not to let the team down. The individual also knows that the leader is there to help and sees active cooperation on their part.

Persuasion – this is an appeal that isn't based on emotion or trust, but on an attempt of the leader to reason based on logic. Consider a request from your manager based simply on asking you to accomplish something and giving you the reason why it needs to be accomplished. Along with persuasion is apprising, where the leader explains how completion of the task will benefit the employee personally.

Inspiration – this occurs when the leader creates motivation based on building an emotional reaction to build conviction. Transformational leaders use inspiration to lead their employees.

Regardless of what leadership style and method of influence you choose, it must come from a sincere place. Additionally, it will greatly help if there is trust between you and whomever you are trying to influence. However, no matter where you are in your ability to lead, you will encounter conflict.

Conflict

The importance of leaders' abilities to identify and resolve conflict cannot be overstated. Conflict exists at all levels in all organizations and can be a result of actual circumstances and occurrences or perceptions of circumstances. What I mean is, conflict can exist and the reason for it is not real. It might only exist in someone's head, but it will have the real result of affecting the team and specifically, that individual's performance and motivation.

Leadership Tip #8 – All human behavior is motivated by one of two things: moving toward pleasure or away from pain.

Any purposeful or reactionary behavior that your employees exhibit is because they are seeking pleasure or avoiding pain. When you find the source of the motivation, you will be better equipped to deal with those factors and mitigate any impacts to your employees. Don't approach the problem from the standpoint of how it affects you as the leader. Be empathetic and approach the problem by asking how your employees are affected and what is causing their unwanted behavior.

Conflicts are best addressed as soon as the leader determines that one exists. Work-based conflicts, such as inequality in tasks being assigned or competition over resources can be resolved through a deeper explanation of the short and long-term organizational goals and re-evaluating the distribution of labor to be equitable. I have always been able to resolve work-based conflicts through objective reasoning with my employees. One thing I do that tends to help is asking them what they would like done. If it is within my power and I agree that it would better the organization, then I do exactly that. If I cannot meet their request, I will candidly explain why and come up with an alternative solution.

Personality-based conflicts are different. These types of conflicts are not easily addressed through logical reasoning and tend to be more emotionally charged than work-based conflicts. Personality conflicts exist between at least two employees who are typically aware that a conflict exists. The first thing I do is set the expectation that the employees talk through the conflict themselves in an attempt to work it out at the lowest level. Sometimes this works, but often it doesn't. This is when the leader should step in and facilitate a discussion much like a mediator. It is important that the leader not take sides, but allow each of the employees to talk through their issues. In a perfect world, we as leaders would be able to solve everyone's problems. However, that is never the case because sometimes there is no solution that both employees will accept. In that case, look for alternatives that will benefit the organization and motivate the employees. Examples of this might be putting them on different shifts, separating their physical work environments, or moving one of them to another department.

With any of these conflicts, my advice is to first consult with your human resources department and your organization's employee handbook before getting involved. Conflict resolution is very situational and you must follow the rules set in place.

Inspections

In order to lead, there must be trust. However, any leader would be foolish to blindly trust that the goals of the organization are being accomplished to the degree and standard that is desired. Ronald Reagan popularized a Russian proverb when discussing U.S. and Soviet Union relations. He said, "trust, but verify."

In this context, you should trust your employees to perform their duties to the utmost of their capabilities, but you should also verify that what they are doing is what you expect. To accomplish this, you will use inspections. By inspecting your employees' work, you show them that you care about what they do, have the opportunity to praise them for good work, and can correct poor work before it becomes a bigger issue and turns into an all-out problem. Don't confuse inspections with micro-management. Allow your employees to accomplish their work and inspect the results as required, but resist any urges to watch them constantly or tell them repeatedly each step they need to take. This will result in resentment and does little to foster independent thinking or grow new leaders.

Build Trust

Successful leaders encourage a climate of mutual trust in which the leader trusts employees and the employees trust their leader. This is extremely important because when trust is present, individuals become willing to accept influence. Trust does not occur overnight. It takes time to develop confidence in someone else's abilities and the mutual respect necessary to promote trust in them.

In order to build trust, you will need to create a positive work environment and show genuine care for your employees. Counsel and develop them with their best interest at heart. This goes back to being an empathetic leader. If you have empathy for your employees, you should understand how to foster trust within your team.

Communicates

The last part of the first competency group of *leads* is communication. Good leaders must communicate effectively, because without communication there will be a breakdown of some sort. Effective communication is a two-way process where the first step of communication is to provide information to others. The second step is to receive information back. However, simply exchanging information is not enough. Information without understanding is worthless -- and a good leader understands the distinction.

In order to communicate effectively, you must ensure there is a shared understanding by providing information that contains context and a purpose behind it. A good tool to do this is to ask your employees to tell you what they heard immediately after you have communicated a message to them. If what they heard is different from what you intended them to hear, find another way to ensure shared understanding. A large part of communication is non-verbal. If your message got lost in a bunch of non-verbal communication (like yelling or being distracted with something else), eliminate the non-verbal noise and communicate again.

Leadership Tip #9 – One of the best tools I like to use is to invite all available employees across my departments to come to a monthly meeting where we discuss ongoing and upcoming projects.

The purpose of this is to foster that shared understanding. I have found myself falling into the trap of thinking that if someone isn't directly involved in a project or event; they don't need to know about it. Well, many employees are curious about what is going on in other parts of the organization. Shared understanding satisfies that curiosity and probably serves to answer some questions related to why they are doing certain things in their support function that might indirectly affect the project or event.

Fosters

In US Army leadership training, the term used here is "develop." I much prefer the term foster, because to foster is to encourage development. It implies that you are creating an environment where everyone can develop and you are continually seeking to improve that environment. Because no one is perfect, there is always room left for improvement. What any effective leader will tell you is that their goal is to make the organization better than it was when they came to it. That is what we should all be doing as leaders.

When you become a facility manager, look to make your organization, your employees, and yourself better than you were when you started. This is how you foster growth and development.

Create a Positive Environment

You have a direct impact on the climate of your organization. The climate refers to the environment and culture in which all employees work. By simply putting on a smile, you are affecting the climate in your immediate vicinity. However, to get the greatest impact, you should be leading your employees and your peers to affect the climate in their immediate vicinity. Here's how to do this:

Take care of people – make sure your employees understand that you care about them and you will do anything to help them learn and grow. Likewise, care for your peers. Enable them to be better at their own jobs in any way you can. This will help the climate of the organization and it will also make them more willing to help you when you need it in the future.

Be fair and inclusive – as you seek to affect the organizational climate, be fair in your interactions. Ensure that your department is free from bias or prejudice and other departments will follow suit. Be inclusive of everyone in your department. Don't play favorites, but treat everyone with the same set of rules.

Be ethical – we've touched on this, but it is important to list here as well. Unethical leaders will ruin the climate of an organization faster than anything. Avoid unethical behavior like the plague.

Be honest and candid – leadership is not necessarily filled with positivity. If you've ever heard the saying, bad news does not get better with age; you will know where I'm going with this. All leaders must communicate news that their employees do not want to hear. Believe it or not, your employees will appreciate you more if you do this in a timely manner, as candidly as possible, and taking the time to answer any questions that they have.

Assess and fix – take a survey of your climate. In some organizations, this is done with formal surveys that every employee must fill out. This can also be done through informal means such as interviews and personal observation. Whichever way you choose, take the information and analyze it. Much like an AAR, compare the climate you meant to foster with the climate you actually fostered and determine where there is room for improvement. Then fix it by implementing a plan for improvement. What next? After the plan is fully implemented and some time has passed, survey the climate again and see if it worked.

Encourage initiative – part of creating a positive environment that encourages development is to encourage your employees to take the initiative. Empowering them to problem solve and letting them implement solutions without your approval is how this is done. To get to this point, there must be trust between you and your employees.

Develop Yourself

As we move through the next section on leadership, I will explain much about leader development. In a general sense, this includes both developing yourself as a leader and developing other leaders around you. Here, I am talking about informal self-study and introspection. With introspection, you are examining your own mental and emotional well-being and preparing yourself for future positions of greater responsibility. I am also talking about formal education, training, and experience. All kinds of self-development come together to develop your leadership abilities and create greater potential within you. The next section on leader development will cover these in-depth.

Develop Others

Similar to self-development, developing those around you is vital to the lifeblood of your organization, because it needs new leaders who will emerge and bring forward new ideas and processes. As a leader, you will develop others by assessing their needs, coaching and mentoring them through their progress, and then developing the team as a whole with these individuals. Developing others will also be covered in-depth in the leadership development chapter.

Achieves

The final group of core competencies is to achieve, which focuses all of our attention on getting results. At the end of the day, results are how we as leaders are judged in most of our organizations. As facility managers, you will definitely be judged on the results you achieve. Lowering costs, saving energy, and finishing projects on time while under budget are all examples of getting excellent results. The degree to which you achieve your goals and deliver results is a direct measure of your effectiveness within the organization. To the same end, the degree to which your team delivers results and contributes to the overall growth and health of your organization is a direct measure of your effectiveness as a leader. It all boils down to how your impact gets the best results possible for the organization. Does it not? Here is how you achieve results:

Provide guidance and direction – it is imperative that you tell your employees what their individual goals are along with their priorities. These should nest within your departmental goals and priorities. Similarly, your departmental goals and priorities should nest within the organization's strategic mission. By nesting, I mean their goals and priorities should support yours. An example would be that your biggest project priority for the week is to finish a renovation for a deadline on Friday. Nested goals for your project team might be to complete punchlist items, install last-minute details required by the deadline, and to show the end users how to work newly added equipment. If one of your project team members busied themselves with completing a design for a different project that didn't have an immediate deadline, their priorities for the week were not nested within yours.

The most basic way to ensure that your goals and priorities are known and followed is by setting SOPs. By definition an SOP lists the standard way of operating. By issuing SOPs, you are telling your employees that absent any additional guidance, the SOP dictates what they do, when they do it, and how they do it. This also frees you up to focus on individual projects and unforeseen circumstances when needs arise.

As you think about providing guidance and direction to your team, do so for both short- and long-term priorities. While it is good to ensure employees understand daily goals, making your employees realize the impact they have on the strategic mission of the organization will keep them motivated and engaged, and will promote employee initiative. Additionally, if they understand the strategic mission, your employees might find a way to accomplish it better, faster, and cheaper.

Adapt to change – rarely do all plans get accomplished without some problem. Recognizing both the problems that arise and the need to change the original plan are signs of great leadership. I've seen leaders before who refuse to deviate from the plan and it tends to hurt them significantly. Don't fall into the trap of thinking that if a contingency wasn't planned then you can't do it. Remember, adaptability is one of the key characteristics of a facility manager. Well, it happens to be important to leadership as well.

Manage resources effectively – as a leader, you will need to put your manager hat on frequently. Likewise, managing resources is key to getting results. These include people, time, money, and supplies. Failure to manage any of them effectively is not going to produce the results you desire.

Give feedback – feedback is essential to achieving desired results. Rarely do our employees perform every task better than we could have imagined. If they do, however, tell them so. Positive feedback is arguably more important than correcting substandard performance. Positive feedback can seem difficult for some leaders, but I will tell you a very easy way to do this. Walk up to your employee, thank them for their performance and tell them why you value their work. It will go a long way.

If you need to correct substandard performance, it is best to do it off to the side, away from everyone else. Some people find it easiest to begin with a positive comment, follow that up with the desired corrective action, and finish with another positive comment. It really just depends on your preference. However you decide to correct the problem, do it in a timely manner. You will lose respect if you allow obvious substandard performance to go uncorrected for any long period of time.

Section Summary

In this section on leadership, we really examined what makes a great leader and why. First, we learned about the attributes, or characteristics that leaders should learn. Second, we learned the core competency groups and how to engage in them to be more effective. These two sides of leadership come together to build the foundation of what a leader is and what a leader does. In the next section, we will learn how to create a program of leader development within your organization.

Section 7: Leader Development

Up to this point, we have looked at what leadership is and what makes a great leader. However, in order to bring it all together we need to explore how to put together a leader development program. It's just not enough to read about leadership through examples, quotes, and philosophical ideas. To change and grow, you need to have a program of development. This holds true in any skill. To be fair, we seem to understand the tangible skill programs in the FM industry. For instance, I'm sure you have been a part of on-the-job training through mentoring or formal instruction in an organization you've worked for. However, how many formal leadership development programs have you been a part of? If you have had the privilege, consider yourself lucky. These programs are not the norm, and in organizations that have them, they often are not open to everyone. Even the Army, which prides itself on leader development, tries to weed out as many people from their leadership programs as possible before they ever begin.

> When I first joined the Army, I was in my senior year of college at the University of Oklahoma -- and I already knew I wanted to be an officer. In fact, the reason I settled on the Army over other branches of the military was because the National Guard had a program where you could sign up for a guaranteed slot at Officer Candidate School (OCS) after graduating from basic training. So that's what I did.
>
> I enlisted in April 2002, but my basic training date wasn't until September. This is when I got my first job in residential construction managing warranty work. Midway through the summer, I received my schedule for OCS that would begin in the spring of 2003. Then I remembered that one of the drill weekends fell on August 23, 2003 – the date my fiancé (now my wife) and I set for our wedding. This was not good.
>
> Now, my wife is more supportive of the military than I ever would be, but this was not going to fly. The only thing I could do was to call the Major over OCS and beg to be let off that weekend without getting kicked out of the school. Keep in mind, this was all happening almost a year and a half earlier, before I ever even went to basic training. When I called the Major and explained the situation, she wouldn't approve or deny my request.

All she would do is tell me how hard it was going to be for me to come directly to OCS from basic training; how no one had ever done it before, and how I should probably not do it. This was not the support I was looking for.

Based on that one conversation, I almost never went to basic training and certainly considered not going to OCS. One five-minute conversation from someone in a position of authority I had never met almost had a profound effect on my leadership development (and not in a good way). I have a major fear of failure and I did not want to embark on such a difficult journey if it was going to be impossible in the end. Luckily, I decided to take the risk. In fact, there were three of us out of the twelve who graduated OCS that had no prior military experience and came straight from basic training.

What would our lives be like without true leaders developing those around them? What would our lives be like if those leaders had never taken the risk to develop themselves? I challenge you to never know the answer to these questions.

Chapter 1: Principles of Leader Development

Whether your immediate aim is to develop personally as a leader or you want to develop other leaders around you, there are certain principles that promote leader development. These are key to developing agile leaders capable of creating a clear vision, accomplishing what should be impossible tasks, and developing subordinate leaders who will assume senior leadership roles in the future.

The principles of leader development are a strong commitment, a clear purpose, a culture of learning, three different kinds of education, and feedback.

A Strong Commitment

Committing to leader development is vital to its success. Understand that this commitment does not end. It is not a short-term quest that can be satisfied with a quick course and a certificate on the wall. Leaders must make life-long commitments to continue their development. There is always something new to learn and a new way to gain influence. Similarly, when leaders commit to their own development, they commit to the development of other leaders. It is not enough to develop our own leadership capabilities because there will always be a need for new leaders to emerge and take our place when the time comes.

A Clear Purpose

The development of any skill must be goal-oriented and have a clear purpose. Leadership is no different. Do not confuse taking a promotion to manager as a sign you are a leader. Leaders define what they need to know and set goals that can be measured and evaluated to determine their progress and manage their growth. Goals can include creating a positive work environment, learning to communicate effectively, understanding what a vision is and how to create one, knowing what skills to be familiar with versus which ones to master, and learning how to counsel employees and develop them to their highest potential.

A Culture of Learning

Leaders never stop learning. The importance of continual education and improvement cannot be understated because our world is continually changing and we must adapt with it. In order to lead our employees, we must adopt an attitude of becoming the perpetual student to let our employees see our desire to learn as often as we can. To do this, we can create a culture of learning for our employees that fosters and encourages education at work and at home. We don't necessarily have to only learn about our vocation, either. Developing leadership includes a well-rounded education, both professionally and personally. In the military, we place a priority on development that occurs concurrently with operations. As leaders perform, they continually develop their subordinates, learn new skills themselves, and perform their organizational requirements in an integrated way that fosters this culture of learning.

Three Kinds of Education

Leadership development occurs in both formal and informal settings. Individuals gain experience, train, and learn by capitalizing on three distinct kinds or levels of education. The first level is the institutional level where leaders develop through formal education such as classes, courses, seminars, etc. The second level is the operational level where leaders gain experience and train through leading others, mentorship, and teaching. The third level is self-development, where leaders find ways to further develop on their own (such as reading books on leadership). The most effective leadership development occurs as a result of the combination of all three of these levels.

Feedback

Leaders routinely give and seek honest feedback. It is an unfortunate truth that many people do not provide honest feedback to their managers, which does not help those managers develop. However, within a culture of learning, honest feedback is both encouraged and expected from managers to employees and from employees back to managers. Once sincere feedback is given, the leader evaluates it and takes action to sustain the things they are doing right and improve the things they are not doing so well. It is this action that makes feedback so important. No one enjoys hearing where they are failing, but don't fall into the trap of resisting feedback or ignoring it.

The importance of each one of these principles cannot be understated, but I feel the need to highlight the fact that leadership development at the operational level is vital. Just like the best way to learn is to teach, the best way to develop as a leader is to lead. This is a scary concept. After years of formal institutional training in the Army, I remember stepping into my first leadership position as a Platoon Leader and not remembering any of what I had learned. Standing in front of 36 Soldiers and giving them orders on what to do, I was clueless. The lessons in formal education came back to me, but the wealth of knowledge I gained from leading others was immeasurable.

Chapter 2: The Leader Development Program

Everyone within your organization either is, or can become, an inspiring leader. Leadership is a skill that can be learned, and true leaders develop themselves and others effectively and efficiently on a continual basis. In my experience, the three best ways to learn as a leader are the following:

<u>Lead</u> – the best way to learn is by doing. Never turn down an opportunity to lead others because you will learn much more quickly and effectively than from any other form of education.

<u>Follow</u> – by following other leaders, we learn from personal experience what works and what does not. We can take these lessons and apply them to our own leadership challenges by improving on them and sustaining the lessons we see working.

<u>Mentor</u> – the value of mentoring others to lead is immense. By offering examples, giving direction, and providing honest feedback, you will grow those around you and aid their development. Similarly, seek quality mentors who will help you grow. Look for willing mentors who have the experience you don't and can share lessons you have not heard before.

To create an effective program, you will need to incorporate these methods of learning with the principles of leader development. The actual structure of your program should be tailored to your organization. However, you should focus on four core areas to achieve the greatest success. ***These four fundamentals are: environment, feedback, learning, and opportunities.***

<u>Environment</u>

First, you must establish the correct environment. Work on encouraging a pro-development culture within your department and let that influence the organization around you. You can do this by actively promoting leadership development. Reward your employees who seek self-development and volunteer to lead small projects. Encourage employees to take calculated risks, own their mistakes, and learn from them. Part of fostering this environment is setting the example yourself. Look again at the leader attributes and competencies from the previous section and work hard to develop them within yourself. Your employees will recognize the effort and will appreciate it. It's been my experience that making an effort to develop will become contagious and others will begin to learn as well. By setting the example with these attributes and competencies, you will encourage their development as leaders.

To establish a learning environment, be open and receptive to your employees' ideas. In meetings or group discussions, don't allow others to belittle anyone and always encourage suggestions and candid thoughts. The learning environment should encourage leaders to use the following process in developing employees:

<u>Identify the problem</u> – leaders must encourage employees to figure out what the problem is and gather all information necessary to solve it.

<u>Develop a foundation</u> – leaders allow employees to identify what knowledge and skills they currently possess that can help solve a problem.

<u>Demonstrate new knowledge</u> – leaders foster learning through demonstration or explanation that will fill the knowledge gap between what the employee knows and what they need to know to solve the problem.

<u>Apply new knowledge</u> – leaders apply what they learn and repeat the new skill or knowledge to ensure it becomes ingrained within them.

<u>Integration of new knowledge</u> – leaders carry the new knowledge with them, uses it, and passes it on to develop others.

How to Establish This Environment

Be a role model and be engaged with your employees. If you are a leader of leaders, encourage them to be visible and present while their employees are working. This will foster confidence and inspire employees to seek guidance and feedback.

Ask employees to evaluate themselves. Challenge them to honestly evaluate what went right and what went wrong with whatever project or task they just completed. Then ask how they could have done it better. If their answer isn't what you would want them to do next time, suggest your alternative. Do this in a way that does not put them down, but allows them to think differently. Once again, encourage employees to learn from their mistakes and not be afraid of them.

Let your employees see you engaged in self-development. Show them that everyone has something to learn and can further develop their leadership abilities. Let them see you make mistakes and how you handle them. Actively listen to their questions and encourage them to ask more.

Be positive in your environment. When an employee comes into your office, stop what you are doing and listen with your full attention. I can't emphasize this enough. It is incredibly annoying and off-putting when an employee enters their supervisor's office with an issue and the supervisor only half-listens while checking email or working on something else. Either give them your full attention or ask them if you can follow-up with them once you have completed whatever it is you are doing. The key here is to ensure you actually do follow-up with them immediately afterward.

How well do you know your employees? Take an interest in more than just their work performance and results they achieve. Ask them about how they think they need to develop, what their goals are, and what they enjoy beyond the workday. Show them that you genuinely care for them, but be cognizant that employees will want to keep some personal issues private. Be sure to respect those boundaries.

Encourage your employees to have a difference of opinion. In order to promote innovation, don't shut them down if they disagree with you. If they are afraid to disagree with you, there is no way you will be able to lead them anywhere. At that point, you are only a manager assigning tasks.

Avoid comparing emerging leaders to others. As you provide mentoring and guidance, you can use personal experience and examples, but judge them based on individual performance. Be objective in your advice.

Establish this environment from the very beginning. If you're new to your position, this is the perfect opportunity to get started. If you've been in your position for a while, it doesn't matter. Start tomorrow and keep the environment going. Here are some suggestions for how the first engagement with your employees should go to set the tone for this new environment:

> "I'm here to help you as much as you allow. I want all of us to do the best we can, not only to accomplish our goals, but to exceed them."

> "When all is said and done and we close out the year, we will measure ourselves on our growth. Are we better than when we started? If the answer is yes, we are headed in the right direction. The answer will be yes."
>
> "Tell me a little about you. What is your experience in your current role and where did you come from? Where do you see yourself going in the future? What do you see yourself doing next? Where do you see yourself 10 years from now?"

The goal here is to establish a basis of trust between you and your employees. You want them to see you as a developmental resource, to understand that this is an environment of learning and growth, and to believe that this culture will foster leadership development through example and action. Let your employees know where your experience is strongest and where you lack experience. No one knows everything and that is okay. Own it and show them you are willing to learn and willing to ask for their help. This will go a long way in developing the kind of trust it will take to lead them.

Plan for Development

In establishing the environment, it is your job as the leader to show how your employees will develop over the course of the year. To do this, help them create an individual plan for development. This will also set the stage for the second fundamental of the program - feedback.

To begin, meet with your employees individually and ask them to identify what they feel their strengths are and where they know they could improve. This will be the basis of their developmental needs and goals for the future. Help them put together an objective plan for improvement by setting clear goals, establishing a timeline to achieve those goals, and setting dates for your follow up with them to track their progress.

The plan for development should include both personal improvement goals as well as professional goals, if you are truly going to develop the whole person. In addition, short-term and long-term goals should be included so that they understand where they are headed in the future. Short-term goals might include attending a certification class or mastering a skill during this calendar year. Long-term goals might include future positions of greater responsibility or completion of professional degrees.

Feedback

There is a reason the subject of feedback keeps coming up throughout these chapters. I want to be certain you understand how important feedback is to both your development as a leader and developing those around you. I cannot emphasize its importance enough. Without feedback, we have nothing. To be fair, if we don't act on the feedback, we still have nothing. However, it seems that where most people get hung up is at the feedback stage. What feedback should I give? How will it be received? Who am I to give them feedback? Will it hurt their feelings? Will they use it to improve or just ignore me? These are all fair questions and they are all questions that I, too, have wrestled with.

The concept of giving honest, timely, and accurate feedback to your employees can be scary. I've counseled many Soldiers, leaders, and employees in my professional career and it still can make me uneasy, depending on the subject of the conversation. That said, you have to push past it. The ability to give feedback well is something that will decisively shape your development as a leader (not to mention, seriously help the recipients of the feedback).

So, when do you give feedback? Now! Give feedback as soon as practical (but you shouldn't interrupt them in the middle of their performance unless it becomes a safety issue). That said, in order for that feedback to be honest and accurate, you must do two things. First, you have to observe your employees in their performance. Then, you need to assess that performance.

Observation and Assessment

First, do not be tempted to make conclusions based on one observation. Sure, there are exceptions to this. For the most part, however, it will take multiple observations to draw accurate conclusions about someone's overall performance. Everyone has a bad day and everyone has taken something they have seen (or heard) out of context. Try to resist the temptation to do that.

My suggestion is to observe your employees in a number of ways. One way is to observe from a distance when they don't expect it. I'm not suggesting you should try and surprise them or look over their shoulders constantly, but they will perform differently when they don't think you are watching. Another way is to help them with the task at hand. Ask them what they want you to do and then show interest in their entire approach to solving the problem or performing their task. The last way is to schedule actual time with them to observe their performance. A good example of this is after they have been shown a new skill and practiced it, making them go through the performance steps before letting them do it alone. Situations will dictate which approach is most appropriate, but the more you can include all three; the more your overall observations will give you a complete picture.

Specifically, in a leader development program, you will observe other leaders through watching their interaction with their peers, managers, and employees (if they have them). Look for patterns of behavior in their communications. Observe how they interact with others during both routine and stressful situations.

After you observe the performance, be sure to take notes so you will remember your immediate thoughts and what you saw. Note what the outcome of the situation was and link it directly to your observation of the leader. Think of this as noting cause and effect. Did the developing leader solve a problem or make the problem worse? In the course of solving the problem, was there anything they might have done differently? It is surprising to see how many leaders don't even realize the changes in emotions that occur in the people they are trying to lead because they get too caught up in trying to communicate. Compile all of this into an assessment of the leader, which you will give to them in the form of feedback.

Deliver Feedback

Consider the experience you have had up until now. What type of feedback have you been given? Has it come from a leader who wanted to develop you and took time to give you day-to-day feedback? Or, has it come from a manager who sits down with you once or twice a year to "evaluate" your performance over the entire period? Which one has made a greater impact on your development?

The most effective form of feedback is daily feedback. Now, I'm not saying to do away with annual evaluations; those have a time and a place. And I'm not saying you literally sit down with every employee, every day. What I am saying is you will see more growth if you develop leaders by providing them with constant feedback as you observe and assess performance. I've already emphasized the importance of timely feedback.

That's because it isn't very effective if you wait four or five months to go over it during a semi-annual review.

The trick to saving time while still providing valuable feedback for development is to make the daily feedback informal and still schedule the formal feedback at quarterly, semi-annual, or annual intervals. Informal feedback could simply be providing praise for something that went well. Similarly, it could be pulling someone aside and offering advice to correct something that didn't go so well.

We also want to focus our feedback on a few things that will make the most impact to the developing leader. First, focus on the attributes and competencies that we already know great leaders must develop. Again, pick just a few so you aren't overwhelming them. Second, focus on the achievement of goals you have previously agreed on in their plan for development. Finally, share your personal experience in leadership development and how that is contributing to the overall strategic direction of the organization.

As you give your feedback, ask the leader what their self-assessment is and what that tells them. Do this before you offer any advice or assessments of your own. This will do a few things. First, it will help to develop their ability to assess others. Second, it will encourage them to continue their personal and professional development on their own. Third, it will give you insight into what they are thinking before you speak. If what they think is vastly different than what you think, perhaps there is another issue you need to address in addition to the feedback you were about to give.
To summarize, these are the steps for providing feedback:

- Observe
- Make assessments
- Approach the leader
- Ask for a self-assessment
- Identify where their self-assessment differs from yours
- Give your feedback, confirming what you agree with and offering suggestions for what you don't
- Ask them how they can sustain what went well and improve what didn't
- Follow-up on their plan for development as appropriate

Learning

Learning is the third fundamental for the leader development program. The trick to enhancing the actual learning of any developing leader is to understand how they learn. Everyone is different and the way each person learns is unique. We've all heard the different methods of learning. From visual learners to tactile learners, there are multiple ways people learn. For me, however, these are ways people best comprehend information. We want to take that one step farther.

Learning is a life-long journey. Maybe I am unique, but I cannot tell you that I am a visual learner in every situation. In some situations, I learn better by physically doing whatever it is that I am learning. In other situations, I can learn better by listening to or reading instructions. My point is this: move past the different ways people comprehend information and look at how we can promote the kind of learning that develops leaders. This kind of learning is engaging, powerful, and long lasting. It's the kind of learning that you won't soon forget and that you will appreciate forever. This kind of learning is best accomplished through mentorship.

Mentorship

Mentorship exists when a leader with greater experience voluntarily develops a leader of lesser experience. A mentor takes the time to engage with their mentee and studies which ways of learning will foster the most development for them personally. Then the mentor becomes a guide to ensure leadership development throughout the mentee's journey.

Now, here's the catch. The mentor-mentee relationship is a special one and it is not well suited for individuals who are in a supervisor-employee or leader-follower relationship because it is hard to marry the two. As a leader, you are responsible for everything we have talked about up until this point. However, as a mentor your focus is almost solely on the relationship you develop with your mentee. This relationship should focus on overall development and not necessarily on the daily feedback on tasks or goals that leaders should focus on. Another reason mentors should not be supervisors of their mentee is that other employees would likely view their interactions as favoritism, which will cause resentment. It would be impossible for FMs to lead all of their employees and be a mentor to all of them at the same time.

That said, leaders should absolutely be mentors to other junior leaders outside of their direct supervisory chain. Leaders should also promote a culture that accepts and invites mentorship within the organization. To do this, set the example and emphasize that mentorship consists of four things.

First, the mentor is there to give feedback that is honest and sincere, but comes from another point of view outside of the mentee's supervisory chain. This feedback includes advice on personal and professional goals, in addition to things the leader does well and things that can be improved upon. Second, the mentor confides in the mentee all of their personal experiences that could help with leader development. This provides context and historical examples that the mentee can apply to their own situation. In addition, this brings the pair close together and fosters a relationship that promotes trust and openness. Third, the mentor motivates and encourages the mentee, helping them to keep their priorities in front of them while taking care of problems that arise along the way. Finally, the mentor acts as a servant leader to the mentee. A servant leader exists when the mentor serves the mentee first and leads them second. As a servant leader, the mentor acts as trusted adviser, counselor, confidant, and sounding board.

There are several things mentors should do to make the most out of the mentor-mentee relationship. These include:

Withhold judgement – this relationship is special and making judgments will only serve to erode the mentee's confidence in their mentor. We all make mistakes as we grow and learn. The mentor's job is to give feedback and advice on how to move forward, not judge the mentee for their past.

Actively listen – it is one thing to hear someone and it is entirely another to listen to them actively. Maintain eye contact, repeat the last few words of what the mentee just said to show you are listening, and then summarize the entire conversation at the end to ensure you understood their message. These are a few active-listening tips that will help you better communicate.

Ask open-ended questions – engage with your mentee by not asking yes or no questions. Ask them to elaborate in order to really understand what they are talking about. Get as much information as possible about a given subject so you can give the best feedback you are capable of giving.

Focus – don't be distracted with texts, phone calls, and emails. When you are communicating with your mentee, ensure that you give them all of your attention. This promotes trust and it will help you be a better mentor.

When done correctly, mentorship is an extremely valuable tool that organizations can use to develop leaders. It obviously helps the organization grow and improve, but it also helps both the mentor and the mentee. The mentor gets a feeling of satisfaction and they learn along with the mentee. The mentee grows from the feedback and experience shared by the mentor. I would love to hear about your successful mentorship programs. Please send me any feedback you have and I will include new ideas in future writings.

Opportunities

The fourth and final fundamental to great leadership development is creating opportunities. This focuses on the practical implementation of the program and might be one that you are already familiar with, depending on your current organization. For our purposes, I'm going to narrow this broad concept to three key drivers to successfully create opportunities. ***These drivers are challenging involvement, supervisory succession, and career management.***

Challenging Involvement

This driver means leaders are constantly challenging junior leaders within the program by giving them new assignments out of their comfort zone, which requires their growth and development in order to succeed. These assignments are by their very nature more complex than the developing leaders are used to. They will probably experience increased pressure and stress, but it is the only way to test their development and create an environment for growth. Facility management is the perfect field in which to do this. There are many sizes and shapes of special projects, repairs, procedures, budgets, and more that we deal with on a frequent basis. We should never be lacking an opportunity to put someone in a position to develop by leading a new initiative.

The key to challenging involvement is to monitor the development progress and make adjustments on an individual basis. The idea is to get them to swim, not sink, and everyone develops at a different rate. Perhaps they meet the challenge and surpass your expectations or perhaps they need more time and encouragement.

Supervisory Succession

We already know that we do not need to be in a position of leadership to be a leader. However, positions of increased leadership responsibility will continue to challenge and develop leaders, which lead to greater growth and development. As a part of your leader development program, you should reward leadership growth by placing these junior leaders into positions of greater authority. The best way to do this is to come up with a supervisory succession plan. All this means is that leaders within your organization need to have a plan for who can step into supervisory positions if the person who currently occupies a position leaves for any reason.

To be clear, automating this (where the technician automatically is promoted to team lead and then automatically promoted to section head, etc.) is not a good idea. This succession plan should be constantly evaluated based on the performance and growth of junior leaders. Ideally, you will have created such a successful leadership development program that most of your supervisory positions can be filled from within the organization. Of course, that never works all of the time because you have to consider such things as the talents of the individuals and desire to promote in addition to their leader development, but it is a great goal.

Career Management

This should go without saying, but all too often we overlook such a basic principle of development. We have to take ownership to actively manage our own career paths. At the same time, supervisors should consider career path options for their employees, while having routine discussions with them regarding where they are in their development and what their desires are for future positions of responsibility.

Leaders within the organization should give advice and share experience about their own career management with junior leaders. This advice is invaluable because they've been there and experienced it. Advice can be tailored to the needs of the individual, but should consider developmental needs outside of the organization (for instance if there is an advanced degree necessary to continue on in their given career path).

Career management goes hand-in-hand with the supervisory succession plan. Based on this plan, what do junior leaders need to do now in order to set them up to assume those positions of greater responsibility?

Chapter 3: Self-development

Self-development lies between the leader development program that fosters operational development and formal education that leaders undergo through structured curriculum. This is a critical piece that cannot be overlooked because it ties the two together. Formal education lays a foundation of knowledge on which to build. Operational development in a work environment allows leaders to grow through real-world experience. However, self-development bridges the gap and fills in the voids that others miss. While this is no doubt an individual responsibility, leaders should encourage self-development and work with employees to help them as they progress.

Self-development has three stages:

> ***Identify developmental needs***
> ***Establish a plan for development***
> ***Learn***

This sounds easy; so let's break it down a little further.

Identify Developmental Needs

To begin on your self-development journey, you need to understand in considerable detail what it is you do and how well you do it. Self-examination is the most basic form of this, but the more feedback (there is that word again) you get from outside sources you trust, the better. Outside sources can give you great insight into how well you lead. Sometimes this can be hard to hear, but it is important to know how others view you because you are trying to develop your ability to lead other people. Makes sense, right?

If your organization has a good leadership development program, this should be fairly straightforward. You are probably already getting daily informal feedback, consistent formal performance reviews, and peer reviews on top of it. So, couple all of that feedback with your own self-assessment and you should have some very strong insights into your strengths and weaknesses.

That said, a lot of organizations fall short, so you might find it challenging to receive honest and sincere feedback. My advice is to ask for it and see what you get. Ask current peers and supervisors you trust, along with those you have worked with in the past. If you're comfortable, ask employees you have personally supervised in the past and see how they viewed you as a manager and leader. That can be eye opening.

One well-known tool many organizations use is a multi-source assessment, also known as a 360-degree assessment. This is essentially a survey that you send to all of the individuals listed above (current and previous supervisors, peers, and direct reports) asking for answers to a series of questions about you. The assessment compiles all of the information into one report for you, which is pretty handy. The downside, however, is that you need a lot of honest responses to average out the opinions and yield an objective report. So if people fail to fill out the survey or don't take it seriously, then you're not really seeing any benefit from it. These can be great tools, but can also fail miserably if they are not implemented well.

Plan for Development

Now that you understand where your weaknesses are, you need a plan to develop in those areas. In doing so, you are going to identify both personal and professional goals and a plan on how to achieve them. For example, one of my professional goals is to become a published author and I'm working on that plan as I type. One of my personal goals is to become a better father. I'm taking time to barbecue with my family this Saturday. It's a small step, but one that leads in the right direction. Also, spending more time with my two boys is on my plan for development.

If you get stuck in establishing goals for your plan, look at the needs around you. Does your organization have a need you can fill? My organization had a need for an organic trainer and presenter at manager meetings. I am one of a couple of people who volunteered to fill that role and it turned out great. To prepare, I spent extra time developing presentations and working on my public speaking, which developed me more as a speaker. Side note – you can never be too experienced at public speaking.

Again, if your organization currently has a leadership development program, you should already be creating an individual plan for development at work. It is completely acceptable to combine these two and include personal goals that you will develop along with organizational goals at work. Remember to include both short-term and long-term goals. One technique that I learned at a recent leadership seminar was to make a list of 50 things I want to achieve before I die. There was no limit on what these things could be and we were encouraged to think really big. At the end of creating this list, it was pretty eye opening to see what I really do want to accomplish when I removed certain boundaries I placed on myself because something might not be "realistic" now.

When you decide on the goals for your development plan, write them down. Each goal must meet five criteria (you may have heard of the acronym "SMART"). ***Goals must be specific, measurable, attainable, relevant, and time-bound.*** Here's why:

> Specific – without specificity we flounder. There is no way we will ever achieve this goal because we really don't have any idea what the goal actually is. Don't create a goal that says you'll make more money. Create a goal that says you will make 10% more salary and 5% more bonus in your next position within three years.
>
> Measurable – you have to know when you achieve a goal and how far away from it you are along the way. Checking the status of your performance is an important part to sticking to any goal, especially one that is long-term.
>
> Attainable – goals must be attainable. Don't set yourself up for failure by putting a goal on your plan that is impossible to achieve.
>
> Relevant – we are specifically talking about leadership development. By being a better father, I am a better leader in my home. That is relevant to my leadership development. Improving my handicap is a goal, but not relevant to leader development.
>
> Time-bound – all goals must be time-bound. If they aren't, it is likely that you will never achieve them. Give yourself milestones and deadlines and hold to them. If you fall behind, catch back up. Be accountable to yourself throughout this journey.

Learn

Without learning, there is no self-development. It's just that easy. My wife teaches nursing school and tells me these stories on a near-daily basis about how students will come into her office and complain about not doing well on tests. Now, to be fair to her, she does not use names or give me any details that would betray their confidence. What she is doing is illustrating a point on how there are so many people who really don't understand how to learn. When these students complain to her, she asks them about their study habits. I'm sure they're all different, but none of them are studying effectively. The flipside to the coin is this. I don't know how many times she tells me the generic story about how she had a student she helped learn how to study who had improved drastically in their testing performance after changing a few things they did in their learning.

I've never been through nursing school. It sounds pretty tough and I tip my hat to all of the graduates that go on to be amazing health care professionals. But if they can change the way they learn to grow and develop through one of the hardest professional programs out there and be successful at the end, there's no reason we can't do that in learning leadership.

Motivation

We have to stay motivated to learn. This is especially true in self-development because there often is no one standing over our shoulder, forcing us to learn (unless you have an amazing mentor). But how do we do that? For me, the idea of self-motivation is kind of an oxymoron. I mean if I had the motivation to self-motivate, then I wouldn't need to self-motivate, right? Well, here are some of the best ways to "self-motivate":

Tie learning to benefits – the first thing you need to understand is that you will get real, tangible benefits from motivating yourself to learn. For me, I love to teach. When I am learning leadership, I actively think about how I can teach what I am learning to others and imagine myself in that situation. I plan exactly how I will pass on the information and get excited about wanting to learn more so I can develop others. Maybe for you, learning to develop as a leader will result in a promotion or your employees performing better. Whatever it is, tie the learning to a reward that you want.

Satisfy curiosity – no one wants to pick up the encyclopedia and start reading without a purpose. Ok, there may be a few people that find that fun, but I certainly don't. I learn much better when I am actually curious about the subject at hand. You can't force yourself to want to be a leader. If you want to learn leadership, you're already curious about it. Drill down to the areas that peak your curiosity the most and those will be the easiest for you to learn. If you're not interested in learning leadership, close this book now and choose something else to do.

Milestones – I mentioned milestones in goal setting above, but really didn't go into them. Milestones are mini-goals within your overall goals. For example, I set goals of finishing each section of this book within a given time frame. The milestones that helped me achieve those goals were writing a set number of words every day. These milestones were still SMART, but they were smaller. The milestone for the number of words was higher on the weekends when I had more time to work on the book and wasn't trying to cram it in after work and family time. Every time I achieved a milestone, I felt a sense of accomplishment and it motivated me to achieve the next one. If you have no milestones and your goals are too far apart, it will feel like you aren't accomplishing anything even if you really are. Milestones are a great way to motivate yourself because you get to achieve them frequently.

Schedule the time – this isn't directly linked to motivation, but it is directly linked to avoiding demotivation. Knowing you have a milestone to achieve and not having the time to do it is completely demotivating. Plan the time to learn by putting it in your schedule and treating it the same way as any other meeting you must keep. You wouldn't miss a meeting with your boss, would you? This is the same (arguably even more important); it's just a meeting with yourself.

Little bites – how do you eat an elephant? One bite at a time. Setting small milestones frequently (i.e., daily) is preferable to larger milestones infrequently (i.e., once a week or longer) even if you're accomplishing the same amount of work on the average. So, I stay more motivated if I set a milestone of writing 300 words every night than I will if I write 2,100 words every Saturday. It's the same number of words, but I have that sense of accomplishment 7 times as often and I feel more connected to my goals.

Review – whenever you have your doubts, review all you have done. Look back at the milestones and goals you have accomplished and put what is left into perspective. This helps me a lot on larger projects where it can be hard to see that light at the end of the tunnel.

Methods of Learning

No, I'm still not going to give you a lesson on visual vs. tactile vs. auditory learning (you're welcome). The following are different methods of learning that will reinforce how to learn. Think of these as tips that will help you learn more effectively. Use the ones that work best for you. Just like my wife gave her students tips to improve how they study, you can use these to improve how you learn.

Use all your senses – I touched on this previously, but I learn distinctive things differently. I can't tell you that I am 100% a visual learner. That's because I learn some things better if I hear them and some better if I do them. If you are reading something, say it out loud, discuss it with someone, search YouTube for a video about it, and then go do it yourself. Include as many senses as possible and you will be able to commit the skill to memory much better.

Space out your learning – this is the same principle as not trying to cram for a test the night before. You can't really learn something if you try and do it all at once. Learn a little piece and then give yourself time to digest and practice it.

Teach what you learn – the best way to learn something is to teach it. I believe this whole-heartedly. In leadership, when you learn things like how to counsel employees through effective communication and how to speak publicly, pass on what you learn and it will reinforce it for you.

Time of day – this goes for learning anything. Know when you are most productive and learn then. For me, I am not a morning person. Therefore, I don't get up at 5:00 a.m. to learn anything. I wouldn't pay attention because my forehead would be in my cereal as I fell asleep at the breakfast table. Know yourself and set aside time to learn at the best time of day to maximize effectiveness and retention.

Practice what you learn – just like teaching a skill, practice greatly helps reinforce what you learn. If you are learning how to effectively give feedback, then go give feedback. Put it into practice and see what works for you.

Think critically – as you learn, don't take everything at face value. Digest the information and really try and understand what you are learning. Dissect all aspects and answer the questions that you think of. Look for other opinions and theories. If you can find a better way to do something, implement the change. Owning the process of learning will greatly help reinforce the skill.

Keep a journal – this is something that I don't do nearly as often as I should. If you keep a journal of everything you learn, it becomes a quick and easy desk reference for you. Most of these skills are perishable, meaning you will forget them or become less proficient in them over time without practice. A journal can speed up the process of trying to reinforce something you learned that might be a bit rusty for you now.

Don't procrastinate – don't put off learning leadership. Beginning to learn a new skill is the hardest part. There are a million reasons we give ourselves as excuses of why we need to wait or why it would be better to start tomorrow. Don't fall into that trap.

This chapter has covered how to learn and stay motivated doing it. I'm sure there are other tips and techniques that have proven successful and I would love to get your feedback on any new ones you have. Send me an email anytime and let me know what you have found that works best for you. Or if any of these haven't worked so well for you, I'd love to know that too. Good luck!

Chapter 4: Activities for Leader Development

Up to this point, I defined what a great leader is in terms of attributes and competencies, described how to set up a leader development program, and gave tips for self-development and motivation. But what's lacking are specifics.

This chapter of leader development will give you detailed questions and activities you can use to develop your own leadership potential and incorporate into your leadership development program. These questions and activities will directly relate back to the leader competencies in the previous section. For each of the three groups of leader competencies, I will give you questions to ask that will give you an understanding of the leader's strengths and weaknesses and where weaknesses might be stemming from. If your answers to the questions indicate you are particularly strong in that competency, then you should focus elsewhere where you aren't so strong.

If your answers indicate a need for improvement, I will list activities you can consider incorporating into your development in three areas: ***feedback, learning, and practice***.

Be as objective as possible when you answer these questions. If you are answering them for yourself, be honest with yourself. No one is perfect. I am far from it. I know I have weaknesses in several of these areas and I'm working to improve them. Understand you will be stronger in some competencies than others and that is expected. Admitting our own weaknesses can be tough, but the ability to do it is valuable. Not only does it say you are ready and willing to develop as a leader, it says you are already humble enough to lead those around you. Don't be afraid to ask for help or advice from those you trust.

Finally, by no means is this an exhaustive list. There are countless ways to improve and develop as a leader. The idea here is to get you thinking about how to tailor your leadership development. I encourage you to come up with new activities. I would love to hear about your ideas and how you implemented them. Now, let's get started.

Leads

Activities for this competency will focus on ***influencing, resolving conflict, building trust, and communicating***. These are the three areas of the leads competency group that I see people struggle with the most and are also the hardest to really quantify and define. There is a major problem I have with most of the leadership publications I've read. They contain a lot of quotes, historical examples, and theories out there, but there isn't nearly as much specific advice when it comes to actual steps to improve. Hopefully, with these activities I can pass along some sound advice for actual things you can implement into your leader development.

Influencing

Here are questions to ask to understand where your strengths and weaknesses lie in this competency:

These Questions Identify Strengths in Influencing

- Do you use the current situation to customize influencing techniques to your individual employees, motivating them to accomplish their goals?
- Do you focus on positive influence, maintaining an optimistic culture?
- Do you only use pressure in time constraints when absolutely necessary?

These Questions Identify Weaknesses in Influencing

- Do you use the same techniques to influence employees every single time, no matter what the situation is?
- Do you act negatively (e.g., glass is half-empty, outwardly frustrated, constantly complaining, etc.), focusing only on personal objectives and not group or organizational goals?
- Do your employees return time and time again for clarification on what you want done?
- Do you put undue pressure and stress on your employees constantly?

If you notice yourself trending to some of the weaknesses, consider if you are doing any of the following:

- Are you taking an empathetic approach to understanding the needs of your employees?
- Is personal gain your primary motivation to get something done?
- Are you failing to empower your employees to make decisions?
- Are you afraid that asking your employees for advice will weaken your authority?

Here are some activities to develop your ability to influence others:

Feedback

- Ask your employees what motivates them and if they feel empowered. Ask them if they are challenged in their duties and what new responsibilities they would like to accept.
- If you are new, speak to the previous supervisor on what they found influenced your employees. What worked and what didn't?
- Ask your peers how they influence their team and compare that to what you are doing.

Learning

- Study the emotions of your employees. Are they stressed? Do they seem happy at work? What is causing additional stress in their lives? Is it personal or business related? Can you help to alleviate any of that stress?
- Re-read the chapter on leadership styles. To really influence your employees, you want to be a transformational leader. You definitely do not want to be autocratic.
- Study what really needs to happen to support the strategic goals of your organization. Take that information and make a priority for your departmental goals. Not everything needs to be done immediately. Take care of the things that need to happen in the order they need to happen.

Practice

- Empower your employees to make decisions. Review the outcomes with them and do not discourage mistakes. Mistakes are how we learn.

- Encourage group participation in problem solving. You want your team to become part of the solution. Help them own it.
- Take time to engage in self-reflection. How do your leaders influence you? What do you consider important in motivation? Are you incorporating these answers into how you influence others?

Resolving Conflict

Here are questions to ask to understand where your strengths and weaknesses lie in this competency:

These Questions Identify Strengths in Resolving Conflict

- Do you use empathy to identify the needs of the organization, team, and each individual on your team?
- Do you actively listen to all of your employees and understand what their position is when conflict arises?
- Do you accept conflict as an opportunity for growth? Do you address it immediately?
- Do you ensure everyone in the conflict understands the position of others involved? Do you understand everyone's position?

These Questions Identify Weaknesses in Resolving Conflict

- Do you avoid addressing conflict at all costs?
- Do you try and negotiate resolution without understanding all points of view and sources of the conflict?
- Do you push the resolution you want personally over a resolution that is beneficial to everyone?
- Do you use the same conflict resolution technique in every situation, regardless of the parties involved?

If you notice yourself trending to some of the weaknesses, consider if you are doing any of the following:

- Are you trying to come to an agreement with all parties? Usually, this consists of give and take from everyone involved.

- Do you meet others halfway in conflict resolution or do you only push your solution?
- Do you ignore conflict because it makes you uncomfortable?
- Do you take conflict personally?

Here are some activities to develop your ability to resolve conflict:

Feedback

- Ask your peers to describe a situation that you have negotiated well. Ask them to describe a situation they have negotiated well. What's the difference?
- Tell your peers how you typically approach conflict resolution and ask them to poke holes in it.
- Role-play several approaches to conflict resolution with someone you trust and record yourself. Review the video and study how you come across. Ask your partner for feedback both after the role-playing and after you watch the video.

Learning

- Learn what the parties involved in conflict really want. Try and find the common ground between them.
- Study how successful negotiators approach conflict. List the things you feel you can incorporate in negotiating, and then review those before you address conflict next.

Practice

- Ask open-ended questions. Don't wait until damaging conflict arises. Anytime there is a difference of opinions, ask the parties open-ended questions about what they are feeling and points they can agree on. Practice finding that middle ground before tensions rise.
- Practice active-listening. This is a skill that will greatly help you in conflict resolution. The ability to truly understand someone else's point of view cannot be overstated.
- Encourage group discussion often. When you sense conflict building, get the team together and address it before it becomes a

bigger issue. Ask for as much input as they are willing to give and support open and candid discussions.

Building Trust

Here are questions to ask to understand where your strengths and weaknesses lie in this competency:

These Questions Identify Strengths in Building Trust

- Do you follow through on everything you say you are going to do?
- Are you honest in your communication? Do you tell the truth, even when it is unpopular?
- Do you show respect for others?
- Do you admit your own mistakes?
- Do you stop gossip when it starts around you?

These Questions Identify Weaknesses in Building Trust

- Do you make empty promises and let go of commitments without doing them?
- Do you betray the confidences of others?
- Do you assign blame to anyone or anything other than you?
- Do you gossip?
- Do you take personal credit for the work of others or the work of your team?
- Do you isolate yourself or make yourself unavailable to your employees?

If you notice yourself trending to some of the weaknesses, consider if you are doing any of the following:

- Are you afraid to give bad news?
- Do you avoid conflict?
- Can you say "no" to requests that you know you won't be able to meet?
- Are you too focused on your own ambitions?
- Do you think you will look weak if you admit your mistakes?

Here are some activities to develop your ability to build trust:

Feedback

- Take a trust self-assessment. You can find these on the Internet after a quick search.
- Encourage feedback from your team on the culture and levels of trust.
- Ask leaders outside of your organization how they build trust. Do they engage in formal group trust-building activities or do they rely only on informal means?

Learning

- Study other leaders and how their actions serve to build trust or erode it. Trust is a funny thing. It is quickly lost and not easily built.
- Observe leaders who are working to rebuild trust. Talk to leaders who have successfully rebuilt trust in an organization. How do you know when this has happened? Ask the employees. Employees of other departments and organizations might be more willing to talk about times of distrust than your own employees.
- Consider your own past. Everyone has experienced distrust in their past. Can you remember a leader you did not trust? What was it about them that made you feel this way?

Practice

- When you get feedback from employees, ensure that they see you acting on that information. Action builds trust.
- When you make a commitment, follow-through on it. Don't make empty promises.
- Learn to say "no." Don't make commitments you will not be able to keep.
- Make sure your feedback is honest. Don't sugarcoat things. It isn't helpful and employees can usually see through it if they are observant.

Communicating

Here are questions to ask to understand where your strengths and weaknesses lie in this competency:

These Questions Identify Strengths in Communicating

- Do you know you are actively listening? Do you understand what active-listening is and do you incorporate those skills into your communication?
- Do you maintain eye contact? Do you summarize what was just said to ensure that you understood the message?
- Do you ask your employees to tell you what they heard you say, ensuring a common understanding of the message?
- Do you use inflection in your tone and gestures to emphasize your points?

These Questions Identify Weaknesses in Communicating

- Do you fail to give your employees your full attention when you are communicating with them? Do emails, phones, texts, tasks, etc., easily distract you?
- Do you speak before thinking and fail to consider the impact of your message? Words mean things.
- Do your employees seem more confused after you deliver a message to them?
- Do you talk down to your employees?

If you notice yourself trending to some of the weaknesses, consider if you are doing any of the following:

- Are you uncomfortable when communicating to individuals or groups?
- Have you prepared what you are going to say ahead of time? Do you find yourself "winging it?"
- Are you confident in your understanding of the content of your message?
- Are you open to feedback on your message? Do you believe you have all the answers and your way is the only way?

Here are some activities to develop your ability to communicate with others:

Feedback

- Encourage open feedback. Actively listen to what is said.
- When misunderstandings occur, ask what led to them. Ask how you could have been clearer and incorporate that into your message next time.
- Ask open-ended questions on your audience's thoughts regarding your topic.

Learning

- Study skilled presenters. Watch TED talks and attend public-speaking events. Practice at home and record yourself doing it. Speak into the camera as though you are speaking to an individual. Then, review it and critique how you did.
- Take a course on communication techniques.
- Observe cultural differences in communication techniques across your organization. Take note of how different cultures react to and understand communication. Incorporate what you learn into your messages when delivering them to a culturally diverse audience.

Practice

- Summarize what you just heard to ensure a common understanding. Do this by saying, "What I heard you say was…"
- If you are delivering the message, ask the person you are communicating with for a summary of what you just said. Perhaps there is a way you could have better delivered your message.
- Ensure your message is in the correct context. Does it relate to individual or organizational goals? Make sure you deliver your message in an appropriate venue.
- Don't speak down to your employees, but speak on their level. Don't try and show them how smart you are. Communicate a message that they understand.

Fosters

Activities for this competency will cover ***creating a positive environment, developing yourself, and developing others***. These activities will help you to encourage the growth and development of leadership in yourself and in those around you.

Create a Positive Environment

Here are questions to ask to understand where your strengths and weaknesses lie in this competency:

These Questions Identify Strengths in Creating a Positive Environment

- Do you encourage teamwork? Do you attribute the results your department achieves to the entire team?
- Do you integrate new employees into the team quickly?
- Do you encourage diversity? Do you make an effort to learn about the varied experiences and situations of your team members?
- Do you encourage job growth and advancement, even if it means losing a valuable team member to a promotion?
- Do you have a calming effect in the face of adversity? Can employees come to you with bad news and expect help solving the problem without judgment?

These Questions Identify Weaknesses in Creating a Positive Environment

- Do you assign blame to individuals? Do you personally take credit for successes?
- Do you hold high-performing employees back because you are afraid to lose their contribution to the team?
- Do you provide preferential treatment to certain employees?
- Do you react negatively to bad news? Are employees afraid of telling you things because of your reactions to them?

If you notice yourself trending to some of the weaknesses, consider if you are doing any of the following:

- Are you not comfortable leading a team? Would you rather be leading individual employees? Would your employees rather work individually than be part of a team?
- Do you trust your team members?
- Do you favor some of the employees on your team for any reason? Are you more comfortable dealing with certain employees than others?
- Does bad news stress you out? Can you remain calm and collected in a demanding situation?
- Do you treat mistakes as learning opportunities?
- Do you find that you are often too busy to listen to employees?
- Are you afraid of change?

Here are some activities to develop your ability to create a positive environment:

Feedback

- Ask your employees if they feel like they are part of the team. Ask them what would make them feel more included.
- Meet with your employees individually. Ask them if they have ever been treated unfairly.
- Brainstorm with your team for solutions to ongoing problems. Promote unity and inclusion in their feedback.

Learning

- Ask your employees what their career goals are. Follow-up with them periodically to see what has changed.
- Read books or articles on team building and cohesion. Ask your peers and the leaders you trust for recommendations.
- Review your communications style with peers and other leaders and ask them how they communicate. Find new ways to encourage open communication among your team.

Practice

- Include your employees in the development of team goals.
- Welcome new employees openly and encourage early involvement with the team.

- Treat everyone with the same respect. Treat them how you want to be treated.
- Encourage leadership development. As you do, know that this will result in some employees moving on to advance their careers. Embrace this as a good thing and have a plan for succession for every key position within your department.
- As you hold periodic (I like monthly) department meetings, ask your employees to update the team on where they are in their tasks and upcoming projects they need to be aware of. This will foster teamwork, get them used to speaking in front of a group, and encourage participation.
- Welcome change. If someone has an idea to make the team better, try it.

Develop Yourself

Here are questions to ask to understand where your strengths and weaknesses lie in this competency:

These Questions Identify Strengths in Developing Yourself

- Do you actively seek a work-life balance?
- Do you remove personal emotions from decision-making?
- Do you eat well and exercise regularly?
- Do you actively learn new skills?
- Do you embrace new technology and systems?
- Do you learn from your mistakes and make changes accordingly?
- Are you aware of what motivates you?

These Questions Identify Weaknesses in Developing Yourself

- Do you have insomnia?
- Do you abuse tobacco, drugs, or alcohol in excess?
- Are you not interested in expanding your knowledge base?
- Do you become overwhelmed with problems, which leads to frustration?
- Do you reject feedback? Do you accept feedback publicly, but make excuses for negative feedback privately?

If you notice yourself trending to some of the weaknesses, consider if you are doing any of the following:

- Do you feel a sense of fulfillment in your personal and professional life?
- Are you stressed by financial troubles or personal relationships?
- Do you find yourself procrastinating tasks?
- Do you feel like there is never enough time in the day?
- Do you feel like you have a lack of experience for your current position?
- Does fear of failure keep you from taking risks or trying to innovate?
- Do you accept that you need personal improvement? (Here's a hint: we all do)

Here are some activities to develop yourself:

Feedback

- Get health exams periodically. Maintaining a healthy lifestyle will help with longevity, stress management, sleep, and stamina.
- Ask your employees who are experts in their areas if there are emerging technologies or trends you need to be considering.
- Ask an experienced problem solver to observe a brainstorming and problem-solving session with your team. Get their thoughts on how you can better manage the next one.
- Get a multi-source or 360-degree assessment.

Learning

- Learn how to live a healthy lifestyle.
- Engage your employees to share their understanding of their jobs with you. This will help you learn and promote trust with them.
- Read outside of the office. You don't have to read only professional books, but expand your knowledge with history, hobbies, or fiction. Read something that interests you. Join a book club if you need accountability or would like to explore what you are reading in more depth.
- Research stress and time management techniques. One of the best articles I've read on time management is *Who's Got the Monkey?* by

William Oncken Jr. and Donald Wass. It was published in the Harvard Business Review in 1999 and you can find it with a quick web search.

Practice

- Exercise regularly (30 mins or more, several times a week). Eat well. Reduce excess alcohol and tobacco consumption. Eliminate any drug abuse.
- Challenge yourself to develop every year.
- Implement lessons learned from others in your profession. Seek out facility managers in similar organizations and share ideas in operations and leadership development.
- Implement stress and time management practices. Good ones I have found are to schedule everything (including personal time and family time). If you can't fit it all in, never multi-task. Do one thing, finish it, do the next, finish that one, etc. Work in a clean environment (keep your desk clear). Finally, learn to delegate.
- Keep a journal specifically for creative thinking and brainstorming. Reflect on what you accomplished each day and list ways you could have done it better.

Develop Others

Here are questions to ask to understand where your strengths and weaknesses lie in this competency:

These Questions Identify Strengths in Developing Others

- Do you use different sources to get information about the development needs of your employees? These sources include your own personal observations, observations from others on the team, your employees' own feedback, etc.
- Do you work with your employees to set up their individual plan for development?
- Do you encourage your employees to learn new skills?
- Do you customize your counseling or mentoring to the individual?

These Questions Identify Weaknesses in Developing Others

- Do you generalize development needs across your department?
- Do you avoid providing negative feedback?
- Do you find yourself doing everything because it would be too hard to teach someone else to do it?
- Are you apathetic toward self-development?

If you notice yourself trending to some of the weaknesses, consider if you are doing any of the following:

- Are you too busy to spend time learning about your employees in order to develop them?
- Are you uncomfortable giving honest feedback?
- Do you view leadership development as a low priority compared to completing the tasks at hand?
- Do you know enough about the development requirements of the career path your employees have chosen?
- Are you afraid that delegation will only result in substandard performance? Do you not want to relinquish control?

Here are some activities to develop others:

Feedback

- Talk to your employees individually at least quarterly to understand where they are in their plan for development and how you can help.
- Ask your employees their thoughts on the development of the overall team.

Learning

- Learn about effective communication techniques to use in evaluations. If you are uncomfortable giving negative feedback, practice this skill.
- Talk to peers and find out what they do to develop those around them.

Practice

- Help your employees set up their plan for development.
- Encourage your employees to engage in self-development. Let them see you doing the same.
- Delegate challenging tasks to your employees. This will develop them and help you with time management.
- Ask your employees to regularly update you on what they have done for self-development. Share what you have done as well. Let them see how important it is to you.

Achieves

At the end of the day, there is a huge emphasis placed on your ability to get results. If you are able to do everything in the above chapters and still fail to meet the goals of your organization, you will not see success in this roll. However, if you are able to go above and beyond what your organization expects you to achieve, you will be able to progressively develop yourself and create or improve your leader development program so that others may benefit from it.

Here are questions to ask to understand where your strengths and weaknesses lie in this competency:

These Questions Identify Strengths in Achieving Goals

- Do you establish clear goals? Do you explain to your employees where you want to be and how you see the team getting there?
- Are your goals SMART? Once you set these goals, do you keep track of them, their progress to completion, and the deadlines you established?
- Do you consider the strengths, weaknesses, and desires of your employees before assigning them new tasks?
- Do your employees clearly understand what contributions are expected from them to both the department and the organization as a whole? Do they feel valued?
- Are you always able to keep track of all people and resources?
- Do you decline taking on tasks that will overburden your team?
- Are you comfortable taking problems to your leaders? Are you comfortable asking for help?

- Do you recognize your team and individuals for excellent performance? Do you provide rewards for surpassing expectations?

These Questions Identify Weaknesses in Achieving Goals

- Do you micro-manage? Do you feel the need to have total control over all aspects of the team's activities?
- Do you commit to projects without having a clear understanding of what is required of your team?
- Do you over-commit? Do you accept more tasks than your team can physically do in the allotted time?
- Do you refuse to recognize or resolve conflict?
- Do you waste time or budget on unnecessary things?
- Do you find it challenging to recognize obstacles to your goals?
- Do you only point out failures such as when your team misses a deadline?
- Do you look for the quickest single solution to a problem or view it from multiple angles and possibilities?
- Do you refuse to change course when the objective changes or a problem arises?

If you notice yourself trending to some of the weaknesses, consider if you are doing any of the following:

- Are you proactive or reactive in your organization?
- Do you identify problems before they occur and have contingency plans for them?
- Do you procrastinate?
- Are you afraid to say "no"?
- Do you fully understand the importance of ensuring common understanding across the team for the problem or task?
- Do you feel disorganized?
- Do you avoid conflict or obstacles until they have reached crisis stage?
- Do you understand the value of recognition?
- Do you fear change?

Here are some activities to develop your ability to get results:

Feedback

- Ask yourself and your team who needs to know about the plans you're making. Make sure there is thorough communication with all stakeholders (both internal and external to your department).
- After every major project, do a thorough evaluation with your team about what was supposed to happen, what actually happened, and how to sustain the successes and improve on the missteps.
- If you are unclear about what is expected from you or your team, ask. Before you accept a task, be clear about the desired result.
- Ask your employees if they have the necessary resources to accomplish their tasks or goals.

Learning

- Study your organization's strategic mission, vision, and values. Ensure your priorities support these.
- Learn your team's strengths and weaknesses. Use them to your advantage. They will benefit from this as well.
- Study your budget and how your team consumes resources. Seek opportunities for cost savings, but recognize the need to provide your team with what they need to accomplish the tasks you have given them.

Practice

- Set SMART (specific, measurable, attainable, relevant, time-bound) goals for your employees and yourself.
- Make regular evaluation of work progress against remaining deadlines a priority. Use a tracking system to do this and hold yourself accountable to update it. The system can be anything from a work order management system to an excel spreadsheet. I've used all kinds. The key is to not let anything surprise you. Routinely review the progress of your team's work. As tasks fall behind schedule, make adjustments to get them back on track.
- Break down processes into steps. Provide responsibilities and expectations for each new task you assign. Ensure thorough understanding by asking your employee for a summary of what you just explained.

- Develop a schedule for your team. Be clear on your expectations, but consider your employees' feedback on the feasibility of your schedule and make adjustments accordingly.
- Partner stronger team members with weaker ones to promote development and knowledge sharing.
- Challenge your team members to accept greater responsibility. This tends to foster motivation and lead to greater work production.
- Balance the workload across your team. If one employee is overwhelmed, do what you can to alleviate the stress and cross-level workload.
- Provide regular and consistent feedback to your team. Be sure to include what they are doing well and how they can improve. Be honest and straightforward in your approach. The purpose of this feedback should fix future problems, not dwell on past problems. This sets the stage for development and does not dwell on past failures.
- Look for alternate solutions to problems. Make contingency plans for high-profile projects and be open to change. Adaptability is key to success in dynamic environments.
- Actively think about maintaining your composure in high-stress situations. Be the calming force in the storm. Be the leader to whom your employees aren't afraid to bring problems.

Section Summary

It is my sincere hope that this practical approach to leadership development will help you in your careers and personal lives. This section has covered all aspects of leader development and gotten pretty in-depth with activities you can use to identify where you should focus in your development program. Nothing frustrates me more than expecting to come away from a book on leadership with steps for improvement and not having anything when I come to the end of it. If you're finishing these sections on leadership and feel that I could expand on any of these concepts (or add new ones for that matter), please feel free to find me at **www.LearningFM.com** and let me know. I'll be more than happy to consider your ideas for future versions of this guide.

Conclusion

The *Complete Guide to Facility Management* contains the basic blueprint of how to establish a successful career in FM and develop yourself and your team to meet the diverse requirements of your organization. I explained the key concepts behind four knowledge domains: Operations & Maintenance, Project Management, Business Finance, and Leadership. All four are vital to your success in facility management, because all four domains serve to round out your development and training.

As I continue my career in facility management, I learn new things daily. I learn these things from the people I work with, from the books I read, from the courses I take and seminars I attend, from the podcasts I listen to, from the subcontractors and service providers I hire, from the members and guests I serve, from my family, from my friends, and everyone in-between. If there is one thing you would allow me to pass on to you after reading this book, it is to never stop learning. Continue to grow in your profession and educate those around you to better understand the massive scope of responsibilities that all FMs share as they support your organization's strategic mission.

Thank you again for giving me the opportunity to pass on what I've learned. I would appreciate any feedback and comments personally at **dan@learningfm.com** or publicly in any of the comment sections on **www.LearningFM.com**. Good or bad, your feedback will help me continue to learn and enable me to improve future versions of this book and future writings.

Good luck in your journey.

Notes

[1] "What is Facility Management?" IFMA. 2017. Accessed February 22, 2017. https://www.ifma.org/about/what-is-facility-management.
[2] "The Four States of Competence Explained." Examined Existence. 2017. Accessed February 22, 2017. http://examinedexistence.com/the-four-states-of-competence-explained/.
[3] National Institute of Building Sciences. 2016. Accessed February 23, 2017. https://www.nibs.org/.
[4] James R. Watson. "Real Property Inventory (RPI) and Asset Management (RPAM)." WBDG. October, 3, 2016. Accessed February 23, 2017. https://www.wbdg.org/facilities-operations-maintenance/real-property-inventory-rpi-and-asset-management-rpam.
[5] Don Sapp. "Facilities Operation and Maintenance." WBDG. October, 3, 2016. Accessed February 23, 2017. https://www.wbdg.org/facilities-operations-maintenance
[6] "What is BIM?" National BIM Standard – United States. 2016. Accessed February 28, 2017. https://www.nationalbimstandard.org/faqs.
[7] "NFPA 101: Life Safety Code®" NFPA. 2015. Accessed March 2, 2017. http://www.nfpa.org/codes-and-standards/all-codes-and-standards/list-of-codes-and-standards?mode=code&code=101.
[8] Ibid.
[9] "OSHA Law & Regulations." United States Department of Labor. Accessed March 2, 2017. https://www.osha.gov/law-regs.html.
[10] "Emergency Action Plan." OSHA. 2017. Accessed March 2, 2017. https://www.osha.gov/SLTC/etools/evacuation/min_requirements.html.
[11] Ibid.
[12] "Learn About PMI." PMI. 2017. Accessed February 24, 2017. http://www.pmi.org/about/learn-about-pmi.
[13] "What is Project Management?" PMI. 2017. Accessed February 24, 2017. https://www.pmi.org/about/learn-about-pmi/what-is-project-management
[14] "PDSA Cycle." The W. Edwards Deming Institute®. 2016. Accessed February 25, 2017. https://deming.org/management-system/pdsacycle.
[15] "Definition of CONTRACT." Merriam-Webster. 2017. Accessed March 24, 2017. https://www.merriam-webster.com/dictionary/contract.
[16] "Tuckman's Team Development Model." The Salvation Army. Accessed March 3, 2017. https://salvos.org.au/scribe/sites/2020/files/Resources/Transitions/HANDOUT_-_Tuckmans_Team_Development_Model.pdf.

[17] "About the FAF." FAF. Accessed March 5, 2017. www.fasb.org/jsp/FASB

[18] Department of the Army. "Leadership." August 1, 2012. ADP 6-22: 1.

[19] John French and Bertram Raven. "The Bases of Social Power." 1959. *Studies in Social Power*: 150-167. Ann Arbor, MI: Institute for Social Research.

[20] "Laissez-faire." Dictionary.com. 2017. Accessed March 30, 2017. http://www.dictionary.com/browse/laissez-faire.

[21] "Confidence." Dictionary.com. 2017. Accessed April 3, 2017. http://www.dictionary.com/browse/confidence.

Printed in Great Britain
by Amazon

76800085R00163